Hogarth's London, pictures of the manners of the eighteenth century

Henry Benjamin Wheatley

HOGARTH'S LONDON

'To the student of History, these admirable works must be invaluable, as they give us the most complete and truthful picture of the manners and even the thoughts of the past century. We look and see pass before us the England of a hundred years ago—the peer in his drawing room, the lady of fashion in her apartment, foreign singers surrounding her, and her chamber filled with gewgaws in the mode of that day, the church with its quaint florid architecture and singing congregation, the parson with his great wig and the beadle with his cane, all these are represented before us, and we are sure of the truth of the portrait.'—THACKERAY'S *English Humourists.*

William Hogarth.
From the Townsley Mezzotint of the portrait
by Wollaston and Hogarth

HOGARTH'S LONDON

Pictures of the Manners of the Eighteenth Century

BY

HENRY B. WHEATLEY, F.S.A.

ILLUSTRATED

LONDON

CONSTABLE AND COMPANY LTD.

1909

AUSTIN DOBSON, Esq., LL D.

DEAR DOBSON,—Some thirty years ago or more Dr. John Percy, F.R.S., the well-known metallurgist and Hogarth collector, after referring to the study of Hogarth's works as too big a subject for one man to deal with, advised me to undertake the division of Hogarth's London. I was pleased with the suggestion and I set to work to collect materials. This was before the publication of your first book on Hogarth, a volume of the greatest interest which has increased in value with each new edition until it is now the chief authority on the subject. From various causes I put the work aside, although I did not relinquish the idea. I have now taken it up again and completed it for publication.

You have done so much towards the elucidation of Hogarth's life and work that your name has become indissolubly linked with that of the great artist and satirist. I am therefore naturally anxious to associate your name with this book, in which an attempt is made to illustrate a side of Hogarth's art upon which you have expressed the opinion that it has not been sufficiently treated. You are so thoroughly master of this literature that I can scarcely hope to put forward anything that is not a commonplace to you. It is, however, a true pleasure to thank you publicly for constant help and to express my respect and esteem for a friend of many years' standing.

You have delighted generations of readers with poetry and prose on a variety of subjects which are as illuminating and convincing as they are charming, and I am proud to range myself among your admirers,—adding that I am always sincerely yours,

HENRY B WHEATLEY.

October 1909

PREFACE

To attempt the illustration of the manners of the eighteenth century as seen in London by the greatest graphic delineator of manners that ever lived, has been my object for several years.

Hogarth was a devoted Londoner, and while illustrating the manners of Englishmen of his time, he drew his subjects from the inhabitants of London with whom he was in daily intercourse. Representations of streets and buildings in all parts of London are to be found in the collection of his works, and most of these are discussed in this book.

It might be thought that enough has already been done,[1] but I hope it will be found that there is still room for a book specially devoted to one branch of Hogarth's work.

I had at first the intention of arranging my materials in topographical order, but on second thoughts I felt that this would scarcely be the fittest manner of treating the subject, because it

---

[1] A short note on the literature which has sprung from the study of Hogarth's works will be found at the end of this book (Chapter xiv)

was not specially the object of the artist to reproduce the topographical features of the Town. Rather is it the general appearance of the streets and the people that filled the streets that make so many of his pictures of such extraordinary interest to us now.

The late Mr. James Hannay well said—'London had been much described before the days of which we are speaking, and especially by the Comic Writers of Charles the Second's time; but there is a depth of philosophical humour in the way that Hogarth and his contemporaries undertake this task, such as had not been brought to bear upon it before. From *their* era dates town literature and town art.'

Hogarth attained great fame in his own lifetime, and was the first English artist to be known and admired abroad. He was, however, admired for one side of his art, while the other side was neglected. His engravings were largely bought, but in many cases his pictures remained on his hands.

The engravings were talked about on every side, and great anxiety was shown in order to find out the inner meaning of the plates and the characters of those who were satirised. Several authors came forward to give the information the public were thirsting to obtain.

The first exhibition of his pictures in the year 1814

was a revelation to the many who knew him only from his engravings ; and from that time to this his fame as a very great painter has continued to increase.

How great an attraction Hogarth's prints afforded to the sightseers of London may be seen in the remarks of the author of a pamphlet, published in 1748, on *The Effects of Industry and Idleness Illustrated*, in which ' the moral of twelve celebrated Prints lately published and designed by the ingenious Mr. Hogarth ' is set forth. The author went the round of the print-shops of London, and found a crowd gathered at all of them, but he was disappointed to find that, instead of alluding to the moral, the crowd gave all their attention to the remarks of those who could point out the individuals from whom the various characters were drawn.

A selection of some of Hogarth's finest pictures and engravings have here been reproduced as illustrating the subjects of the different chapters. In the preface to the valuable Catalogue of the British Museum Satirical Prints, the late Mr. F. G. Stephens wrote, ' The Collection of " Hogarths " in the British Museum is incomparably the largest and most select in existence ; the same may be said for the copies, piratical as well as legitimate, which abound in the national depository.

'But with regard to the copies, even the Print Room and the Library do not contain all the English examples. . . . It may be said that every nation which has attained Civilisation continues to produce such copies. In a very large number of cases these copies bear names differing from those Hogarth gave.' I have been greatly indebted to the descriptions in this Catalogue for much information and for numerous references to the literature of the time.

In conclusion, I wish to express in this place my cordial thanks to Mr. Austin Dobson for his valuable suggestions; to the Earl of Portsmouth, Mr. D'Arcy Power, Mr. George Peachey, Mr. Robert Grey, Treasurer of the Foundling Hospital, and Mr. J. L. Spiers, Curator of the Soane Museum, for kind assistance; and to the Duke of Newcastle, John Murray, Esq., the Governors of St. George's Hospital, the President and Council of the Royal Academy, for allowing their pictures to be reproduced; and especially to the authorities of the National Gallery, the British Museum, and the Soane Museum for assistance in respect to the reproduction of pictures and engravings.

CONTENTS

CHAPTER I

INTRODUCTION

CHAPTER II

HOGARTH'S LIFE AND WORKS

CHAPTER VI

CHURCH AND DISSENT

CHAPTER VII

PROFESSIONAL LIFE

CHAPTER VIII

BUSINESS LIFE

CHAPTER IX

TAVERN LIFE

CHAPTER X

THEATRICAL LIFE

CHAPTER XI

HOSPITALS

CHAPTER XII

PRISONS AND CRIME

CHAPTER XIII

THE SUBURBS

CHAPTER XIV

LITERATURE OF HOGARTH

LIST OF ILLUSTRATIONS

CHAPTER I

INTRODUCTION

To those who live in the twentieth century a study of the manners of the eighteenth century is singularly fascinating, as that is near enough for its aims to be understood and its philosophy to be sympathised with, and yet distant enough to be fresh and piquant to those of a later age.

It may be said to have been, not so very long ago, the Cinderella of the Centuries, inasmuch as many writers have not tired in declaiming against it. Mr. Frederic Harrison is its most valiant defender, and completely answers the unmeasured abuse of Carlyle.[1] He justly styles it 'the turning epoch of the modern world,' and asserts that although it was an age of prose, it was not prosaic. We are just at the right distance from this period to judge it without bias. At present the nineteenth century is too near us to be treated historically. Therefore we ought to understand the eighteenth century better, and to admire it in spite of its glaring faults. We know it better than most other centuries, because

---

[1] 'The age of prose, of lying, of sham, the fraudulent bankrupt century, the reign of Beelzebub, the peculiar era of Cant'

A

its authors have painted the manners and social life of their times more minutely than the authors of previous periods have done theirs. It was specially a friendly social century, and as we read the pages of Fielding, Richardson, Boswell, Walpole, Cowper, Fanny Burney, and Jane Austen we follow the life of the time in all its phases with breathless interest.

What is most striking in this body of literature is that all classes are depicted. We never tire of reading of the men and women who were divided by artificial barriers into different worlds. What did Walpole's world know of Johnson's world? what did Cowper care for either?

There was, however, one man who did more than all the others put together to help us to understand the life of the eighteenth century—at all events how it was lived by Londoners, for he appeals to the eye as well as to the intellect; and that man was Hogarth. He was seldom absent from London, and no day passed without his eye finding something to record—a line if not a picture, perhaps a thumbnail sketch for future enlargement. Hogarth was immediately recognised by his contemporaries as a great pictorial satirist, and it was not long before his engravings became well known abroad. It has, however, taken longer for his other great qualities to be universally acknowledged.

Horace Walpole had a great admiration for Hogarth, and he was one of the first to set the fashion of collecting Hogarth's prints. In commencing the chapter on this great artist in his *Anecdotes of Painting* (vol. iv. 1771), he writes : ' Having dispatched the herd of our painters in oil, I reserved to a class by himself that great and original genius, Hogarth ; considering him rather as a writer of comedy with a pencil, than as a painter. If catching the manners and follies of an age *living as they rise,* if general satire on vices and ridicules, familiarized by strokes of nature, and heightened by wit, and the whole animated by proper and just expressions of the passions be comedy, Hogarth composed comedies as much as Molière ; in his " Marriage à la Mode " there is even an intrigue carried on throughout the piece. He is more true to character than Congreve ; each personage is distinct from the rest, acts in his sphere, and cannot be confounded with any other of the *dramatis personæ.*'

Carrying on his comparison of Hogarth with the great French dramatist, Walpole writes : ' Molière, inimitable as he has proved, brought a rude theatre to perfection. Hogarth had no model to follow and improve upon. He created his art and used colours instead of language.'

Mr. Austin Dobson has drawn attention to an article in the *Gray's Inn Journal*, Feb. 9, 1754, apparently written by Arthur Murphy, in which Walpole's description of the painter as a ' writer of comedy with a pencil' is forestalled. Replying to Voltaire, who had been accusing the English of a lack of genius for Painting and Music, the author of this article wrote: 'Hogarth, like a true genius, has formed a new school of Painting for himself. He may be truly styled the Cervantes of his art, as he has exhibited with such a masterly hand the ridiculous follies of Human Nature. . . . He may be said to be the first, who has wrote Comedy with his pencil. His "Harlot's Progress," and "Marriage à la Mode" are, in my opinion, as well drawn as anything in Molière, and the unity of character which is the perfection of Dramatic Poetry, is so skilfully preserved, that we are surprised to see the same personage thinking agreeably to his complexional habits in the many different situations in which we afterwards perceive him.'

Mr. Dobson also quotes from a literary case in July 1773, when Lord Gardenstone, a Scottish judge, after defining Hogarth as 'the only true original author which this age has produced in England,' went on: 'I can read his works over and over . . . and every time I peruse them I discover new beauties, and feel fresh entertainment.'

Fielding was one of Hogarth's greatest admirers. The first time we find their names united was in 1731, when Hogarth engraved a frontispiece for Fielding's *Tragedy of Tragedies*. In the preface to his first novel, *Joseph Andrews*, the novelist takes the earliest opportunity of introducing a brilliant criticism of the artist's insight in his own remarks on the Ridiculous: 'He who should call the ingenious

Hogarth a burlesque painter, would, in my opinion, do him very little honour: for sure it is much easier, much less the subject of admiration, to paint a man with a nose, or any other feature of a preposterous size, or to expose him in some absurd or monstrous attitude, than to express the affections of men on canvas. It hath been thought a vast commendation of a painter, to say his figures seem to breathe; but surely, it is a much greater and nobler applause, that they appear to think.' In *Tom Jones* the references to Hogarth are continually occurring as illustrations of some of the characters.

Three great writers, about the same time, claimed the highest position in his art for Hogarth: Coleridge in 1809, Charles Lamb in 1811, and Hazlitt in 1814. Hazlitt classes Hogarth with the Comic Writers, and Lamb says: ' His graphic representations are indeed books. They have the teeming, fruitful, suggestive meaning of *words*. Other pictures we look at—his prints we read.'[1] Coleridge beautifully expresses his appreciation of that sense of beauty which many ignorantly denied to Hogarth. He writes in *The Friend* (No. 16, Dec. 7, 1809): ' One of those beautiful female faces which

[1] A great friend of Charles Lamb was amusingly enthusiastic on Hogarth's art. This was Martin Burney, son of Admiral James Burney, and nephew of Dr. Charles Burney. Barry Cornwall (B. W. Procter) in his Memoirs of Lamb (1866) thus refers to Martin ' The last time I saw Burney was at the corner of a street in London, when he was overflowing on the subject of Raffaelle and Hogarth. After a long and prolonged struggle, he said he had arrived at the conclusion that Raffaelle was the greater man of the two.'

Hogarth, in whom the satyrist never extinguished that love of beauty which belonged to him as a Poet, so often and so gladly introduces as the central figure in a crowd of humorous deformities, which figure (such is the power of true genius!) neither acts nor is meant to act as a contrast; but diffuses through all, and over each of the group a spirit of reconciliation and human kindness; and even when the attention is no longer consciously directed to the cause of this feeling, still blends its tenderness with our laughter; and thus prevents the instructive merriment at the whims of nature or the foibles of our fellow-men from degenerating into the heart poison of contempt or hatred.'

Walter Savage Landor wrote to John Forster: 'What nonsense I see written of Hogarth's defects as a colourist. He was in truth far more than the most humorous, than the most pathetic, and most instructive, of painters. He excelled at once in composition, in drawing and in colouring; and of what other can we say the same? In his portraits he is as true as Gainsborough, as historical as Titian.'

The need of acknowledging the realism of Hogarth's art is very important for our present purpose, as half the value of it to us would be lost if we did not understand the truthfulness of his work. We have the authority of Walpole for this.

In a letter to Sir David Dalrymple (Lord Hailes), Dec. 11, 1780, he writes, 'I believe, Sir, that I may have been overcandid to Hogarth, and that his spirit and youth and talent may have hurried him into more real caricatures than I specified; yet he certainly restrained his bent that way pretty early.'[1]

Although so just and full of praise, for one side of Hogarth's art, Walpole was singularly blind to his merits on the technical side, for he says, 'As a painter he had but slender merit.' The distinction of his paintings was strangely ignored in his own time, and was not generally acknowledged until 1814, when fifty of his original pictures were exhibited at the British Institution. Richard Payne Knight, the writer of the preface to the Catalogue, ventured to praise the high qualities of his work, and he somewhat timidly wrote, 'His pictures often display beautiful colouring as well as accurate drawing.'

When the public had the opportunity of seeing Hogarth's original pictures, and were able to criticise them as distinct from his engravings, they began to realise that the painter was a great master worthy to rank with the chief of his predecessors; they found that, besides being a writer of comedy with a pencil, he was a brilliant artist in colour as well as in draughtsmanship.

During a severe illness when James Whistler was little over twelve years old, he had the opportunity of studying a large volume of Hogarth's engravings. His mother relates that he said on one occasion, 'Oh how I wish I were well, I want so to show these engravings to my drawing master,

[1] *Letters*, ed. Cunningham, vol. vii. p. 472.

it is not every one who has a chance of seeing
Hogarth's own engravings of his originals,' and
then added, in his own happy way, ' And if I had
not been ill, mother, perhaps no one would have
thought of showing them to me.'

Mr. and Mrs. Pennell remark: ' From this time
until his death Whistler always believed Hogarth
to be the greatest English artist who ever lived,
and he seldom lost an opportunity of saying so.
The long attack of illness in 1847 is therefore
memorable as the beginning of his love of Hogarth,
which became an article of faith with him.' [1]

In an article by Mr. Sidney Colvin (*Portfolio*, iii.
p. 153), Hogarth's high qualities as a painter are
ungrudgingly praised:

' Hogarth, in his best works, catches with a
perfect subtlety the colour of rich or poor apparel,
indoor furniture and outdoor litter, the satin, bows,
jewels, ribbons of the bride, the fur coat and hose
and waistcoat of the beau, lace, silk, velvet, broad-
cloth, spangles, and brocade, rich carpets, rich
wall hangings, the look of pictures on the wall;
or, on the other hand, the coarse appurtenances of
the market-place or the street crossing: he catches
them, and their tone and relations in the indoor
or outdoor atmosphere with a perfect subtlety
and sense of natural harmony. And not only so,
but without a school, and without a precedent
(for he is no imitator of the Dutchmen) he has

---

[1] *Life of J. M Whistler*, by E R. and J. Pennell, 1908, vol. 1. p 21.

found a way of expressing what he sees with the clearest simplicity, richness and directness.'

Sir Walter Armstrong, in his Essay prefixed to Dobson's folio edition of his *Hogarth*, has done full justice to Hogarth's claim to a high place as a painter. He styles him a creator of beauty, a master of grace and a perfect craftsman, affirming that his 'supreme achievement as a painter lies in the completeness with which he gave artistic expression to ideas which were not essentially pictorial in themselves.'

Now his position as a painter has been completely established, and we can forgive the ill-judged remarks of Walpole, in the spirit of which, by the way, he was supported by the opinion of many of his contemporaries.

While pointing out Hogarth's high position when he followed his natural bent, we have regretfully to acknowledge that he had his limits, and it is necessary to refer to the mistake he made when he endeavoured to essay a style entirely unsuited to his genius, although even in his religious subjects there are merits which have been unfairly overlooked.

Mr. Dobson quotes the painter's extraordinary utterance respecting the great style of history painting, where he appears to value the Scripture scenes at St. Bartholomew's Hospital (1736) more than such pictures as the 'Harlot's Progress.'

Hogarth in his autobiography writes—'I have endeavoured to treat my subjects as a dramatic writer: my picture is my stage, and men and women my players, who by means of certain actions and gestures, are to exhibit a dumb show. Before I had done anything of much consequence in this walk, I entertained some hopes of succeeding in what the puffers in books call the great style of History painting; so that without having had a stroke of this grand business before, I quitted small portraits and familiar conversations, and with a smile at my own temerity, commenced history painter, and on a great staircase at St. Bartholomew's, painted two Scripture stories, " The Pool of Bethesda " and " The Good Samaritan," with figures seven feet high.' [1]

It is impossible with any success to compare Hogarth with other painters, as he stands absolutely alone. Mr. Dobson writes : ' He was an exceptional genius, not to be conveniently ticketed off, by any preconceived theory respecting his race, his epoch, or his environment.'

We can now pass on to consider Hogarth as a delineator of manners and an illustrator of London Topography.

The manners and morals of a period form complex subjects for consideration. In order therefore to obtain any true understanding of the time, it is necessary to sort out the various subjects into classes, and when we have done this we shall find

[1] *Anecdotes of W. Hogarth, written by Himself* Edited by J. B. Nichols. London, 1833, p. 9.

how completely the works of Hogarth cover the ground in respect to the manners and life of the eighteenth century. The plan of this work is to deal with these subjects in separate chapters, but here a more general view of the whole field may be taken.

The first thing to note is the similarity of aims among all classes of Society during a large part of the century. What has been styled *The* World was the pervading influence in the eighteenth century. Even then there were several Worlds, but they all had points of contact one with another. Now in the twentieth century the World has become too large to hang together, and the one is disintegrated into the many, all of these having different orbits. In the eighteenth century good society met in London, in Bath, and abroad. Its members renewed old acquaintanceship at the different seasons in different places. But we must not generalise overmuch, for there are shades of difference which must be accounted for. The literary world of Johnson was very different from the fashionable world of Horace Walpole, and there were few points of contact between them, but there were some.

For our present purpose that remarkable picture of Old London in Gay's *Trivia* is a help to the understanding of our subject, for Gay painted the very London that Hogarth loved and depicted, but he only drew the exterior of the streets, while Hogarth delineated the humours both of the insides and outsides of the houses.

We ought to understand the eighteenth century because it has a special fascination for us, although it has strongly marked features which are often repulsive.

The characteristic qualities are strength and unity of aims.   No period exhibits more remarkably these qualities, shown at the beginning of the century in calm chequered by Rebellion, and at the end in the fire of Revolution.   Both of these characteristics had their evil side, the strength developed into coarseness, and the unity was largely a unity of want of refinement.   There is no evidence in Walpole's Letters that the higher classes, who might be expected to have exhibited good manners (if not morality) were any better than other classes. In some respects they were much inferior to the middle classes.   It is always dangerous and unjust to make sweeping charges against a whole nation, but all we read and all we see of the eighteenth century—at all events parts of it—seem to point it out as one of the worst-mannered periods in our history.   There is much to disgust us in Hogarth's pictures of life, but the worst of all are the 'Four Stages of Cruelty,' which are simply appalling in their atrocity.

The Restoration period is sometimes considered to be one of the worst in our annals, but there is some reason to think that after the Revolution there was exhibited a depth of turpitude in public and private life that had not been so widespread before. Great intellectual vigour and goodness within well-defined limits were also distinguishing features of the age ; among its many faults hypocrisy was not to be numbered.   One of the striking faults of the century was its hatred of enthusiasm and its distrust of ideals, yet in studying its history we see the gradual emergence of a new spirit and a new life from the dull apathy of the early years to the burning hopes and faith in the future as exhibited in the midst of troubles at the end of the century.

In referring to Hogarth's reproduction of the striking contrasts of his age, Mr. Dobson says : 'He has peopled his canvas with its *dramatis personæ*, with vivid portraits of the more strongly marked actors in that cynical and sensual, brave and boastful, corrupt and patriotic time.'

The truth of Hogarth's pictures of his age has been acknowledged by all, and by no one more completely than by Horace Walpole, who was one of the best of judges. Of the painter's interiors he wrote : 'It was reserved to Hogarth to write a scene of furniture.   The rake's levee-room, the nobleman's dining-room, the apartments of the husband and wife in "Marriage à la Mode," the alderman's parlour, the poet's bedchamber, and many others, are the history of the manners of the age.' [1]

Hogarth is styled a moralist, and in his great work, the 'Marriage à la Mode,' he is truly that.   He has taken as his subject a life-history, which must

---

[1] Walpole's *Anecdotes of Painting*, 1876, vol. iii. p. 7.

have been repeated in every age, but he has treated it with so much of the power and insight of genius that he points a moral which we feel to be that of a drama worthy of the greatest tragic writer. In the 'Progresses,' and 'Industry and Idleness,' he also shows himself a moralist, but in a more conventional manner.

In some of his other works there is rather too evident a zest and interest in the incidents of a vicious life to allow the moral to be so strongly marked. He was in these more the moralist in the sense of an exhibitor of manners.

Mrs. Oliphant speaks of his unimpassioned tragedy, and Mr. Dobson elaborates this point with his usual insight. He writes: 'He was a moralist after the manner of eighteenth century morality, not savage like Swift, not ironical like Fielding, not tender-hearted like Johnson and Goldsmith; but unrelenting, uncompromising, uncompassionate. He drew vice and its consequences in a thoroughly literal and business-like way, neither sparing nor softening its features, wholly insensible to its seductions, incapable of flattering it even for a moment, preoccupied solely with catching its fugitive contortion of pleasure or of pain.'

In order to obtain an idea of the chief features of the manners of the eighteenth century, it has been thought well to arrange the particulars under certain headings, which it is hoped will comprise all that need be discussed in this connection.

The headings of the chapters of this book are the following, and some general remarks may here be set down, leaving discussion of the various points for the chapters themselves.

High Life seems at first sight to be outside of Hogarth's ken, but his knowledge of human nature helped him to picture correctly a life which he had not lived. His many portraits were largely chosen from among the aristocracy, and the follies of the upper classes were as patent to the satirist as were those of men and women in a less exalted sphere. The picture of the nobleman in the 'Marriage à la Mode' is as successful a portrait as Hogarth ever painted.

The delineation of *Low Life*, however, was more congenial to Hogarth's taste, and he gloried in the humours which were to be found on all sides—in the streets, in the prize-fighter's amphitheatre, in the cockpit, the prison, and the brothel.

Such a view of the streets of London as we see in 'The Four Times of the Day' is not elsewhere to be seen. The dangers of the streets must have been appalling, and yet Gay, who points out some of the dangers, apostrophises

> 'Happy Augusta! Law-defended town!
> Here no dark lanthorns shade the villain's frown,
> No Spanish jealousies thy lanes infest,
> Nor Roman vengeance stabs th' unwary breast;
> Here tyranny ne'er lifts her purple hand,
> But liberty and justice guard the land,
> No bravos here profess the bloody trade,
> Nor is the Church the murd'rer's refuge made.'

There can be little doubt that the inhabitants of London who walked in the streets after dark took care to possess means of protection, and those who were defenceless kept within-doors.

The man of quality had his sword which he could ordinarily use with skill, and others were proficient with their fists.   Johnson was a powerful man, and was well able to take care of himself as we know from several recorded adventures, especially the one in Grosvener Square when he caught the man who had stolen his handkerchief and knocked him down before the thief knew where he was.

Swift paints a sorry picture of the state of the streets in his description of a City Shower, and Gay advises the walker to wear strong shoes.   It was evidently a serious matter for men in decent apparel to walk the streets, for they were subject to the drippings of roofs as well as the splashing of passing carts and coaches :

> ‘When dirty waters from balconies drop,
> And dextrous damsels twirl the sprinkling mop,
> And cleanse the spatter'd sash, and scrub the stairs ;
> Know Saturday's conclusive morn appears.’

The streets were cleansed in the middle ages, but they were evidently neglected in the eighteenth century.

Political Life is well represented by Hogarth. He drew the tradesman-politician reading his paper, and a sitting of the House of Commons ; the Humours of a Country Election, and the unfortunate print of ‘The Times,’ which made enemies of some of his former friends and caused much ill-will to be poured out upon the artist.

In *Church and Dissent* we see the picture of the deadest time in the religious life of the country, when congregations slept and churchman and dissenter were alike the butt of the wits.

Professional Life is well represented by the lawyers, the doctors and the soldiers as well as by the artists and the authors, but none of these classes was flattered.

Business Life is seen in Hogarth's shop bills. In his pictures the creaking sign-boards are visible on all sides, and carts and drays lumber along the streets.

This was the time of street cries, and artists have left us pictures of the men and women following peripatetic trades, all with their distinctive cries. Sleep fled from the eyes of the weary when these commenced their work in the early morning.

> 'Successive cries the season's change declare,
> And mark the monthly progress of the year.
> Hark, how the streets with treble voices ring,
> To sell the bounteous product of the spring!
> Sweet-smelling flowers, and elder's early bud,
> With nettle's tender shoots, to cleanse the blood:
> And when June's thunder cools the sultry skies,
> Ev'n Sundays are profan'd by mackerel cries.'[1]

The streets were doubtless noisier in the eighteenth century than now (although some of us complain of the present condition of things), and we are shown in the 'Enraged Musician' how difficult

[1] *Trivia*, Book II.

B

was the life of the intellectual worker in the midst of the turmoil around him. In his *Voyage to Lisbon* Fielding declared that to look at this picture was enough to make a man deaf.

Tavern Life was a special feature of the century, and here social life flourished. Hogarth has perpetuated the names of many of the London taverns and coffee-houses which were largely patronised.

Theatrical Life is painted very effectively in Hogarth's works. The playhouses and many of the actors, with Garrick at their head, are shown. The pictures of the *Beggar's Opera,* which was said to be the first great popular success known to the English stage, exhibit to us the audience on the stage, apparently very much in the way of the actors. This evil was not done away with altogether until Garrick made some of his chief improvements.

In *Hospitals,* which found a true friend in Hogarth, we obtain a glimpse of the better side of human nature in the eighteenth century.

Prisons and Crime, on the other hand, show us some of the worst evils of the age, and the impotence of the system of police to deal effectively with Crime. Pickpockets and cheats were found on all sides.

The Suburbs in the eighteenth century were at the very doors of the City, although they have long since been swallowed up. The citizen walked with his family in the afternoon and evening to the tea-gardens of Hoxton, Islington, Hampstead, Tottenham Court and Marylebone, and the humours of these places are to be found displayed in Hogarth's works. The general effect of the scenes painted by Hogarth and described by Gay is to impress upon us the evils of the time, and to leave us unimpressed by much good which must have existed, although it is left unnoticed.

London has always exerted a great influence over its children, for it is a city of unique and indescribable charm. The Londoner is spoiled for living in other places, and however far he may have wandered, he is forced eventually to return to London, as the one place in which life is lived in all its completeness.

Hogarth was a thorough Londoner. He was born in Bartholomew Close, lived in London all his life, and died in Leicester Square. He is known, with Londoners like himself, to have made a cockney tour from London to Sheerness and back again, but this five-days' trip comprised nearly the whole of his travels, and his life was spent chiefly between Leicester Square and Chiswick. From boyhood to his latest hour he never tired of exhibiting the life around him, and he may be said to bring that life before our eyes in a way no other artist before or since his time has ever done. From the East to the West, from the North to the South, the London of Hogarth's day can be traced topographically in his pictures and sketches.

Mr. Dobson points out the need of a Commentary to illustrate some of the intricacies of Hogarth's London Topography,[1] and it is hoped that this book

[1] 'If the chief circumstances of the painter's career should remain unsupplemented, there will always be a side of his work which must

may to some extent carry out the object he has in view.

It may be well here to set down a short indication of the extent of the topographical illustrations.

Hogarth's picture of the streets is singularly vivid, the kennels and the cobbled roads, the creaking sign-boards and the oil lamps and the attendant inconveniences are all brought before our eyes. The traffic, consisting of heavy carts and carriages and the lighter chairs with their chairmen, made the art of walking the streets as expounded by Gay in his *Trivia* a specially difficult one.

The localities represented in Hogarth's pictures may be divided into the City, the West End and Westminster, and the Suburbs; and there is little that goes to the making of the Great London of the eighteenth century which is unrepresented in this gallery. This London was large in itself, although when compared with the London of to-day it may seem small to us.

Taking the City first, there is the district round Fleet Street, and that round the Bank. Newgate is shown in the scene from the *Beggar's Opera*; the Old Bailey ('Industry and Idleness,' Plate 10);

continue to need interpretation. In addition to delineating the faults and follies of his time, he was pre-eminently the pictorial chronicler of its fashions and its furniture. The follies endure; but the fashions pass away. In our day—a day which has witnessed the demolition of Northumberland House, the translation of Temple Bar, and the removal of we know not what other time-honoured and venerated landmarks,—much in Hogarth's plates must seem as obscure as the cartouches on Cleopatra's Needle. Much more is speedily becoming so, and without guidance the student will scarcely venture into that dark and doubtful rookery of tortuous streets and unnumbered houses—the London of the eighteenth century.'

Bridewell in the ' Harlot's Progress,' Fleet Prison in the ' Rake's Progress ' ; Temple Bar in the eleventh plate of *Hudibras* ('Burning of the Rumps') is Wren's Bar (1672), of a later date than the scene itself (1660) ; Hanging Sword Alley, Water Lane, Fleet Street in ' Industry and Idleness' ; Chick Lane, West Smithfield in the same series ; Little Britain Gate (King's Arms), and the Cock Lane Ghost in ' A Medley.'

Round the Bank we find the Lord Mayor's Show in Cheapside ('Industry and Idleness,' Plate 12), the Bell in Wood Street ('Harlot's Progress,' Plate 1), Old London Bridge through the Window ('Marriage à la Mode,' Plate 6), Fishmongers Hall ('Industry and Idleness,' Plate 8), the base of the Monument on Fish Street Hill in the same series, Plate 6, and Bedlam, Moorfields ('Rake's Progress,' Plate 8). West of the City there are still more scenes as in St. Giles's, Soho, Covent Garden, Drury Lane, St. Martin's Lane, and last and best of all, St. James's Street ('Rake's Progress,' Plate 4)—an admirable view of London's premier street. In the Suburbs we see Tyburn in the execution of the Idle Apprentice at the Triple Tree (Plate 11), Marylebone Church ('Rake's Progress,' Plate 5), Tottenham Court in the 'March to Finchley' and Sadler's Wells (Evening). This is only a selection of places in London represented in Hogarth's pictures and prints, but it is sufficient to show the wealth of illustrations which is to be found in the wonderful variety of his works.

CHAPTER II

HOGARTH'S LIFE AND WORKS

FROM one point of view the life of Hogarth may be said to have been uneventful, but when we consider the amount of varied work which he carried on with a single-minded aim throughout a long life, as well as the sterling character of the man himself, which enabled him to carry out all his undertakings with decision, we shall find his life full of stirring events and replete with interest.

The main object of this work is to direct special attention to the illustrations of London life and manners to be found in Hogarth's work, but in order to show the relation of this part to the whole, it is necessary to set down the leading particulars of his life, and mark his position in the world in respect to friends and enemies, completing this chapter with a chronological notice of his most famous productions.

William Hogarth was born in Bartholomew Close, West Smithfield, on the 10th of November 1697, and baptized on the 28th of the same month at the parish church of St. Bartholomew the Great.[1]

[1] Hogarth's two sisters—Mary, born Nov. 23, 1699, and Ann, born Oct. 1701, were baptized—Mary also at St Bartholomew's on Dec 10, and Ann at St. Sepulchre's on Nov. 6

His father, Richard Hogarth, was the third son
of a yeoman farmer who lived in the vale of
Bampton, about fifteen miles north of Kendal. He
was educated at Archbishop Grindal's Free School
at St. Bees, and afterwards kept a school in his
native county of Westmorland. This proving unsuccessful, he removed to London.[1] He married
Anne Gibbons, and he and his wife were living in
Bartholomew Close when their distinguished son
was born. Afterwards he kept a school in Ship
Court, on the west side of the Old Bailey. The
house, with others, was pulled down in 1862 to make
room for the warehouse of Messrs John Dickinson
and Co., paper-makers, which was built on the site.

He was also employed as a hack writer and
corrector of the press to Mr. Downinge the printer,
whose acquaintance he probably made when he was
living next door to him in Bartholomew Close. He
appears to have been a man possessed of much out
of the way learning, for he made large additions to
Littleton's *Latin Dictionary*, but these marginal
additions were never printed, and his interleaved
copy remained in the possession of his son. In 1689
he published *Thesaurarium Trilingue Publicum*,
a copy of which is in the possession of Mr. Austin
Dobson, and in 1712 was issued his little work
entitled *Disputationes Grammaticales*.

[1] 'He came to London in company with Dr. Gibson, the late Bishop of
London's brother, and was employed as corrector of the press, which in
those days was not considered as a mean employment.'—John Ireland,
Hogarth Illustrated, vol. iii. p. 6

Richard Hogarth made scarcely enough to live upon, and he was able to give his son little or no education.   As his son himself says in his autobiographical sketch (John Ireland, 1798), 'My father's pen, like that of many other authors, did not enable him to do more than put me in the way of shifting for myself.'

There has been much discussion as to the origin of the family, and some have, with very little cause, supposed the surname to come from France.   There is a village in Westmorland named Hogarth, but doubtless the family originally came from Berwick, or even further north.   The name Hoggert has been found in Scotland as early as 1494, and an Aberdeen family of the name has been traced. There was a George Hogarth in London in the reign of Elizabeth.   The name was originally pronounced hard and the final *h* was not sounded, as Swift rhymes it in his satire on the Irish Parliament entitled 'A Character, Panegyric and Description of the Legion Club, 1736.'   These lines are more than interesting as proving this point, and are worth transcribing in full:

'How I want thee, humorous Hogarth !
Thou I hear a pleasant rogue art.
Were but you and I acquainted,
Every monster should be painted ;
You should try your graving tools
On this odious group of fools ;
Draw the beasts as I describe them :
From their features, while I gibe them,

Draw them like, for I assure you,
You will need no *car'catura*;
Draw them so that we may trace
All the soul in every face'

There was little likeness between father and son, but Thomas Hogarth of Troutbeck, an uncle of William, known as Auld or Ald Hoggart, was a rustic dramatist and satirist.   He is referred to by Nichols as an original genius, but his Remains are very commonplace.   Nevertheless some of his *Remnants of Rhyme*, selected from an old MS. collection of his writings preserved by his descendants, were published at Kendal as late as 1853.[1]

From boyhood to his latest hour William Hogarth devoted himself to the study of the life around him, and he never tired of exhibiting that life in his pictures and engravings.   Moreover, to the end he ceaselessly strove to excel.   He himself refers in his autobiography to this early bent: 'As I had naturally a good eye, and a fondness for drawing, *shows* of all sorts gave me uncommon pleasure when an infant; and mimicry, common to all children, was remarkable in me.   An early access to a neighbouring painter drew my attention from play; and I was, at every possible opportunity, employed in making drawings.   I picked up an acquaintance of the same turn, and soon learnt to

[1] Professor G. Baldwin Brown, in Appendix iv to his interesting little book on Hogarth (1905), quotes one of Ald Hoggart's songs (Momus and Marina), and says that a selection of Hoggart's poems has been reprinted by Mr. George Middleton, Ambleside.

draw the alphabet with great correctness. My exercises when at school were more remarkable for the ornaments that adorned them than for the exercise itself.'[1]

As a boy he was in the habit of making pencil sketches on his thumb-nails of whatever struck him. This practice he continued, and J. Ireland says that when he came home he copied the sketch on paper and kept it for future use. He adds, 'Several of these sketches I have seen, and in them may be traced the first thoughts for many of the characters which he afterwards introduced into his works.'[2]

His schooldays were soon brought to an end, and he entered in 1712 into an apprenticeship to Ellis Gamble, a silver-plate engraver in Cranbourne Alley, which ended about 1718. Mr. Dobson points out that Gamble was probably a connection of the Hogarth family, as there is a notice in 1707 of the marriage of a Sarah Gambell to Edmund Hogarth in Colonel Chester's *London Marriage Licenses*, 1521-1869.

Hogarth must have done much good work when in the employment of Gamble, although he himself refers to his engraving on silver as causing him to have to do with 'the monsters' of heraldry instead of learning 'to draw objects something like nature.'[3]

---

[1] John Ireland's *Hogarth Illustrated*, 1798, vol. iii p 4

[2] *Hogarth Illustrated*, vol iii. p 12 (note).

[3] There is a list of prints of coats-of-arms from those engraved by Hogarth in John Ireland's *Hogarth Illustrated*, vol iii. p 369 ; and another in J. B. Nichols's *Anecdotes*, 1833, p. 292.

DESIGN ON A SILVER TANKARD, BY HOGARTH.

John Thomas Smith in his Life of Nollekens says,
' I am inclined to believe it very possible that some
curious specimens of Hogarth's dawning genius
may yet be rescued from future furnaces,' and he
mentions two silversmiths who collected articles
of the artist's handicraft. Panton Betew, of Old
Compton Street, Soho, was intimate with Hogarth,
and frequently purchased pieces of plate engraved
with armorial bearings by him. Richard Morison,
a silversmith in Cheapside, took off twenty-five
impressions of the coat-of-arms of Sir Gregory Page
engraved on a silver tea-table by Hogarth. These
impressions he not only numbered, but also attested
each by his signature. Morison after taking the
impressions melted the plate, which he had bought
at Sir Gregory's sale. J. T. Smith is wrong in
stating that the engraving was on a large silver dish.
Another of his works was an elegant design engraved
on a large silver tankard used by the members of
the weekly club (of which Hogarth was a member)
held at the Spiller's Head in Clare Market. A copy
of this was given by Samuel Ireland in his *Graphic
Illustrations* (1794). One of the earliest of Hogarth's
works to be catalogued is a reproduction of

'Sir Plume, of amber snuff-box justly vain,
And the nice conduct of a clouded cane,'

in the *Rape of the Lock*, taken from the lid of a
gold snuff-box supposed to have been engraved
about the year 1717. How successfully Hogarth
engraved the heraldic subjects he undertook, may

be seen from the very fine etching of the arms of
the Duchess of Kendal, mistress of George I.,
also reproduced by Samuel Ireland.   In spite of his
success, he felt truly that for him there was no
future in silver-plate engraving, and in his autobiography he writes : ' Engraving on copper was, at
twenty years of age, my utmost ambition.'   He
probably practised this art while he was still with
Gamble, for he engraved a charming little book-
plate as well as a bold and effective shopbill for his
master.[1]

An anecdote which John Thomas Smith relates
in his *Nollekens* comes in at this time, and shows
Hogarth's kindly nature—' I have several times
heard Mr. Nollekens observe that he frequently
had seen Hogarth, when a young man, saunter
round Leicester Fields with his master's sickly
child hanging its head over his shoulder.'

Richard Hogarth, then residing in Long Lane,
West Smithfield, died at that place in May 1718.
Soon afterwards his son William set up in business
for himself.   His shop card is inscribed ' W.
Hogarth, Engraver.   Aprill ye 23, 1720.'   A copy
on which Hogarth had written ' Near the Black
Bull, Long Lane,' was seen by John Ireland.   From
this address it might be assumed that he continued
for a time to live with his mother and sisters, but

---

[1] The name of 'Ellis Gamble of Leicester Fields, Goldsmith,' is among
the list of bankrupts in 1733 printed in *Gentleman's Magazine*, vol. iii.
(1733), p. 48.

Nichols's copy (*Genuine Works*, ii. 20) has the inscription—'At y° Golden Ball y° Corner of Cranborne Alley, little Newport Street.   April y° 29, 1720.'

In the new business which he started by himself Hogarth began to design and engrave plates for the booksellers and printsellers, and he continued the making of book-plates which he apparently commenced when he was an apprentice of Gamble. In the preface to the British Museum Catalogue of the Franks Collection of Book-plates (1903, vol. i.), it is stated that 'perhaps the most interesting plates of the eighteenth century are the four engraved by Hogarth, viz. Gamble; the two states of the plate of John Holland, the Herald painter; George Lambart (*sic*); and a plate engraved for some member of the Paulet or Powlett family.   The impressions of the Gamble and Lambart plates are believed to be unique, and to be the same from which [Samuel] Ireland made his well-known copies.'

Hogarth's own plate, which consists of a monogram of his initials W. H. in a Jacobean frame, is not here mentioned.   The late Mr. Walter Hamilton, Treasurer of the Ex-Libris Society, adopted and copied Hogarth's plate as his own, the initials being the same.

In his autobiography Hogarth writes: 'The instant I became master of my own time, I determined to qualify myself for engraving on copper. In this I readily got employment; and frontispieces to books . . . soon brought me into the way.   But the tribe of booksellers remained as my father had left them, when he died . . . of an illness occasioned partly by the treatment he met with from this set of people . . . so that I doubly felt this usage.'

Hogarth found his proper sphere in 1721 when he produced his two earliest satirical engravings—'An Emblematical print on the South Sea Scheme,' and 'The Lottery.' He thus early commenced what was to be the main feature of his life-work, but these prints were wanting in the chief merits of his later productions, which stand easily at the head of their class. They did not catch the popular taste, and he continued his work for the booksellers for some years.

The late Mr. Frederic George Stephens, in the British Museum Catalogue of Satirical Prints (vol. ii. p. 15), says, 'Hogarth, the originator of English art in its modern and current phase, began about 1725 to do for English artistic satire almost as much as he afterwards did, technically and intellectually, for English painting. In fact Hogarth created modern English satire : he needed no help from inscriptions or textual side of any kind, and after 1725 only once employed the former ; he drew and there is no mistaking his meaning.'

Mr. Stephens goes on to refer to the two prints of 1721 : 'The first work of this designer is, however, strikingly enough, cumbrous, and its humour is far-fetched . . . "The Lottery" is hardly less cumbrous, but its humour is spontaneous.'

Hogarth

J. fecit

S.ʳ JAMES THORNHILL

Etch'd by S.ʳ Iohn...

Impression

Publish'd March 1798 by H. Baldwin...

PORTRAIT OF SIR JAMES THORNHILL.

Hogarth was twenty-eight years of age in 1725, so that this date fairly coincides with what he himself says: 'Owing to this and other circumstances, by engraving until I was near thirty, I could do little more than maintain myself; but even then I was a punctual paymaster.'

He is reported to have said of himself on one occasion, 'I remember the time when I have gone moping into the city with scarce a shilling in my pocket; but as soon as I had received ten guineas there for a plate I have returned home, put on my sword, and sallied out again with all the confidence of a man who had ten thousand pounds in his pocket.'

The great turning-point in Hogarth's life was his attendance at the painting-school of Sir James Thornhill, in the Piazza at the east corner of James Street, Covent Garden, which was established in 1724. Hogarth appears from his autobiography to have been early moved by Thornhill's painting, which he wished to emulate. He writes: 'I soon found this business in every respect too limited. The paintings of St. Paul's Cathedral and Greenwich Hospital, which were at that time going on, ran in my head, and I determined that silver-plate engraving should be followed no longer than necessity obliged me to it.'

From this it became certain that Hogarth would take the very first opportunity of obtaining the advantage of instruction from an artist he so much admired. He is said to have gained the good graces of his master by 'Masquerades and Operas, Burlington Gate,' also called by Hogarth 'The Taste of the Town' (1724), in which he attacked the feeble Kent. This was followed in the following year by the severe satire of Kent's altar-piece at St. Clement Danes. Kent was the *bête noire* of Thornhill, and Hogarth completely sympathised with him in his dislike. Kent was a bad painter, a passable architect, and a good landscape gardener.

The plates which Hogarth designed for books had their merits, but they are distinctly uninteresting, and this was probably caused by reason of the artist not having a free hand, and being interfered with by the booksellers. In 1726 Hogarth produced the most important of these in a series of illustrations to *Hudibras*, which he specially mentions in his autobiography as representative items in this department of his work. He must have been peculiarly interested in the pleasant task of illustrating the wonderful poem of so congenial a spirit as Butler's. The history of these illustrations is a very curious one, and can only be stated briefly here, but as we have little or no information besides what is contained in the books themselves, there are many points which are difficult to understand. The whole subject, consisting largely of the relative chronology of the engravings, the paintings and the drawings, requires full investigation. *Hudibras* was first published in 1663-64, and the first edition

'adorned with cuts' was printed for John Baker
in 1710 with a correct portrait of Butler. In the
following year another edition with plates from the
same designs was issued by R. Chiswell. In 1716
another edition 'adorned with cuts' was printed
for T. Horne [and others]. This contains the
same plates as the previous edition, but they
are somewhat varied, and a correct likeness of
Butler. It is not stated who was the artist who
produced these plates. In 1726 appeared the
edition which was illustrated by Hogarth, printed
for D. Browne [and others]. The plates were
founded upon those in the former illustrated editions,
but were considerably altered, and not always for
the better. The portrait which serves as frontispiece is not that of Butler, but a copy of White's
mezzotint of Jean Baptiste Monnoyer the painter.
This edition was reprinted in 1732 and 1739, and
each of these reprints contains a correct portrait of
Butler. All these are printed in duodecimo, and
there are sixteen small prints by Hogarth.

Early in the year 1726 (February 24) Hogarth
issued twelve large prints entirely different from the
small ones and of an altogether superior character.
The title-page is as follows: 'Twelve Excellent
and most Diverting Prints; taken from the celebrated Poem of Hudibras, wrote by Mr. Samuel
Butler. Exposing the Villany and Hypocrisy of
those Times. Invented and Engraved on Twelve
Copper-Plates by William Hogarth . . . Printed

and sold by Philip Overton, Printer and Map-
seller at the Golden Buck near St. Dunstan's Church
in Fleet street ; and John Cooper in James street
Covent Garden, 1726,' [1] and are humbly dedicated
to William Ward, Esq., of Great Houghton in
Northamptonshire, and Mr. Allan Ramsay of
Edinburgh.

There must be some secret history respecting these
illustrations of which at present we know nothing.
It is an extraordinary circumstance for Hogarth to
bring out almost simultaneously two sets of illustrations—one published with the text by the booksellers,
and the other without text by printsellers. It
would seem as if the smaller set had been in hand for
some time before publication, and the artist being
discontented with it as being mostly an adaptation
of other men's work had set to work on his own
account and with a free hand to produce something
worthier of the great classic of which he might be
truly proud. These twelve larger prints must have
taken a considerable time ' to invent and engrave,'
and their publication can scarcely have been considered as a friendly act by the publishers of the
small prints.

They do the greatest credit to Hogarth's invention
and skill, and form without question the most important piece of work which up to this year, 1726,
he had produced. In some subsequent editions of

[1] The author possesses a series of the first impressions of these prints
which form a fine (in fact a magnificent) volume.

Hudibras the small series of prints were repeated, and in one at least Hogarth's name is omitted. The plates were enlarged and slightly varied by J. Mynde for Dr. Zachary Grey's octavo edition.

Some pictures of incidents in *Hudibras* attributed to Hogarth were exhibited at the Winter Exhibition of the Royal Academy (1908).

Mr. Dobson mentions four series of paintings of subjects from *Hudibras* on the authority of J. B. Nichols (*Anecdotes*, 1833, pp. 349-50).

1. A set, since sold in November 1872 at the death of Mrs. Sawbridge, the owner of East Haddon Hall, Northamptonshire, is supposed to have been painted by Hogarth subsequent to the issue of the large series of prints. Mr. Dobson points out that the proprietor of East Haddon in 1726 was the William Ward to whom Hogarth dedicated the prints, and that therefore it is probable that the pictures were painted from the prints by commission.

2. A set belonging to John Ireland and believed by him to be Hogarth's originals, but thought by others to be by Heemskirk. These, Mr. Dobson informs me, now belong to Mrs. G. E. Twining, of Dulwich.

3. A set of twelve designs on panel belonging in 1833 to J. Britton and believed by him to be Hogarth's. Sir Thomas Lawrence pronounced them to be by Vandergucht.

4. A set belonging in 1816 to Mr. W. Davies,

bookseller in the Strand. Attributed to Francis Le Piper or Lepipre. Several drawings in illustration of *Hudibras* attributed to Hogarth were exhibited at Whitechapel in 1906. There are also specimens of the same series at Windsor Castle.[1]

Three painted sketches illustrating scenes from *Hudibras*, cantos II. and III., were lent to the Royal Academy Winter Exhibition of Old Masters, 1908 (Nos. 97, 98, and 101), by Mrs. Howard Stormont.

In connection with these illustrations, an instance of Hogarth's familiarity with *Hudibras* may be seen in the print of ' Cunicularii or the Wise Men of Godliman in Consultation ' :

> 'They hold their Talents most adroit
> For any Mystical Exploit.'—*Hudib.*

which was published in December 26, 1726, at the time when the mind of the public was much exercised by the impostures of Mary Tofts, the rabbit-breeder. It is referred to here on account of an interesting fact recorded by John Nichols in his *Biographical Anecdotes* (1785, p. 23). ' In the year 1726, when the affair of Mary Tofts, the rabbit-breeder of Godalming, engaged the public attention, a few of our principal surgeons subscribed their guinea a-piece to Hogarth, for an engraving from a

---

[1] John Ireland writes (*Hogarth Illustrated*, 1793, vol. i p. xxxii): ' Seven of the drawings are in the possession of Mr. Samuel Ireland, three are in Holland , and two are said to have been in the collection of a person in one of the northern provinces about twenty years ago, but are now probably destroyed. Thus are the works of genius scattered like the Sybill's leaves '

ludicrous sketch he had made on that very popular
subject.'   Some further notice of this print will be
found in Chapter vi. in connection with the prints
'Enthusiasm Delineated,' and 'Credulity, Superstition and Fanaticism: a Medley.'

In 1728 Hogarth found it necessary to go to law
with a tradesman, who refused to pay for work done
for him.   The artist in December 1727 agreed with
Joshua Morris, an upholsterer, who kept a shop in
Pall Mall at the sign of the Golden Ball, to furnish
him with a design on canvas, representing the
element of Earth as a pattern for tapestry,
apparently a very intractable subject.   Morris
when he received the work was so dissatisfied with
it that he rejected it and refused payment.   He
had previously been uneasy on being told that
Hogarth 'was an engraver and no painter.'

Hogarth sued him for the money, and the suit
was tried before Lord Chief-Justice Eyre at Westminster on May 28, 1728.   Nichols prints the
defendant's case in his *Biographical Anecdotes*, and
says that the suit was determined in favour of
Hogarth.[1]   Mr. Dobson writes : 'As to the fate of
the *Element of Earth* history is silent.   It is not
likely, however, that it was more fortunate than
some of Hogarth's subsequent efforts in the " grand
style." '

[1] This is the statement in the third edition (1785).   In the second edition
(1782) it is written : 'What was the event of the suit we do not learn, but
it is probable that Hogarth was non-suited.'   Between these two dates the
author may be supposed to have learned the truth.

One of the artist's witnesses to ability was Sir James Thornhill, who was interested in his future son-in-law as a pupil and a critic of his arch-enemy Kent. Hogarth returned his good offices by gaining the affections of the painter's daughter. He felt sure that his suit would not receive the sanction of Thornhill, so he took the matter in his own hand, and running away with his sweetheart was married at old Paddington Church on March 23, 1729, as appears by the parish register.

It is supposed that the young couple had the active sympathy of Lady Thornhill, and there is no doubt that it was not long before the pair were forgiven. In 1730, Hogarth was certainly engaged with his father-in-law in the production of the well-known picture entitled ' The House of Commons,' which contains portraits of the Speaker Onslow, Sir Robert Walpole, Sidney Godolphin, Colonel R. Onslow, Thornhill and the two clerks.

There is a tradition that Hogarth was engaged at the time of his marriage in preparing for his first great series of pictures, ' A Harlot's Progress,' which are dated 1731. The judicious placing a few of the sketches in the way of the father-in-law caused him to exclaim, ' The man who did those can afford to keep a wife.' For a time Hogarth and his wife went to live at South Lambeth, but Thornhill soon seems to have relented, and we find that at the time of engraving of the ' Harlot's Progress ' Hogarth was domiciled in the Piazza with his father-in-law,

LADY THORNHILL

Pub.d for S. Ireland May 1 1799

PORTRAIT OF LADY THORNHILL.

who found the assistance of a competent artist in some of his pictures of use to him. According to Nichols, when Thornhill painted an allegorical ceiling, illustrating the story of Zephyrus and Flora, at Headley Park, Hants, the figure of a satyr was put in by Hogarth, some of whose work is also to be seen in the staircase pictures painted by Thornhill at the house No. 75 Dean Street, Soho.

About this time Hogarth appears to have been initiated into Masonry, probably through the influence of Thornhill, who was Senior Grand Warden in 1728. The dates are rather uncertain, but Hogarth was certainly a Grand Steward in 1735.

Mr. G. W. Speth gives, in a note on the picture of Night, some particulars of Hogarth's Masonic career. In the Grand Lodge Register he appears as a member of the lodge meeting at the ' Hand and Apple Tree,' Little Queen Street. This lodge was constituted 10th May 1725, met in 1728 at the 'King's Arms,' Westminster, in 1729 at the ' Vine,' Holborn, and was erased in 1737. It cannot be determined whether he remained a member of the lodge till its erasure or at what period he joined it. The Grand Lodge Register shows that he was also a member of the' Corner Stone Lodge' in 1731. This name, however, was not assumed till 1779. It started in its career in 1730 at the ' Bear and Harrow' in Butcher Row, and its list of members shows it has been one of the most distinguished lodges of the day.[1]

When Hogarth lived at South Lambeth he renewed his acquaintance with Jonathan Tyers, who re-founded Vauxhall Gardens in 1732, and helped him with advice as well as more material services. He presented Tyers with his picture of Henry VIII. and Anna Bullen in 1729, which was hung in the Rotunda. While preparing for the opening of the gardens, Tyers became very depressed respecting the probable success of his undertaking. Hogarth suggested that the gardens should be opened with a Ridotto al fresco, which took place on Wednesday, the 7th of June 1732, and proved a great success. Several years afterwards he allowed Francis Hayman to copy his 'Four Times of the Day.' In consequence Hayman's pictures at Vauxhall were often mistaken for the work of Hogarth.

In return for all his valuable assistance, Tyers presented Hogarth with a free pass (gold ticket) to admit a coachful (six persons) to the gardens. Mrs. Hogarth had it after her husband's death, and in 1856 it was in the possession of Mr. Frederick Gye, who bought it for £20. It was subsequently sold at Sotheby's for £310. The design of the pass was attributed to Hogarth, but Mr. Warwick Wroth thinks that probably it was the work of Richard Yeo.

We have now come to the parting of the ways.

---

[1] *Transactions of the Lodge Quatuor Coronati*, vol. ii, 1889, p. 116

Life School at Hogarth's Academy in Peter's Court.

The artist was beginning to be recognised, but he was only recognised as 'an ingenious designer and engraver.' Sir James Thornhill died on May 13, 1734, and in an obituary notice after a mention of his only son it is added, ' He left no other issue but one daughter, now the wife of Mr. Wm. Hogarth, admired for his curious miniature conversation paintings.' This is about the earliest mention of the paintings, and these were soon to be eclipsed by his brilliant satires which gave him a European reputation. His marriage had stirred him to greater endeavours, and he had begun to mount the ladder of success.

On the death of Thornhill, the properties connected with the art school formed by him in a room built at the back of his house came into the possession of Hogarth, and were transferred to the studio in Peter's Court, St. Martin's Lane, which Roubiliac had left. ' Thinking,' Hogarth remarks, ' that an academy conducted on proper and moderate principles had some use, [I] proposed that a number of artists should enter into a subscription for the hire of a place large enough to admit thirty or forty people to draw after a naked figure.' Hogarth did not approve of the plan adopted by Thornhill of admitting all who required admission without payment, and he writes: ' I proposed that every member should contribute an equal sum to the establishment, and have an equal right to vote in every question relative to the society. As to electing presidents, directors, professors, etc., I considered it as a ridiculous imitation of the foolish parade of the French Academy.' He adds, writing in 1762 : ' To return to our own Academy ; by the regulations I have mentioned, of a general equality, etc., it has now subsisted near thirty years, and is, to every useful purpose, equal to that in France or any other ; but this does not satisfy.'

Hogarth disapproved of the formation of the Royal Academy (which was largely formed by the members of his own society), and ' refused to assign to the society the property which I had before lent them. I am accused of acrimony, ill-nature, and spleen, and held forth as an enemy to the arts and artists. How far their mighty project will succeed, I neither know nor care ; certain I am it deserves to be laughed at, and laughed at it has been.'

After his marriage Hogarth had to undertake work which was likely to be more profitable than what he had previously been engaged in, so he took in hand the painting of portraits and conversation pieces, but these did not pay him so well as he expected. He writes in his autobiography: ' I then married and commenced painter of small conversation pieces, from twelve to fifteen inches high. This having novelty, succeeded for a few years. But though it gave somewhat more scope to the fancy, was still but a less kind of drudgery ; and as I could not bring to act like some of my brethren and make it a sort of a manufactory, to be carried on by the help of background and drapery painters, it was not sufficiently profitable to pay the expences my family required. I therefore turned my thoughts to a still more novel mode, viz. painting and engraving modern moral subjects, a field not broken up in any country or any age.'

Joseph Mitchell, for whose opera, *The Highland Fair*, Hogarth designed a frontispiece, wrote in 1730 'A Poetical Epistle to Mr. Hogarth, an eminent historical and Conversation Painter,' in which he introduced this couplet:

'Large families obey your hand,
Assemblies rise at your command.'

These family pictures were styled respectively Conversations and Assemblies. A Conversation was a group of persons, generally of one family, and an Assembly was a still larger collection of persons; but now that the special meaning of the two words is lost there has been some confusion in the use of the terms. Thus the picture which was sold on June 3, 1905, by Messrs. Christie, amongst Lord Tweedmouth's collection, and was exhibited at the Winter Exhibition of the Royal Academy in 1906 by Mr. C. Morland Agnew, was catalogued as an Assembly at Wanstead House, although it was described on the frame as 'A Conversation.' This picture is further alluded to in Chapter III.

Most of these Conversation pieces were painted within a few years of the painter's marriage, although it has been difficult to fix the date of many of them. Samuel Ireland engraved in the *Graphic Illustrations* (1799) a 'Conversation in the Manner of Vandyck,' from a painting which he bought from Charles Catton, R.A. It was said to be painted by Hogarth to prove he could do as good work as Vandyck, a pretension which was disputed by his colleagues in the Academy of St. Martin's Lane. Ireland declares that the picture was painted about 1740. He illustrates his narrative by the well-known and amusing anecdote of John Freke, the famous surgeon.

'Hogarth one day dining with some friends, amongst whom was Cheselden, a surgeon of great eminence, was told, that it had been asserted by Mr. Freke, a surgeon, in a public company, that Dr. Greene, the musician, was as eminent and skilful a composer as Handel. On which Hogarth replied : That Freke is always shooting his bolt absurdly : Handel is a giant in music ; Greene is only a light Florimel kind of composer. True, said another of the company, but that same Freke declared you were as good a portrait-painter as Vandyck. There he was in the right, adds Hogarth, and so I am, give me my time and let me choose my subject.'

His composition of these small pictures with numerous figures taught him the great art of arranging his materials with skill—an art which he can scarcely be said to display in his illustrations of books except in the case of the plates to *Hudibras*.

He thus taught himself to become pre-eminent in the orderly arrangement of a multitude of details in his pictures, where the less important accessories are always subordinated to the main theme of the composition.

Hogarth himself admirably describes the ideas he had formed in his own mind as to the plan of composition of his great series of moral satires: ' The reasons which induced me to adopt this mode of designing were, that I thought both writers and painters had, in the historical style, totally overlooked that intermediate species of subject, which may be placed between the sublime and grotesque. I therefore wished to compose pictures on canvas, similar to representations on the stage, and farther hope, that they will be tried by the same test, and criticised by the same criterion. . . . Ocular demonstration will carry more conviction to the mind of a sensible man, than all he would find in a thousand volumes; and this has been attempted in the prints I have composed. Let the decision be left to every unprejudiced eye; let the figures in either pictures or prints, be considered as players dressed either for the sublime,—for genteel comedy, or farce,—for high or low life. I have endeavoured to treat my subjects as a dramatic writer; my picture is my stage, and men and women my players, who by means of certain actions and gestures, are to exhibit a *dumb show.*'

During the period between 1728 and 1735, which

saw his marriage and the death of his father-in-law, Hogarth did an immense amount of work, both in painting and engraving, and doubtless much of his progress in painting was due to what he learned from his association with Thornhill.

His time was chiefly employed in the production of illustrations to books, conversation pieces, the six pictures and plates of the 'Harlot's Progress' (1731-2), and such important pictures and engravings as the 'Committee of the House of Commons examining Bambridge' (1729), 'Scene in the *Indian Emperor*' (1731), 'Southwark Fair' (1733), and 'A Midnight Modern Conversation' (1733). These pictures will be considered in later chapters. 'The Rake's Progress' was undertaken in 1735, and the 'Four Times of the Day' in 1738. He had therefore already proved to the world what a great and original artist he was, although it was not until the year 1745 that he produced his masterpiece—the six pictures of the 'Marriage à la Mode.'

This was the turning-point in Hogarth's career. He had been gradually preparing himself for the position which he knew he was capable of occupying, and now the world was ready to acclaim him victor. He exhibited a rare instance of the union of the man of business with an original genius. He entirely made his own career by continued progress and experience, and by so working as to cause everything to lead to the desired end.

With the brilliant power of original conception,

but escaping the impetuosity of genius, he was willing
to work continuously in the most laborious manner
to perfect himself in whatever he undertook.
Genius has been denied to him by some, but it is
safe either to claim or deny because it is impossible
to define genius. Whatever else it may be,
originality is its very essence, and there never
lived a man with a more original mind than Hogarth.
In his own particular line the world has never seen
his equal, and probably never will.

Though success came, it was not unalloyed.
Annoyance and persecution followed the man during
the remainder of his life. The popularity of his
work caused him to become the prey of the pirates
who instantly copied and spoiled the sale of his
original engravings; for instance, Steevens tells us
that he had seen eight piratical imitations of the
'Harlot's Progress.' The earliest and best of these,
published by Bowles, contained verses on the
different scenes. Hogarth saw the advantage of
these, and added verses written by Chancellor
Hoadly to the plates of the 'Rake's Progress.'

The evils of this widespread practice of piracy
were so great that it became imperative to take
action in the matter. In concert with George
Vertue, Gerard Vandergucht, Pine, and Lambert,
besides several others, he petitioned Parliament for
leave to bring in a bill to vest in designers and
engravers an exclusive right to their own works
and to restrain the multiplying of copies without

their consent. Hogarth applied to William Huggins,
author of the oratorio of *Judith,* who drafted the
bill on the statute of Queen Anne in favour of
literary property. It was not satisfactory in
practice, and as Mr. Stephens says, 'gave, although
it did not secure, copyright to artists.' In a cause
which came before Lord Hardwicke in Chancery,
he determined that no assignee, claiming under an
assignment from the original inventor, could take
any benefit by the Act. According to Sir John
Hawkins, Hogarth lamented to him 'that he had
employed Huggins to draw the Act, adding that
when he first projected it, he hoped it would be such
an encouragement to engraving and printselling
that printsellers' would soon become as numerous
as bakers' shops, which hope, notwithstanding the
above check, does at this time seem to be pretty
nearly gratified.'

In the *London Daily Post,* June 27, 1735, there is
a special reference to the acts of the pirates.
'Certain Printsellers in London, intending not only
to injure Mr. Hogarth in his Property, but also to
impose their base imitations on the Publick, which
they being oblig'd to do only [by] what they could
carry away by memory from the sight of the
Paintings, have executed most wretchedly both in
Design and Drawing, as will be very obvious when
they are expos'd.'

The 'Rake's Progress' was printed by Boitard on
one very large sheet of paper, and came out about

a fortnight before the genuine set. Hogarth's originals were kept back until 'Hogarth's Act' (8 Geo. II. cap. 13) received the Royal Assent on May 15, 1735. His attempt to issue cheap sets in order to drive out the pirates was not successful. In spite of the faults of the new Act, Hogarth seems to have been fairly satisfied with the result as an improvement upon the previous lawless condition of things.

He wrote in his autobiography: 'After having had my plates pirated almost in all sizes, I in 1735 applied to Parliament for redress, and obtained it in so liberal a manner, as hath not only answered my own purpose, but made prints a considerable article in the commerce of this country; there being now more business of this kind done here, than in Paris, or any where else and as well. The dealers in pictures and prints found their *craft* in danger by what they called a new-fangled innovation. Their *trade* of living and getting fortunes by the ingenuity of the industrious has I know, suffered much by my interference; and if the detection of this band of public cheats, and oppressors of the rising artists, be a crime, I confess myself most guilty.'

Hogarth commemorated the passing of the Act by publishing a small print with emblematical devices entitled 'Crowns, Mitres, Maces, etc,' and the following inscription quoted from Nichols's *Biographical Anecdotes*:

D

In humble and grateful acknowledgment
of the grace and goodness of the Legislature
Manifested
In the Act of Parliament for the Encouragement
Of the Arts of Designing, Engraving, &c.
obtained
By the Endeavours, and almost at the sole Expence,
Of the Designer of this Print in the Year 1735 ;
By which
Not only the Professors of those Arts were rescued
From the Tyranny, Frauds, and Piracies
Of Monopolizing Dealers,
And legally entitled to the Fruits of their own Labours,
But Genius and Industry were also prompted
By the most noble and generous Inducements to exert themselves ;
Emulation was excited,
Ornamental Compositions were better understood ;
And every Manufacture, where Fancy has any concern,
Was gradually raised to a Pitch of Perfection before unknown,
Insomuch, that those of Great-Britain
Are at present the most Elegant
And the most in Esteem of Any in Europe.

This etching was converted into a receipt for the subscription to the Election Series, and inscribed 'Designed, Etch'd and Publish'd as the Act directs by Wm. Hogarth, March 20th, 1754.'

On a scroll is written, 'An Act for the Encouragement of the Arts of Designing, Engraving, and Etching, by vesting the Properties thereof in the Inventors and Engravers, during the time therein mentioned.' [1] About this time the engravings of Hogarth began

[1] After Hogarth's death his widow was granted (7 Geo. III. cap 38) a further exclusive term of twenty years in the property of her husband's works. Mr. Stephens remarks respecting this, 'Even "Mrs. Hogarth's Act," which became law many years after this date, did little more than declare the wishes of Parliament.'—*B M. Catalogue*, vol. iv. p. 55.

to attract crowds around the shop windows which contained them, and besides these the frequent satires on the artist were eagerly sought after.

Mr. Stephens writes of a rather later date : 'His figure was so well known that everybody recognised it in "A Stir in the City," where he appears in a crowd before the Guildhall.' [1]

It seems strange, after Hogarth had mastered the secret of success by a series of carefully considered steps, each of which led him higher on the ladder of fame, that he should for a time have turned aside to follow a style of art that was not in accord with his taste and practice. He makes in his auto-biography a sort of ' Apologia ' for doing this, although he is far too modest in the opening sentence as to the importance of the two ' Progresses' already published : 'Before I had done anything of much consequence in this walk, I entertained some hopes of succeeding in what the puffers in books call the great style of history painting ; so that without having had a stroke of this grand business before : I quitted small portraits and familiar conversations, and with a smile at my own temerity, commenced history painter, and on a great staircase at St. Bartholomew's Hospital, painted two Scripture stories, " The Pool of Bethesda," and " The Good Samaritan," with figures

---

[1] A further proof of Hogarth's popularity is to be seen in the note of publication of this print, 'Sold by John Smith at Hogarth's Head opposite Wood Street, Cheapside.'—*B.M. Catalogue,* vol III p. 911.

seven feet high. These I presented to the Charity, and thought they might serve as a specimen, to show that were there an inclination in England for encouraging historical pictures, such a first essay might prove the painting more easily attainable than is generally imagined. But as religion, the great promoter of this style in other countries, rejected it in England, I was unwilling to sink into a portrait manufacturer, and still ambitious of being singular, dropped all expectations of advantage from that source, and returned to the pursuit of my former dealings with the public at large. This I found was most likely to answer my purpose, provided I could strike the passions, and by small sums from many, by the sale of prints, which I could engrave from my own pictures, thus secure my property to myself.'

We here see that Hogarth was not altogether satisfied with the result. Although he condemns the attitude of Protestantism towards the inclusion of religious pictures in churches, he must have felt that such painting was uncongenial to him. He did, however, return to the painting of religious subjects after 1736, for in 1748 he painted 'Paul before Felix' for the Honourable Society of Lincoln's Inn ; in 1751 'Moses brought to Pharaoh's Daughter' for the Foundling Hospital, and in 1756 the altar-piece for St. Mary Redcliffe, Bristol. The latter consists of three compartments: the centre division, which is much the largest, represents the Ascension, and has not been engraved. The subject of the right compartment is 'The Sealing of the Sepulchre,' that of the left 'The Three Maries visiting the Sepulchre.' The two side pictures were engraved by Isaac Jenner.

Some further remarks will be found in subsequent chapters on the pictures at St. Bartholomew's and Foundling Hospitals and at Lincoln's Inn, but as those at Bristol have nothing to do with London life a few words respecting them may be added in this place. Hogarth received £525 for these pictures, but they have never been favourites, and by some have been unconditionally condemned. They were presented by the Vestry of St. Mary Redcliffe to the Fine Arts Academy of Clifton in 1857.

A writer in the *Critical Review* (June 1756), just after the completion of the altar-piece, remarks 'that the purchasing such a picture for their church does great honour to the opulent city for which it was painted, and is the likeliest means to raise a British School of Artists,' although he adds, 'It would be a just subject for public regret if Mr. Hogarth should abandon a branch of painting in which he stands alone, unrivalled and inimitable, to pursue another in which so many have already excelled.' Britton in his *Historical and Architectural Essay on Redcliffe Church*, 1813, says of the pictures 'they possess much merit, and may be viewed with advantage by the young artist, but in the forms and expressions of the figures, and in their attitudes and grouping, we seek in vain for propriety, dignity or elegance.' This is too severe a criticism, and the chief objection to Hogarth's religious pictures is that they are not conceived with the spirituality and the lofty aim which we expect in religious subjects, but we know Hogarth was not capable of throwing into his work. It is necessary to remember, however, that few if any painters of the eighteenth century rose to this height.

Professor Baldwin Brown in his book on Hogarth has some admirable remarks on this subject. He writes : ' The blunderers in the matter of historical painting were not Hogarth or his predecessors, but the later men of the period after Reynolds, who took themselves seriously as professed votaries of the " grand style." . . . Reynolds's own efforts in the grand style are theatrical and unreal, while Haydon and other men of genius who broke their hearts over unsuccessful efforts, were stumbling in the dark with no guidance but a noble ambition. . . . If Hogarth's work in this style is cold and uninspired, at any rate it is better than the blundering efforts of some of his successors in the school.'

Hogarth appears to have lived nearly the whole of his working life in Leicester Square and its immediate neighbourhood. Although he occasionally frequented the lowest haunts of London life for the purposes of his art, he was no Bohemian. He lived a quiet and respectable life, and kept a comfortable home for his wife and himself.

John Thomas Smith in his *Nollekens* absurdly
attacks his moral character, and sets down in his
Table of Contents the entry 'Immorality of
Hogarth.' In justification of this he writes:
'Great as Hogarth was in his display of every
variety of character, I should never think of
exhibiting a portfolio of his prints to a youthful
inquirer ; nor can I agree that the man who was so
accustomed to visit, so fond of delineating, and
who gave up so much of his time to the vices of the
most abandoned classes, was in truth a " moral
teacher of mankind." My father knew Hogarth
well, and I have often heard him declare, that he
revelled in the company of the drunken and the
profligate : Churchill, Wilkes, Hayman, etc., were
among his constant companions. Dr. John Hoadly,
though in my opinion it reflected no credit on him,
delighted in his company ; but he did not approve
of all the prints produced by him, particularly that
of the first state of " Enthusiasm Displayed " (*sic*)
which had Mr. Garrick or Dr. Johnson seen, they
could never for a moment have entertained their
high esteem of so irreligious a character.'

It is quite possible to condemn several of Hogarth's
prints without agreeing with this sweeping condemnation, which contains nothing that can justify
a charge of immorality. The character of the
friends who will be specially mentioned later on is
sufficient answer to such an unwarrantable attack.
When a boy, as we have already seen, Hogarth was

apprenticed to Ellis Gamble in Cranbourne Alley. After living for a short time with his family in Long Lane, he set up for himself in 1720, apparently at the corner of Cranbourne Alley by Little Newport Street, but we have no evidence as to how long he remained there.

After his marriage he moved about for a time; but in 1733 he had taken the house at the south-east corner of Leicester Fields, which was rebuilt a few years ago.

Here he remained for the rest of his life, with the villa at Chiswick as his country house. His widow remained in the Square after her husband's death. Taking up again the chronology of Hogarth's life, we find that after finishing his Scripture pictures at St. Bartholomew's Hospital he occupied himself with success in painting portraits. His grand portrait of Captain Coram at the Foundling Hospital was painted in 1739, that of Martin Folkes, P.R.S., in 1741, and his own portrait in the National Gallery in 1745, the year of the publication of the 'Marriage à la Mode,' his masterpiece, which was preceded in 1738 by the 'Four Times of the Day,' the most interesting of his London prints. Other great works by him which should be mentioned here are the 'March to Finchley' (1750), and the Four Pictures of an Election (1755). To these must be added the twelve prints of 'Industry and Idleness' (1747).

Comparatively early in his career, Hogarth's prints were known on the Continent; in fact he was

FRONTISPIECE TO "CATALOGUE OF PICTURES." 1761.

little over thirty years of age when his pictures were copied on fans and pottery and reproduced for the benefit of foreigners. The 'Midnight Modern Conversation' (1733) was the first English print to be re-engraved and republished abroad; and a passage in one of Walpole's Letters to Sir Horace Mann (Dec. 15, 1748), referring to 'The Gate of Calais' (1749), seems to show that the Governor and the people about him were acquainted with Hogarth's fame, and in spite of the satire enjoyed the humour of his sketches.

Hogarth went to France, and was so imprudent as to take a sketch of the drawbridge at Calais. He was seized and carried to the Governor, where he was forced to prove his vocation by producing several caricatures of the French; particularly a scene of the shore, with an immense piece of beef landing for the 'Lion d'Argent, the English inn at Calais, and several hungry friars following it. They were much diverted with his drawings, and dismissed him.' This occurrence was immediately after the Peace of Aix la Chapelle. There are three versions of the story, the first by the painter himself, another in Nichols's *Biographical Anecdotes,* and the third as above.[1] Hogarth was ready on all

[1] The original picture of Calais Gate was bought from the painter by the Earl of Charlemont. It was sold in 1874 for £945 and formed part of the Bolckow collection until May 1891, when it was bought by Messrs. Agnew for 2450 guineas It was afterwards in the collection of the Duke of Westminster, who in July 1895 presented it to the National Gallery. The picture was engraved and published in March 1749, and entitled 'O the Roast Beef of Old England, etc.'—DOBSON

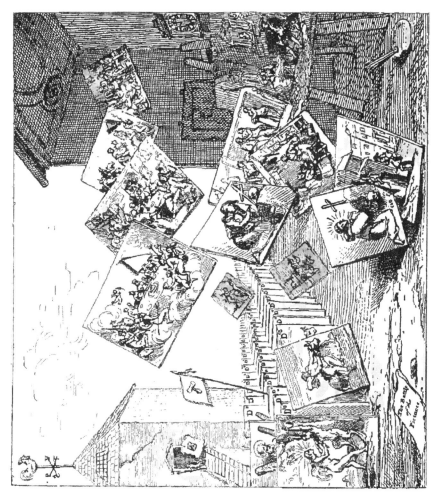

"THE BATTLE OF THE PICTURES." 1745.

Ticket for the auction of "A Rake's Progress," etc.

Hogarth was indignant with and intemperate in his language towards the connoisseurs from the time he first began to paint, and it must be allowed that he had cause. His first pictorial attack was contained in ' The Battle of the Pictures,' prepared in the beginning of the year 1745, as a ticket for the sale of his paintings which was arranged to take place at this time. Above the design is engraved : ' The bearer hereof is entitled (if he thinks proper) to be a bidder for Mr. Hogarth's pictures, which are to be sold on the last day of this month ' (February 1744-5).

It is the old battle between the Moderns and the Ancients, which fired Swift in the *Battle of the Books.* In this print there are at the left of the plate three rows or battalions of old pictures, true and false, ready to be sold, and above them there is a flag with an auctioneer's hammer displayed. The outside of the saleroom is surmounted by a vane having the four points of the compass lettered p, u, f, s. The weathercock is intended as a play upon the name of the fashionable auctioneer Cock, of the Piazza, Covent Garden. Some of the ancient pictures are flying in the air, attacking and injuring some of Hogarth's works, but the Moderns are not allowed to be beaten, and in the end the damage to each side is about equal. An old ' St. Francis ' injures the modern ' Noon,' and a copy of the antique mural painting styled ' The Aldobrandini Marriage ' makes a serious rent in one of the scenes in the tragedy of the ' Marriage à la Mode,' but

Hogarth's pictures have their opportunity and are enabled to injure some of the Black Masters.

If the English painter was mad before the sale, he must have been madder when he found what ridiculous prices his pictures fetched.

It is strange that Hogarth, who was business-like in his work, should be so thoroughly unbusiness-like in so important a matter as the selling of his pictures. He published rules and regulations respecting the biddings, which must have been singularly irritating to those who proposed to be purchasers. The biddings were to remain open from the first to the last day of February. No person was to bid on the last day, except those whose names were before entered in the book. The printed proposals conclude with this note: 'As Mr. Hogarth's room is but small, he begs the favour that no persons, except those whose names are entered in the book, will come to view his paintings on the last day of sale.'

The miserable result of the sale of nineteen of Hogarth's chief pictures under these absurd conditions was the realisation of £427, 7s. 0d.

'Harlot's Progress,' six at 14 guineas each, .	£88	4	0
'Rake's Progress,' eight at 22 guineas, . .	184	16	0
'Morning,' 20 guineas, ...	21	0	0
'Noon,' 37 guineas, . . .	38	17	0
'Evening,' 38 guineas, . . .	39	18	0
'Night,' 26 guineas, . . .	27	6	0
'Strolling Players,' 26 guineas, . . .	27	6	0
	£427	7	0

At this sale it was announced that the six pictures of the 'Marriage à la Mode' would be sold in the same manner as soon as the plates then being taken from them should be completed.

The sale was delayed until June 1751, when these masterpieces were obtained by the highest bidder for £126 or twenty guineas each, that is, a little more than the 'Harlot's Progress,' and less than the 'Rake's Progress.' As the frames, which cost the painter four guineas each, were included, the actual receipt was only sixteen guineas each. The purchaser was Mr. Lane, of Hillingdon near Uxbridge, who was the only attendant in Leicester Square on June 6 (the last day of sale), with the exception of Hogarth himself, and his friend Dr. James Parsons. It was announced that the highest written offer was £120, on which Lane offered guineas, with the expression of a desire that they should wait until the fixed hour of closure in case a purchaser willing to give more should arrive.

The painter allowed his hatred of the picture-dealer to injure the value of his property by ruling that 'no dealers in pictures were to be admitted as bidders,' thus greatly limiting the possibility of competition. Surely some of these men would have had the wisdom to prevent the sale of such precious works of art at so low a price.

Hogarth satirised the Society of Dilettanti and 'Athenian' Stuart in his print 'The Five Orders of Perriwigs as they were worn at the late Coronation,

measured Architectonically,' in 1761, which, oddly
enough, is intended to make fun of a book, the first
volume of which was not published until the following year, viz. *The Antiquities of Athens measured
and delineated* by James Stuart and Nicholas
Revett, 1762.   The explanation of this anticipation
of the book is given in the History of the Society
(1898), where in a note we read, ' It would appear
that even before the publication of the work, Stuart
had expatiated freely upon its merits and those of
the artists concerned.'

John Ireland quotes from Hogarth's MSS. the
following passage, which shows the object of his
satire : ' It requires no more skill to take the
dimensions of a pillar or cornice, than to measure a
square box, and yet the man who does the latter is
neglected, and he who accomplishes the former
is considered as a miracle of genius, but I suppose
he receives his honours for the distance he has
travelled to do his business.'   Stuart took all this
in good part, and was willing that the public should
think that he himself was pleased even with the
adverse criticism of a genius.   J. T. Smith in his
Nollekens says his parlour in his house on the
south side of Leicester Square 'was decorated
with some of Hogarth's most popular prints, and
upon a fire-screen he had pasted an impression of
the plate called the " Periwigs," a print which Mr.
Stuart always showed his visitors as Hogarth's
satire on his first volume of *Athenian Antiquities.'*

As Statues moulder into Worth _Dr. H._

To Nature and your Self appeal,
Nor learn of others, what to feel. Anon:

"TIME SMOKING A PICTURE." 1761.
Subscription Ticket for Sigismunda.

Horace Walpole, in a letter to George Montagu,
Nov. 7, 1761, referring to a copy of the ' Periwigs,'
which he sent, writes, ' The Athenian head [the
barber's block] was intended for Stuart ; but was
so like, that Hogarth was forced to cut off the nose.'
A curious satire on Hogarth's satire entitled ' A
Sett of Blocks for Hogarth's wigs,' was published in
October 1762.[1]

To return to the subject of Hogarth's warfare
against the ' Black Masters,' which about this time
became a specially deadly struggle owing to the
personal interests introduced by the malignant
criticism of his painting of ' Sigismunda,' in 1759.
He kept up the feud until his death, for the tailpiece ' Finis ' or ' The Bathos or Manner of Sinking,
in Sublime Paintings, inscribed to the Dealers in Dark
Pictures,' was his last published work (March 3, 1764).

' Time Smoking a Picture ' (1761) was the
subscription ticket for the print of ' Sigismunda,'
which did not appear until many years after
Hogarth's death.

Time as an aged man seated on a fragment of a
statue, is seen puffing smoke from his pipe against
the surface of a landscape painting on an easel

[1] Mr F G Stephens gives a very full account of this etching in the
B.M. Catalogue (vol. iv. p. 11), and quotes the Advertisement below the
design. ' In about seventeen years will be compleated in six volumes folio,
price fifteen guineas, the exact measurements of the Perriwigs of the
ancients ; taken from the Bustos and Basso Rilievos of Athens, Palmira,
Balbec and Rome ; by Modesto, Perriwig-meter from Lagado. N.B. None
will be sold but to Subscribers.' A description of ' a Sett of Blocks ' will
be found in the same catalogue (vol. iv. p 137).

before him, and near the easel is a large jar of varnish. Time's scythe is seen to have pierced the canvas, so that here are figured the various causes for the dark character of some of the pictures of the old masters that have been looked upon as giving added value to them. Mr. Stephens says of the original print, 'In order to enhance the characteristic depth of tone in the representation of the picture on which Time is operating, Hogarth mezzotinted the landscape, and etched the remainder of the work. This distinction of parts is not observable in copies from this print.'[1] This subscription ticket contains a very effective attack upon the artist's enemies, who had greatly increased in consequence of the painting of 'Sigismunda.'

The story of this picture is so well-known that any notice of it here must be brief, but as it formed one of the most important incidents in this quarrel that embittered Hogarth's later years, the case must be stated.

We have Hogarth's own narrative of the origin of the painting of 'Sigismunda weeping over the heart of her murdered lover Guiscardo,' from Dryden's version of Boccaccio's story. Sir Richard Grosvenor urged Hogarth to paint him a picture, which was undertaken with reluctance, although the choice of a subject was left to the artist. Having been disgusted at the high prices paid for the old masters at Sir Luke Schaub's sale, and especially at

[1] *B.M. Catalogue*, vol. iv. p. 43.

£400 being realised for a picture of 'Sigismunda' attributed to Correggio, but believed to be by Furini, Hogarth chose the same subject and at once put himself in competition with the Italian in order to prove that he could paint a better picture. While it was being painted the patron expressed himself pleased with it, but subsequently he changed his mind in consequence of adverse criticism which was aroused by the enemies of Hogarth, who himself expressed himself strongly on the subject. He wrote: 'As the most violent and virulent abuse thrown on " Sigismunda " was from a set of miscreants, with whom I am proud of having been ever at war, I mean the expounders of the mysteries of old pictures; I have been sometimes told they were beneath my notice. This is true of them individually, but as they have access to people of rank, who seem as happy in being cheated, as these merchants are in cheating them, they have a power of doing much mischief to a modern artist.'

The correspondence between Grosvenor and Hogarth has been printed in the third volume of John Ireland's *Hogarth Illustrated*, and it does not do much credit to Sir Richard Grosvenor's courtesy or good taste. Hogarth fixed the price of the picture at £400, for which sum the old picture sold, but he gave Sir Richard the option of refusing it. He only asked him to make up his mind, as Hoare the banker wanted a picture painted. In answer Sir Richard did not give his real reason for being

disappointed with the picture, but wrote: 'If he
[Mr. Hoare] should have taken a fancy to the
" Sigismunda," I have no sort of objection to your
letting him have it; for I really think the performance so striking and inimitable, that the
constantly having it before one's eyes would be too
often occasioning melancholy ideas to arise in one's
mind, which a curtain's being drawn before it would
not diminish in the least.'

This letter was not likely to give much satisfaction to Hogarth, and he settled the matter as
soon as he could by giving the picture to his wife and
desiring her not to sell it for less than £500.   What
hurt the painter in this most unfortunate affair was
the disgusting manner in which his enemies described 'Sigismunda' as a representation of a vile
woman, although they knew well enough that the
figure was taken from his beloved wife.   But if
Wilkes and Churchill mixed abuse of the picture with
their attack upon the painter on political grounds,
Robert Lloyd, their friend and his, wrote:

> ' While Sigismunda's deep distress,
> Which looks the soul of wretchedness,
> When I [*i.e.* Time], with slow and soft'ning pen,
> Have gone o'er all the tints agen,
> Shall urge a bold and proper claim
> To level half the ancient fame;
> While future ages yet unknown
> With critic air shall proudly own
> Thy Hogarth first of every clime,
> For humour keen, or strong sublime,
> And hail him from his fire and spirit,
> The Child of Genius and of Merit.'

Walpole, who chose to praise the older painting in extravagant terms and in contrast to abuse Hogarth's picture most unjustly, adopted the same image respecting the strange woman in an exaggerated form. We have the privilege of seeing the picture in the National Gallery and knowing how ludicrously untrue Walpole's criticism is: 'Hogarth's performance was more ridiculous than anything he had ever ridiculed.' Hogarth wishing to vindicate his fame by the production of a good engraving of the picture, engaged Ravenet to undertake the work, but afterwards it appeared that Ravenet was under articles not to work for any one except Mr. Boydell for three years then to come, so the subscription was stopped and the money returned to the subscribers.'[1] The following notice (dated January 2, 1764) was issued: 'All efforts to this time to get the picture finely engraved proving in vain, Mr. Hogarth humbly hopes his best endeavours to engrave it himself will be acceptable to his friends.'

Under the painter's direction, a drawing in oil was made by Edward Edwards, A.R.A., and from this, Basire made an outline; but it was not until 1793 that Dunkarton's mezzotint was published. In 1795 appeared Benjamin Smith's engraving.

The vicissitudes of the picture itself are interesting. Mrs. Hogarth kept it during her lifetime as her

[1] In a MS. volume in the British Museum (Add. MSS. 22,394), there is a list of subscribers' names to a Print of Sigismunda and Guiscardo, March 2, 1761. Most of the names are struck through with the note 'money returned.' In one or two cases there is a note 'money refused'

husband wished, and at the sale of her effects (1790) it was bought by Alderman Boydell for £58, 16s. It was sold again in 1807 for £420, and was bequeathed to the National Gallery in 1879 by Mr. James Hughes Anderdon.

In 1762 Bonnel Thornton opened an Exhibition of Sign Paintings at 'the large Room the Upper End of Bow Street, Covent Garden, nearly opposite the Playhouse Passage,' in which Hogarth took some interest. This was a freak and a joke on the part of Thornton, but as it gave an opportunity for a gibe at the buyers of old pictures, Hogarth entered into the joke with deadly earnest intention. John Nichols (*Biographical Anecdotes*) was informed that Hogarth 'contributed no otherwise towards this display, than by a few touches of chalk. Among the heads of distinguished personages finding those of the King of Prussia and the Empress of Hungary, he changed the cast of their eyes so as to make them leer significantly at each other. This is related on the authority of Mr. Colman.'[1]

The catalogue of the Exhibition presents many evidences of Hogarth's hand both in the notes and various satirical touches such as 'Portrait of a justly celebrated Painter, though an Englishman

[1] These two portraits are numbered in the Catalogue 53 and 54, but Nichols is not accurate in the description, which stands thus in the Catalogue—'53, an Original Portrait of the present Emperor of Russia. 54, Ditto of the Empress Queen of Hungary. Its antagonist Drawn by Sheerman' Colman was a good authority for the information, as he was an intimate friend of Bonnel Thornton.

and a Modern,' or this note, ' N.B. that the merit
of the Modern Masters may be fairly examined into,
it has been thought proper to place some admired
works of the most eminent old masters in this room,
and along the Passage thro' the Yard.' Several
of the paintings are stated to be by Hagarty.

In the *St. James's Chronicle* for Tuesday, 23rd of
March 1762, there was published a notice of the
forthcoming exhibition :—' The Society of Sign-
painters are preparing a most magnificent Collection
of Portraits, Landscapes, Fancy Pieces, Flower
Pieces, History Pieces, Night Pieces, Sea Pieces,
Sculpture Pieces, etc. etc., designed by the ablest
Masters and executed by the best Hands in these
kingdoms. The Virtuosi will have a new opportunity of displaying their taste on this occasion by
discovering the different stile of the several masters
employed and pointing out by what hand each
piece is drawn. A remarkable cognoscente who
has attended at the Society's great Room with his
glass for several mornings, has already piqued himself on discovering the famous Painter of the Rising
Sun, a modern Claude Lorraine, in an elegant
Night-piece of the Man-in-the-Moon. He is also
convinced that no other than the famous artists
who drew the Red Lion at Brentford, can be
equal to the bold figures in the London 'Prentice,
and that the exquisite colouring in the piece called
Pyramus and Thisbe must be by the same hand
as the Hole-in-the-Wall.'

The public seem to have supposed that the whole announcement was merely intended as a hoax, but this soon proved to be a mistake by the opening of the exhibition in April. The hours of admission were from nine till four. The price of the tickets, which included a catalogue, was one shilling. It is said that the names of the sign-board painters given in the catalogue were those of the journeymen in Baldwin's printing office where it was printed.

The exhibition naturally created a sensation, and the newspapers of the day were full of correspondence respecting this very original show. Churchill refers to it in his poem of *The Ghost* (Book iii.):

> 'Of sign-post exhibitions, raised
> For laughter more than to be praised,
> (Though by the way we cannot see
> Why praise and laughter mayn't agree)
> Where genuine humour runs to waste,
> And justly chides our want of taste,
> Censured, like other things, though good,
> Because they are not understood.'

The exhibition was an admirable subject for the pictorial satirists, and the chief of the prints of the time alluding to it was 'A Brush for the Sign-Painters. *Iustitia Rubweel Inv. et del. Aquafortis Sculp. Price 6d.*,' which was published in April. In these satires Hogarth and his works occupy prominent positions. Advantage is taken of several of the items in the catalogue which bear some allusion to Hogarth.[1]

[1] See *British Museum Catalogue*, vol. IV pp. 48-50.

It is unfortunate that we know so little as to Hogarth's connection with this exhibition. As has already been pointed out, his hand is to be suspected in many of the descriptions in the catalogue, but at the same time he allowed many allusions to himself to appear, which were eagerly taken up by the critics; thus No. 2 is ' A crooked Billet formed exactly in the Line of Beauty,' and No. 5 ' The Light Heart. A Sign for a Vintner. By Hagarty. [N.B. This is an elegant Invention of Ben Jonson, who in *The New Inn or Light Heart*, makes the landlord say, speaking of his Sign :

> An Heart weighed with a feather, and outweighed too ;
> A Brain—child of my one and I am proud on 't.']

This is alluded to in ' A Brush for the Sign-Painters,' where there is a signboard on an easel showing a caricature of Sigismunda bearing the inscription ' The sign of a Heavy Heart.' Below the figure is a caricature of the ' Line of Beauty,' designated ' A Lame Principle.'

In the King's Library at the British Museum is a small pamphlet strangely printed as follows, to form a sort of companion to the exhibition :

First Leaf.

Gentlemen and Ladies | are desired | to tear off this Leaf, | which | will serve as a Ticket to introduce | them to the | London | Printed for W Nichol at the Paper-Mill, in | St Paul's Churchyard | MDCCLXII |

Second Leaf.

Ha! Ha! Ha! | and | in due Time | they | will gain admission to the |

Third Leaf.

He! He! He!

Pages 7-24 a succession of short paragraphs plentifully supplied with dashes.

It is impossible not to charge Hogarth with inconsistency in his action connected with the training of artists, because although he did great things by means of his school in St. Martin's Lane, yet he set himself in opposition to the natural outcome of his own work in the establishment of an ' Academy for the Better Cultivation, Improvement and Encouragement of Painting, Sculpture, Architecture, and the Arts of Design in General.' His opposition to this scheme set many of his fellow-artists against him, and of these enemies Thomas and Paul Sandby were prominent.

Hogarth's reasons for his opposition in this matter are set out by himself in manuscripts which were printed by John Ireland in the third volume of *Hogarth Illustrated.*

He further stated that ' Many of the objections which I have to the institution of this Royal Academy, apply with equal force to the project of the Society for the encouragement of Arts, Manufactures, and Commerce, distributing premiums for drawings and pictures ; subjects of which they are totally ignorant, and in which they can do no possible service to the community.'

Hogarth had been a member of the Society, and chairman of one of the committees ; therefore at one time he had approved generally of its action, but subsequently he changed his mind, and parodied the inscription of 'Arts Promoted.' He was quite consistent, for he had early satirised the Dilettanti Society. It would be improper to leave this instance of Hogarth's individualism without notice, but this is not the place to discuss it fully.

By entering fully into Hogarth's quarrel with the advocates of the Black Masters, we have passed over the period of the publication of the *Analysis of Beauty*, in 1753, which first caused his enemies to swarm around him and satirise him on his own ground.

It is now therefore time to turn back a few years, and to point out briefly the position that this remarkable book occupies in the author's life. Wilkes chooses in his vindictive remarks to refer to the *Analysis* as attributed to Hogarth; such a sneer is, as he must have known, perfectly groundless. Men of learning such as Townley and Morell gave what literary help to the author he required for the production of his book, not that he himself was without considerable ability in expressing in suitable terms the view he wished to present to his readers. Hogarth had long thought over the central idea and drawn the line of beauty in his own portrait (1745), thus appropriating the symbol to himself.

The idea was elaborated in his own mind and grew out of the teaching of the ancient philosophers.

This is seen from a passage in the book itself, quoted by Mr. Dobson, where Hogarth gives his version of a story from Pliny: 'Apelles having heard of the fame of Protogenes went to Rhodes to pay him a visit, but not finding him at home asked for a board, on which he drew a *line*, telling the servant-maid, that line would signify to her master who had been to see him; we are not clearly told what sort of a line it was that could so particularly signify one of the first of his profession: if it was only a stroke (tho' as fine as a hair as Pliny seems to think), it could not possibly, by any means, denote the abilities of a great painter. But if we suppose it to be a line of some extraordinary quality, such as the serpentine line will appear to be, Apelles could not have left a more satisfactory signature of the compliment he had paid him. Protogenes when he came home took the hint, and drew a finer, or rather more expressive line, within it to show Apelles when he came again, that he understood his meaning. He soon returning was well pleased with the answer Protogenes had left for him, by which he was convinced that fame had done him justice, and so correcting the line again, perhaps by making it more precisely elegant, he took his leave. The story thus may be reconcil'd to common sense, which, as it has been generally receiv'd could never be understood as a ridiculous tale.' Matthew Prior versified this tale, from which the following lines are taken:

' Piqued by Protogenes's fame
From Co to Rhodes Apelles came
To see a rival and a friend,
Prepar'd to censure or commend

. . . .

Does squire Protogenes live here?
Yes, sir, says she, with gracious air,
And court'sy low, but just call'd out
By lords peculiarly devout.

. . . .

And sir, at present would you please,
To leave your name?   Fair maiden, yes,
Reach me that board.   No sooner spoke
But done.   With one judicious stroke,
On the plain ground Apelles drew
A circle regularly true.

. . .

Again at six Apelles came,
Found the same prating civil dame,
Sir, that my master has been here,
Will by the board itself appear
If from the perfect line he found
He has presum'd to swell the round,
Or colours on the draught to lay,
'Tis thus (he order'd me to say)
Thus write the painters of this isle :
Let those of Co remark the style.'

Horace Walpole related the same story in *Ædes Walpolianæ*, and made the line a straight one.

John Ireland printed the following anagram containing an amusing prediction which he found among Hogarth's papers in the handwriting of his friend Townley :—' From an old Greek fragment. There was an ancient oracle delivered at Delphos, which says, " That the source of beauty should never be again rightly discovered, till a person should arise, whose name was perfectly included in the name of Pythagoras ; which person should again restore the ancient principle upon which all beauty is founded.

| Πυθάγορας, | | | | PYTHAGORAS |
| "Ογαρθ, | . | . | . | HOGARTH.'[1] |

The Analysis of Beauty was no ordinary book, although it may have outlived any utility it once possessed, and it attracted no ordinary attention. A work which was translated into German, Italian and French,[2] and was praised by such men as Burke, Lessing and Goethe, must be treated as something out of the common run. Doubtless Hogarth was possessed of a brilliant idea and saw its boundless possibilities, but he had not the philosophic grasp of mind to save him from confusion in the presentment of his case.

Burke's *Essay on the Sublime and Beautiful* was first published in 1756, three years after the publication of the *Analysis*, but it contains no allusion to the book. In the second edition, published in 1757, Burke mentions Hogarth's work with approval.

The German translation contained a preface by Lessing, and the book was enthusiastically welcomed by him in the *Vossische Zeitung* in 1754. Mr. Bosanquet says that in his preface the great German

---

[1] *Hogarth Illustrated,* vol. iii p. 146
[2] *German* Zergliederung der Schoenheit, die schwankenden Begriffe von dem Geschmack festzusetzen, von C Mylius. Berlin, 1754. *Italian :* L'Analisi della Bellezza, con figure. Livorno, 1761. *French :* Analyse de la Beauté de Guillaume Hogarth. Paris an XIII (1805).

authority ' lays his finger on the point of difficulty in its conception, viz. the question of determining on general grounds, the degree and kind of curvature that constitutes beauty of line.' The same writer further remarks that 'Hogarth's undulating line supplied Goethe with a name for the tendency which he ranks as the polar opposite of the characteristic.' [1]

The French translation, which was made by Henri Jansen, librarian to Talleyrand, contains also a translation of Nichols's *Biographical Anecdotes,* and was published in two volumes. It will be seen that Hogarth had done a considerable thing, but unfortunately he had made many enemies, and these men, waiting for the opportunity to attack, chose the subject of this book as the battle-ground for which they had long sought. The author, however, preferred censure to neglect, and cared little for attacks so long as these did not touch his private life.

His friends stood by him and lauded his discovery. Laurence Sterne was one of these, who highly praised the *Analysis* in the second volume of *Tristram Shandy,* and Bishop Warburton expressed his opinions in a letter to the author thus : ' I was pleased to find from the public papers that you have determined to give us your original and masterly thoughts on the great principles of your profession. You owe this to your country, for you

---

[1] *History of the Æsthetic,* 1892, pp. 207-208.

are both an honour to your profession, and a shame to that worthless crew professing virtu and connoisseurship, to whom all that grovel in the splendid poverty of wealth and taste are the miserable bubbles.'

Hogarth's enemies—both literary and artistic critics—forgot their manners and good sense. Benjamin West's opinion of the book is therefore worth something. He said in answer to J. T. Smith's question as to his opinion of the *Analysis*— 'It is a work, my man, of the highest value to every one studying the Art. Hogarth was a strutting, consequential little man, and made himself many enemies by that book ; but now that most of them are dead, it is examined by disinterested readers, unbiassed by personal animosities, and will be yet more and more read, studied, and understood.'

A satirist must expect to be satirised, but Hogarth was more bitterly attacked than he deserved to be because, although he was very severe in his satire, he was never personal except under severe provocation, as in the quarrel with Wilkes and Churchill.

The pictorial satires are fully dealt with by F. G. Stephens in the British Museum Catalogue. Some of these satires were contemptible and produced by unknown men, but it is specially painful to find so distinguished a man as Paul Sandby attacking in so violent and unkind a manner his brother artist.

'Burlesque sur le Burlesque,' published December

1, 1753, is full of violent ridicule of Hogarth's work and represents various insulting ways of disposing of the *Analysis of Beauty*. 'Pugg's Graces etched from his original Daubing' contains an infinity of abuse, an item of which is an open book inscribed 'No Salary, Reasons against a Publick Academy,' 1753, and 'Reasons to prove erecting a Publick Academy without [space] a wicked Design to introduce Popery and Slavery in to this Kingdom.' Beneath a figure of a decrepit old man whose person is curved to ridicule Hogarth's 'line' is this scurrilous inscription :

'Behold a wretch who Nature form'd in spight,
    Scorn'd by the Wise ; he gave the Fools delight,
    Yet not contented in his Sphere to move
    Beyond mere Instinct, and his Senses drove
    From false examples hop'd to pilfer fame
    And scribl'd nonsense in his daubing name
    Deformity her self his figures place,
    She spreads an Uglines on every face,
    He then admires their ellegance and grace,
    Dunce Connoisseurs extol the author Pugg,
    The senseless, tasteless, impudent Hum Bugg.'

Another of Sandby's discreditable productions is 'The Author run mad,' an etching showing Hogarth in a lunatic asylum, clad in a fantastic dress, wearing a crown of straw, and holding an ink-bottle as a crown stuck on his head, one of his legs being bound with straw, his palette hanging round his neck, his mahlstick being curved to resemble the 'Line of Beauty.'[1]   Among the multiplicity of references

[1] Mr. Stephens's description in the *British Museum Catalogue of Satires*, vol. iii. p. 894.

to the painter in this plate there is a special attack
on his paintings of religious subjects with this
epigram :

'Shou'd we thy Study'd Labours trace
In search of Beauty—Air or Grace
   Are they to us ye Rule ?
Has Phara's daughter got them all ?
Are they in Felix seen ? or Paul
   or at Bethesda's pool ? '

It is not necessary to describe the whole series of
these deplorable exhibitions of rancour which are fully
analysed in Mr. Stephens's British Museum Catalogue,
but astonishment must be expressed that an artist
so capable of appreciating the beauty of the ' March
to Finchley ' could caricature that picture as ' The
Painter's March from Finchly,' or throw mud upon
a man he knew to be an honour to English art,
and style him a ' Mountebank Painter,' and
inscribe on his print such lying words as these :
' This arrogant Quacking Analist who blinded by
the darkest ignorance of ye principles of painting,
has spoke so foolishly of the works of ye greatest
masters—is hereby challeng'd to produce one piece
of his either in painting or on Copper plate, that
has ye least grace, beauty or so much knowledge
in Proportion as may be found in common signs in
every street—O Will thy impudence is the certain
consequence of thy ignorance.'

Hogarth was not without friends to support him
against these attacks by satirising his opponents,
but he himself did not retaliate, for he was too proud

to descend to such methods. We have, however, the good fortune to be able to read in his autobiography his own admirable expression of the natural disgust he felt at the unworthy treatment he had received. He wrote:

'I have been assailed by every profligate scribbler in town, and told, that though words are man's province, they are not my province; and that though I have put my name to the *Analysis of Beauty*, yet (as I acknowledge having received some assistance from two or three friends) I am only the *supposed* author. By those of my own profession I am treated with still more severity. Pestered with caricature drawings, and hung up in effigy in prints; accused of vanity, ignorance and envy; called a mean and contemptible dauber; represented in the strangest employments and pictured in the strangest shapes; sometimes under the hieroglyphical semblance of a satyr, and at others, under the still more ingenious one, of an ass.

'Not satisfied with this; finding that they could not overturn my system, they endeavoured to wound the peace of my family. This was a cruelty hardly to be forgiven; to say that such malicious attacks, and caricatures, did not discompose me, would be untrue; for to be held up to public ridicule would discompose any man; but I must at the same time add, that they did not much distress me. I *knew* that those who venture to oppose received opinions, must in return have

F

public abuse: so that feeling I had no right to exemption from the common tribute, and conscious that my book had been generally well received, I consoled myself with the trite observation, that every success or advantage in this world must be attended by some sort of a reverse; and that though the worst writers and the worst painters have traduced me; by the best I have had more than justice done me. The partiality with which the world have received my works, and the patronage and friendship with which some of the best characters in it have honoured the author, ought to excite my warmest gratitude, and demands my best thanks; it enables me to despise this cloud of insects; for happily, though their buzzing may tease, their stings are not mortal.'

In 1753, the date of the publication of the *Analysis of Beauty*, most of Hogarth's great works had been produced, although he had still to paint his fine series of four pictures of the 'Election' (1755), and the 'Lady's Last Stake' (1759), so that his maligners had no excuse in respect to any incompleteness in the brilliant harvest of the greater portion of his life. Mr. William Sandby, in his account of Thomas and Paul Sandby (1892), makes the best of Paul Sandby's libels and praises them highly, but in spite of artistic design they form a pitiable instance of unjust defamation of a great man.

It is said that Hogarth proposed to draw up a

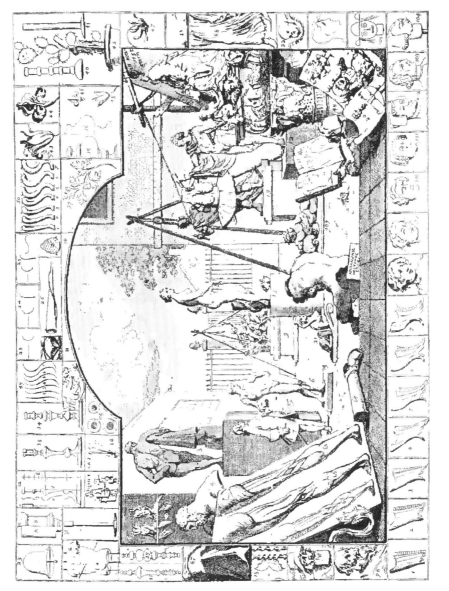

A STATUARY'S YARD. (THE ANALYSIS OF BEAUTY, PLATE I.) 1753.

succinct history of the Arts in his own time, as a
sort of supplement to the *Analysis*: some notes for
this were printed by John Ireland in his *Hogarth
Illustrated* (vol. iii.) in connection with dispersed
portions of autobiography, but nothing continuous
has survived, and nothing to prove the intention of
publication except the well-known 'No Dedication,'
of which a facsimile will be found in John Ireland's
Hogarth Illustrated, 1798 (vol. iii.). The manuscript
(which is in the Morrison Collection of Autographs)
was lent to the Guelph Exhibition (1891) by the
late Mr. Alfred Morrison :

'The No-Dedication ; not dedicated to any Prince
in Christendom, for fear it might be thought an
idle piece of arrogance ; not dedicated to any man
of quality, for fear it might be thought too assuming ;
not dedicated to any learned body of men, as
either of the Universityes or the Royal Society, for
fear it might be thought an uncommon piece of
vanity, nor dedicated to any one particular friend,
for fear of offending another ; therefore dedicated to
nobody ; but if for once we may suppose nobody
to be everybody, as everybody is often said to be
nobody, then is this work dedicated to everybody,—
'By their most humble and devoted
'W. HOGARTH.'

The year 1762 is an ominous date in the life of
Hogarth, for in that year he made the grievous
mistake of producing a political print entitled

'The Times, Plate 1,' in which Lords Chatham and Temple were satirised and ridiculed, and thus he made dangerous enemies of two former friends— Wilkes and Churchill.

Hogarth was no politician and had not previously interfered in politics, of which he knew little or nothing. Mr. Stephens seems to think he shows definite opinions in the pictures of the Election, but there is every reason to believe that he chose the characters he thought the most effective, without any bias from his own opinions. One would have expected sufficient patriotism in Hogarth to save him from treating Pitt's thoroughly deserved pension as discreditable to the great statesman, but it may be that he was one of those who yearned for peace after 'expensive' wars. We need take no account of the turbulent Temple, although he was greatly admired by Wilkes and Churchill.

It may be supposed that Bute was ready to pay liberally for the support of Hogarth, which he so much required, but it is quite incorrect to say that he received a pension. He had received the appointment of Serjeant Painter to the King in succession to his brother in-law, John Thornhill.

The following lines 'To the Author of the Times' are quoted in John Ireland's *Hogarth Illustrated* (vol. iii. p. 216):

> 'Why, Billy, in the vale of life,
> Show so much rancour, spleen and strife?
> Why, Billy, at a statesman's whistle,
> Drag dirty loads, and feed on thistle?

PORTRAIT OF JOHN THORNHILL. (BROTHER-IN-LAW OF HOGARTH.)

Did any of the long-ear'd tribe
E'er swallow half so mean a bribe ?
Pray, have you no sinister end,
Thus to abuse the nation's friend ?
His country's and his monarch's glory.'

In his autobiography Hogarth catalogued under four headings the chief causes of complaint against him : the first three are too absurd for words and require no refutation from the painter, although he condescends to answer them. He writes : ' The chief things that have brought much obloquy on me are, first, the attempting portrait painting. Secondly, writing the *Analysis of Beauty*. Thirdly, painting the picture of Sigismunda ; and fourthly, publishing the first print of the Times.'

Of the last count in the indictment he says : ' The anxiety that attends endeavouring to recollect ideas long dormant, and the misfortunes which clung to this transaction, coming at a time when nature demands quiet, and something besides exercise to cheer it, added to my long sedentary life, brought on an illness which continued twelve months. But when I got well enough to ride on horseback I soon recovered. This being at a period when war abroad and contention at home engrossed every one's mind, prints were thrown into the back-ground ; and the stagnation rendered it necessary that I should do some *timed thing*, to recover my lost time, and stop a gap in my income. This drew forth my print of "The Times," a subject which tended to the restoration of peace and unanimity, and put the opposers of these humane objects in a light, which gave great offence to those who were trying to foment destruction in the minds of the populace. One of the most notorious among them, till now rather my friend and flatterer, attacked me in a *North Briton,* in so infamous and malign a style, that he himself when pushed even by his best friends, was driven to so poor an excuse as to say he was drunk when he wrote it. Being at that time very weak, and in a kind of slow fever, it could not but seize on a feeling mind. My philosophical friends advise me to laugh at the nonsense of party-writing—who would mind it ? —but I cannot rest myself :

> " Who steals my purse, steals trash ; 'tis something, nothing ;
> 'Twas mine, 'tis his, and has been slave to thousands :
> But he that filches my good name,
> Robs me of that which not enriches him,
> And makes me poor indeed."

Such being my feelings, my great object was to return the compliment, and turn it to some advantage.'

Paul Sandby and others renewed their caricatures of Hogarth on account of 'The Times, No. 1,' but these the artist could treat with contempt. It was the virulent defamation of his moral character, contained in No. 17 of the *North Briton* by Wilkes, which embittered his last days. He could neither forget nor forgive the references to his wife or such passages as this : ' The public never had the least share of his regard, or even good will. Gain and vanity have steered his little light bark quite through life. He has never been consistent but to those two principles.'

Mrs. Hogarth gave Samuel Ireland a worn copy of this number, which had been purchased by her husband and carried in his pocket many days to show his friends.

We cannot but regret that the print of ' The Times, Plate 1,' was ever published, as it has no particular merits and the consequences of its appearance were disastrous. We can understand the disgust of Wilkes and Churchill at the position taken by Hogarth, but nothing can excuse their rancorous writings. The passage above from the auto-biography is of the greatest interest as expressing Hogarth's feelings of the necessity of peace, and we have such confidence in his inherent truthfulness that we do not doubt that his words describe correctly his own feelings. Possibly many of the public held similar opinions.[1]

Mr. Saunders Welch, who appreciated the delicacy of Hogarth's feelings, tried to persuade him not to publish his satirical print against Wilkes and Churchill (' The Times '). He observed ' that the mind that had been accustomed for a length of years to receive only merited and uniform applause, would be ill calculated to bear a reverse from the bitter sarcasms of adversaries whose wit and genius

---

[1] This subject is more fully discussed in Chapter v. on Political Life.

would enable them to retort with severity such an attack.'

Hogarth took his revenge when he drew the sinister portrait of Wilkes and the caricature of Churchill, which have added to the artistic wealth of the world, and proved that his powers of satire continued to be as great and brilliant as they had ever been, but nevertheless the contemplation of this enmity makes an unhappy ending to the story of Hogarth's life.

There is little to record of work done after these wonderful portraits, which gibbeted these men for all time. The artist was indeed revenged for the libels of the authors.

Hogarth was broken down although he still worked, and the end came suddenly on October 25, 1764. He was conveyed in a weak condition from Chiswick to London, and soon after going to bed in his house in Leicester Square, he died in the arms of Mrs. Mary Lewis, who was called up to attend to him. The cause of death was the bursting of an aneurism. The last thing he did was to write a rough draft of an answer to an agreeable letter received from Benjamin Franklin.

The house in Leicester Square has been rebuilt, and his residence can no longer be seen except in engravings, but the Chiswick house, thanks to Lieut.-Colonel Shipway, who bought it in 1902, and as Mr. Dobson says, preserved it to the nation,[1]

[1] It has now been definitely transferred to the Middlesex County Council (*Evening Standard*, April 29, 1909).

can be visited as a museum sacred to the memory
of Hogarth.   Not far off is the pleasant churchyard,
with its important-looking monument, upon which
can still be read Garrick's epitaph :

'Farewel, great painter of mankind,
    Who reach'd the noblest point of Art,
Whose pictur'd morals charm the mind,
    And through the eye correct the heart

If genius fire thee, reader, stay ;
    If Nature touch thee, drop a tear ;
If neither move thee, turn away,
    For HOGARTH'S honour'd dust lies here '

Garrick submitted his first draft of the epitaph
to Johnson, and the latter rather severely criticised
it in a letter to the former, dated December 12, 1771.
He considered 'pictured morals' a beautiful expression which he wished retained, but he praised
little else.   It will be seen from the following
emendation by Johnson that Garrick availed himself of the valued suggestion :

'The Hand of Art here torpid lies
    That traced the essential form of Grace ;
Here Death has closed the curious eyes
    That saw the manners in the face.

If Genius warm thee, Reader, stay,
    If Merit touch thee, shed a tear ;
Be Vice and Dulness far away !
    Great Hogarth's honour'd dust is here.'

Dr. Townley wrote a laudatory inscription to
Hogarth's memory which was printed in the *Public
Ledger* of November 19, 1764, and will be found in
John Ireland's *Hogarth Illustrated* (vol. iii.).

In closing this chapter we may record his chief characteristics. Rough and unpolished, he had a kindly heart; honest and truthful, he did his duty through life. He was considerate to his friends and thoroughly companionable, full of talk on subjects interesting to him, although, when Horace Walpole asked him to meet Gray at dinner, the dilettante found the two men equally silent and unsympathetic.

He was light-hearted, and equal to playing the fool when with congenial spirits, as he did when on that memorable Frolic on the Thames and Medway in May 1732, in the company of John Thornhill, Samuel Scott, painter, William Tothall, draper, and Ebenezer Forrest, attorney.

To his enemies he was ever on his guard, as he was thoroughly convinced that they were malignant, and therefore dangerous. No doubt he had a good opinion of himself, but he had reason for this opinion. This, and a consequential air, are forgivable sins where there are ever present virtues to counterbalance them, as was certainly the case in respect to Hogarth.

We know that the charge made by some of his enemies that he was filled with greed for money was ridiculously untrue. He was the most industrious of men, and his main object was to make a comfortable home for his wife and himself, and there is no evidence that he lived extravagantly, although he was generous.

Hogarth pinx.   *Ryder sc.*

Mrs *HOGARTH.*

Pub.^d for S.Ireland June 7, 1797.

PORTRAIT OF MRS. HOGARTH.

He made his chief income from the sale of his prints, the sale of some of which was considerable, but here he was robbed on all sides by piratical printsellers. He made but little out of his splendid paintings, partly because the market price of English pictures was not high, but partly on account of his adopting an ill-judged mode of selling them, as we have already seen.

He was able to leave Mrs. Hogarth little but the stock of his plates and engravings, and, living as she did twenty-five years after her husband, she became straitened in her means, so that she was glad to accept a pension of £40 from the Royal Academy.

CHAPTER III

HIGH LIFE

THE popular idea of Hogarth's genius is probably that he possessed little understanding of High Life, and that the study of Low Life was his forte. There is some truth in this, because he delighted to paint strong exhibitions of character which are more commonly to be found among classes who do not hide their feelings. Although it may be said that the incidents of low life are the chief objects of his pencil, it is equally true that he took all human nature under his charge, and when he did paint scenes of high life, he showed himself equally at home as in those of low life. Nothing finer than some of the episodes in the 'Marriage à la Mode' has ever been produced, and in the first picture the figure of the Earl is superb in his haughty grandeur. In the 'Rake's Progress' we see the man's attempt to shine in so-called good society, but perhaps at no time in our history were a large portion of the upper classes so essentially vulgar as in the eighteenth century.

Although we are delighted with the vivid pictures

in the pages of Horace Walpole of those who moved
ın the highest circles of society, we are not able
to say that we are edified. Walpole himself was
fastidious, but his records of the proceedings of his
friends prove that theır doings must be largely
condemned as being as low in taste as in morals.
There is plenty of evidence of exclusiveness, but
little of refinement.

The fashionable parts of town are shown in many
of Hogarth's pictures, as St. James's Street in the
fourth plate of the 'Rake's Progress,' Lord
Burlington's house in Piccadilly in the 'Taste of
the Town' and in the 'Man of Taste,' and in St.
James's Park—Rosamond's Pond, Spencer House,
and the Treasury are all pictured by him.

The Park continued to be the resort of Fashion
in the eighteenth, as it had been in the seventeenth
century. It was thronged before dinner between
twelve and two, and from seven till midnight in
the summer. On Sundays the Park was crowded
by another class, who were busy on week-days.
'Taste in High Life' is pure caricature, but in the
'Lady's Last Stake' we find an elegant West End
interior quite perfect in its design, with a terrible
story told in a strong but reticent manner. It
exhibits as fine an instance of harmony as any
picture ever painted by Hogarth. Everything is
in keeping, and nothing is exaggerated. Well might
Horace Walpole write: 'The very furniture of
his rooms describe the characters of the persons to

whom they belong : a lesson that might be of use to comic authors.' [1]

In his Portraits and Conversation Pieces, Hogarth exhibited High Life from the King (George II.) and his family downwards. Many of these require some special notice.

It was in the painting of these that he attained that dexterity of treatment and brilliancy of composition, which stood him in good stead in his more original work. We can therefore trace in these pictures the growth of the painter's art; but this could not have been done before the days of exhibitions, as the pictures passed into the hands of those for whom they were painted. We have to bear this in mind when we feel surprise at the neglect of the public for Hogarth's eminent powers as a painter. All knew the engravings and admired them, but few were acquainted with the pictures.

The best known of these Conversations is that styled indifferently the 'Wanstead Assembly,' or 'A Conversation at Wanstead House.' This, belonging to Lord Tweedmouth, was sold by auction by Messrs. Christie on June 3, 1905, when it was bought by Messrs. Agnew for 2750 guineas. The picture is thus described in the catalogue :

'An Assembly at Wanstead House. Containing portraits of Richard Child, first Earl of Tylney, and many of his friends and relations. Interior of a saloon : twenty-six full-length figures ; on the

---

[1] *Anecdotes of Painting in England*, 1876, vol. iii. p. 7.

left [right] a gentleman and two ladies seated at a table, drinking tea ; in the centre, a party of four people playing cards ; on the right [left] a girl and two boys ; one of whom is riding a poodle, the other ladies and gentlemen stand about, while the servant lights the candles in a chandelier. Said to be the earliest known picture by the painter. Painted for Lord Castlemain in 1728 ' [25 in. by 29½ in.].

The date here given is certainly wrong, for in a memorandum of Hogarth's with the heading, ' Account taken, January 1, 1731, of all the pictures that remain unfinished—half-payment received,' there is this entry, ' An Assembly of twenty-five figures, for Lord Castlemaine, August 28, 1729.' [1]

The picture must therefore have been finished after 1731, and the extra figure added. The painter himself describes the picture in the above memorandum as an Assembly, but on the old frame was the inscription : ' A Conversation at Wanstead House.' This same picture was exhibited at the Winter Exhibition of the Royal Academy, 1906 (No. 20), with a similar description to that in Christie's Catalogue, but the words ' right ' and ' left ' are as given between brackets in the above quotation.

J. B. Nichols (1833) describes the picture thus : —' The Wanstead Assembly, painted for Lord Castlemain. This was the first picture that brought Hogarth into notice. It was exhibited in the British

[1] John Ireland's *Hogarth Illustrated*, vol iii p 23

Gallery in 1814, and was then the property of W. Long Wellesley, Esq. It was in the catalogue of his effects in 1822, but was bought in by the family.' Elsewhere he writes: 'A beautiful small painting, a family group, was at Tilney House, Wanstead, and was in the catalogue of Mr. Wellesley's effects in 1822, but was bought in by the family.' [1]

Much confusion has arisen in this case owing to the fact that a picture described as the 'Wanstead Assembly' was known to be in the possession of Mr. William Carpenter of Forest Hill. When he died he left it to the South London Art Gallery, and on examination it turned out to be the dance in the *Analysis of Beauty*, one of the *Happy Marriage* set, and not executed until 1750 or thereabouts. (Cf. A. Dobson's *Hogarth*, 1907, pp. 196, 198, 310.)

It may be well to add here a note as to Wanstead and its proprietors in order to clear up the difficulty as to the names and titles of the proprietors.

The history of the Manor of Wanstead, Essex (six miles from Whitechapel Church), commences before the Norman Conquest, and the manor is registered in Domesday. Coming to later times, Pepys visited Sir Robert Brooke at Wanstead House on May 14, 1665. Two years after this the property was sold to Sir Josiah Child, the great merchant and banker, who spent large sums of money upon it, planting walnut-trees and making fishponds, as

---

[1] *Anecdotes of William Hogarth*, pp. 350, 376

Evelyn, who visited him on March 16, 1682-3, tells us in his *Diary*. Sir Josiah's son, Sir Richard Child, was created Viscount Castlemaine in 1718, and Earl Tylney of Castlemaine in 1731, both titles in the Peerage of Ireland. He it was who pulled down the old mansion about 1715, and erected a new Wanstead House from the design of Colin Campbell, which was pronounced by con-temporaries to be 'one of the noblest houses not only in England, but in Europe.' The reception-rooms were very magnificent, and the walls hung with pictures.

It was one of these rooms that is depicted in Hogarth's painting. On the death without issue of John, second Earl Tylney, in 1784, the manor passed to the Earl's sister, from whom it devolved to her granddaughter, Catherine, the daughter of Sir James Tylney Long. During Miss Tylney Long's minority the house was the residence of the Prince de Condé (father of the Duc d'Enghien), and occasionally of Louis xviii. The hand of Miss Tylney Long was much sought after, and she unfortunately married a very worthless man—the Hon. William Wellesley Pole, who added his wife's name to his own and became William Pole Tylney Long Wellesley. The authors of the *Rejected Addresses* thought the names would make a good line, and introduced them in their first parody—'Long may Long Tilney Wellesley Long Pole live.' Wellesley Pole soon dissipated the heiress's wealth, and in June

G

1822 the contents of Wanstead were sold by auction by George Robins. The sale occupied thirty-two days, and realised £41,000. No purchaser for the mansion being found, it was pulled down and the materials sold. The family portraits were reserved, but in 1851 these too were sold by Messrs. Christie and Manson in consequence, as the catalogue states, 'of the non-payment of expenses for warehousing room.'

Wellesley Pole was Viscount Wellesley from 1842 to 1845, and in the latter year he succeeded his father as Earl of Mornington. He died in poverty on the 1st July 1857, at lodgings in Thayer Street, Marylebone.

There is considerable difficulty in fixing the date of these several conversation pieces, but it will be seen from the various pictures of distinguished families which are known, that Hogarth was well patronised when he undertook this branch of work.

A picture of 'The Devonshire Family' was exhibited at the Guelph Exhibition in 1891 by the late Duke of Devonshire. The scene is at Chiswick, and the persons represented are Lady Caroline Cavendish, William, fourth Duke of Devonshire, Lord George Cavendish, and Lord Frederick Cavendish. The same picture was shown in the Winter Exhibition of the Royal Academy, 1908.

Mr. Dobson mentions a single portrait of the fourth Duke, signed 'W. Hogarth, Pinx^t 1741,' which in 1833 was in the possession of the Hon.

Charles Compton Cavendish, at Latimers, Bucks. Another ducal family is said to have been painted by Hogarth. In the Winter Exhibition of the Royal Academy (1908) was a picture lent by Mr. C. Newton Robinson and described as the Walpole family.

A picture of the Shelley family belonging to Sir G. A. C. Russell, Bart., of Swallowfield Park, Reading, contains portraits of Lady Shelley, wife of Sir John Shelley, and sister to Holles, Duke of Newcastle, Mr. and Mrs. Richard Shelley, their two daughters Fanny and Martha Rose (who married Sir Charles Whitworth), Captain the Hon. William Fitz-William, Mr. Richard Benyon, Governor of Fort St. George, and Mrs. Beard.

A very interesting picture, containing the two heads of the Fox family and others styled ' A Conversation,' belonging to the Earl of Ilchester, is at Melbury House, Dorchester. Starting from the left, Mr. Villemain, a clergyman in black gown and bands, is seen standing upon a chair, rather insecurely placed, with a telescope to his eye; next, sitting at a table, is Stephen, first Earl of Ilchester, then next to him is Henry, first Lord Holland, with a plan of a building in his hands. John, first Lord Hervey, points to the plan, both standing. To the right of these two is Charles, second Duke of Marlborough (died 1758), sitting, and to the extreme right is the standing figure of the Right Hon. Thomas Winnington. The scene is a terrace by the side of a river with a large gate at the back. Hogarth painted a separate portrait of Lord Holland, which was exhibited at the Royal Academy Winter Exhibition, 1908, by Mary Countess of Ilchester. Hogarth told the subject that he would paint him a good portrait. Hogarth, in mentioning his appointment in 1757 to the office of Serjeant Painter to the King, wrote in his autobiography that, as he had to paint some portraits of the royal family, the position might be worth to him two hundred per annum.

The picture of ' George II. and his family,' which belonged to Samuel Ireland, and is now in the National Gallery of Dublin, is reproduced in his *Graphic Illustrations* (vol. ii. p. 137). The portraits are those of George II., Queen Caroline, the Prince of Wales (Frederick), the Duke of Cumberland, the Princess of Hesse, etc. The King is much too youthful in appearance. The Corporation of York possess a portrait of Queen Charlotte by Hogarth, who also painted portraits of two Dukes of Cumberland—William Augustus (third son of George II.), K.G., and Captain-General of the Army (d. 1765); and Henry Frederick (third brother of George III.), as a boy. He was created K.G. in 1767, and died in 1790. The former picture is in the Jones Collection at the Victoria and Albert Museum, South Kensington; the latter was exhibited in 1888 by the late Sir Charles Tennant, Bart.

Hogarth also painted separate portraits of many distinguished noblemen. One of Henry Pelham-

Clinton, second Duke of Newcastle, K.G. (1720-94), was exhibited at the Grosvenor Gallery in 1888 by Sir John Pender. One of George Parker, second Earl of Macclesfield, President of the Royal Society, and a prominent promoter of the change of the style, was exhibited in 1882 by the Earl of Macclesfield. A picture of Captain Lord George Graham (who commanded the *Diana* frigate at the reduction of Quebec) in his cabin, was exhibited in the Royal Naval Exhibition in 1891.

A portrait of Gustavus Lord Viscount Boyne is now in the National Gallery of Ireland. One of Horace Walpole in his youth was exhibited at the Guelph Exhibition in 1891, and at Whitechapel by Mr. H. S. Vade Walpole. Another portrait of Walpole at the age of ten was at Strawberry Hill, and Mr. Dobson tells us it belonged in 1856 to Mrs. Bedford, and in 1866 was bought by Mr. H. Farrer for £213, 3s. The stated age dates this picture as painted in 1727. A picture of George William, sixth Earl of Coventry, and his wife (the beautiful Maria Gunning) was exhibited at the Guelph Exhibition in 1891 by the Earl of Coventry.

Laurence Shirley, Earl Ferrers, was painted by Hogarth, but as he was executed at Tyburn on May 5, 1760, he does no honour to this list.

The two children of William, fourth Lord Byron, with a dog were painted by Hogarth, and the picture was originally at Newstead. It was sold in 1870 for £57, 15s. by Lord W. G. Osborne. A portrait of Frances Lady Byron was exhibited in 1814 by the Earl of Mulgrave, and is now at Lowther Castle. An engraving, 'W. Hogarth pinx^{t}, I. Faber fecit,' was published and 'sold by Faber at the Golden Head in Bloomsbury Square' in 1736. Samuel Ireland in the *Graphic Illustrations* (vol. ii. p. 102) gives an engraving by T. Ryder from a sketch of Lady Pembroke made by Hogarth from recollection about 1740. He gave no particulars of the drawing, nor any justification for the attribution. The Lady Pembroke of 1740 must have been Mary, eldest daughter of Richard, fifth Viscount Fitzwilliam, who married Henry, ninth Earl of Pembroke, in 1733.

This is a goodly list of aristocratic patrons (and possibly there were more that have not been recorded), which is quite sufficient to prove that Hogarth had many opportunities of association with people of high social position. We have no information as to how cordial the relations between Hogarth and these patrons may have been, and it is therefore pleasant to refer to Lord Charlemont's friendly communications with the painter.

The portrait of Lord Charlemont does not appear to have been painted for the Earl, as it was in the possession of Samuel Ireland, who published an etching made by Joseph Haynes in 1782. 'The Right Hon. James Caulfield, Earl of Charlemount,' etc., 'From an Original Portrait by Hogarth in the possession of Mr. Samuel Ireland.'

'The Lady's Last Stake' 1759

The picture entitled 'The Lady's Last Stake,' or 'Picquet,' or 'Virtue in Danger,' already referred to, is one of the artist's most charming works. Hogarth has himself given an account of its origin : ' While I was making arrangements to confine myself entirely to my graver, an amiable nobleman (Lord Charlemont) requested that before I bade a final adieu to the pencil, I would paint him one picture. The subject to be my own choice, and the reward,— whatever I demanded. The story I pitched upon, was a young and virtuous married lady, who, by playing at cards with an officer, loses her money, watches and jewels ; the moment when he offers them back in return for her honour, and she is wavering at his suit, was my point of time.

' The picture was highly approved of, and the payment was noble ; but the manner in which it was made, by a note inclosed in one of the following letters, was to me infinitely more gratifying than treble the sum.' The first letter was dated from Mount Street, 19th August 1759, and in it Lord Charlemont expresses his thanks for the picture, for which he says ' I am still your debtor, more so indeed than I ever shall be able to pay.' He also says : ' I have not been able to wait upon you according to my promise, nor even to find time to sit for my picture ; as I am obliged to set out for Ireland to-morrow.'

The second letter is so pleasing that it must be copied *in extenso*.

'DUBLIN, 29*th January* 1760.

'*To Mr. Hogarth.*

'DEAR SIR,—Inclosed I send you a note upon
Nesbitt, for one hundred pounds; and considering
the name of the author, and the surprising merit
of your performance, I am really much ashamed
to offer such a trifle in recompence for the pains you
have taken, and the pleasure your picture has
afforded me. I beg you would think that I by no
means attempt to pay you according to your merit,
but according to my own abilities. Were I to pay
your deserts, I fear I should leave myself poor
indeed. Imagine that you have made me a present
of the picture, for literally, as such I take it, and
that I have begged your acceptance of the inclosed
trifle. As this is really the case, with how much
reason do I subscribe myself,—Your most obliged
humble servant,   CHARLEMONT.'

John Ireland adds to Hogarth's own description
of the picture : 'It may fairly be considered as a
moral lesson against gaming. The clock denotes
five in the morning. The lady has lost her money,
jewels, a miniature of her husband, and the half of
a £500 bank note, which by a letter lying on the
floor, she appears to have recently received from him.
In fine,—all is lost, except her honour ; and in this
dangerous moment she is represented perplexed,
agitated and irresolute.' [1]

---

[1] *Hogarth Illustrated*, vol. iii. p. 198 (note).

The picture was exhibited at Spring Gardens in the year 1761, with the title of ' Picquet, or Virtue in Danger.'

Mrs. Piozzi (Hester Lynch Salusbury, 1741-1821) asserted that she sat for the portrait of the heroine, but Mr. Dobson points out that, as her accounts of the circumstance differed, we cannot consider them to be conclusive. Doubtless Hogarth did remark to her when he was painting the picture, 'Take you care, I see an ardour for play in your eyes and in your heart; don't indulge it.' When Abraham Hayward published Mrs. Piozzi's autobiography, he prefixed an engraving from this picture to the second volume at the suggestion of Lord Macaulay.

Lord Charlemont's conduct towards Hogarth was very different from that of Sir Richard Grosvenor, who certainly acted meanly in the rejection of ' Sigismunda,' and the painter himself alluded in his autobiography to the contrast. He writes, in commenting on Lord Charlemont's letters: ' This elevating circumstance had its contrast, and brought on a train of most dissatisfactory circumstances, which by happening at a time when I thought myself as it were, landed, and secure from tugging any longer at the oar, were rendered doubly distressing.'

The acceptance of £100 as ' a noble payment ' for such a picture shows how little grasping the painter was, and it also illustrates how largely he was guided by sentiment. He rated the 'Sigismunda' at £400 (four times the price of 'Picquet'), because the so-called Correggio was sold for that sum, and because his interest in the picture increased as the prejudice against it was increased by the active exertions of his enemies. The atrocious libels written on the female figure hurt him the more in that the original of it was his own wife. Therefore he requested her not to sell the picture during her lifetime for less than £500, which he had sufficient experience of the sale of his pictures to know was the same as to request her to keep the picture in her own possession for life.

There, however, is something to be said for Sir Richard Grosvenor who, having been pleased with 'Picquet,' pressed Hogarth with much vehemence to paint another for him, and received a picture which was certainly very different in subject. 'Picquet' remained in the possession of Lord Charlemont's family at the Villa Marina near Dublin for many years.

It was sold at Christie's in 1874 for £1585, 10s., and is now in the possession of Mr. J. Pierpont Morgan.

Lord Charlemont was a Viscount when his portrait and this picture were painted, but he was created an Earl in December 1763. As all lovers of Hogarth must feel interest in Lord Charlemont, it will interest them to learn, on the authority of an old edition of Debrett's *Peerage*, the remarkable reason for this creation—the revival of an order given by James I. one hundred and forty years before: 'It appearing from the rolls of the Court of Chancery that James I. by letters under his sign manual, dated at Westminster, July 16, 1622, directed the chief governor of Ireland to cause letters patent to pass under the great seal, containing a grant of the dignity of an earl to the first Lord Charlemont (Toby Caulfield), but which was never put in execution.' Hogarth's Earl died on August 4, 1799.

We now come to consider two of the great series of pictured morals—the 'Marriage à la Mode,' and the 'Rake's Progress.'

Some have attempted to show points of connection between Dryden's comedy of *Marriage à la Mode* and Hogarth's pictures owing to similarity of title, but there is certainly no likeness between the two. The names of the characters in the play sufficiently disprove this—Polydamas, Usurper of Sicily, Leonidas, Argaleon, Hermogenes, Eubulus, Rhodophil, Palamede, Palmyra, Amalthea, Doralice, Melantha, Philotis, Belisa, Artemis.

It is almost equally difficult to see any hint of the incidents in the *Clandestine Marriage* (1766) in the series of plates illustrating the 'Marriage à la Mode,' although Garrick in his prologue alludes very cleverly to the connection:

'To-night, your matchless Hogarth gives the thought,
  Which from his canvas to the Stage is brought,

And who so fit to warm the Poet's mind,
As he who pictur'd Morals and Mankind?
But not the same their characters and scenes;
Both labour for one end, by different means:
Each as it suits him, takes a separate Road,
Their one great Object, MARRIAGE-A-LA-MODE,
Where titles deign with Cits to have and hold,
And change rich blood for more substantial gold,
And honour'd Trade from interest turns aside
To hazard happiness for titled Pride.'

All the pictures of the series are of Interiors, and all these interiors are of London houses. They form Hogarth's masterpiece and his chief illustration of High Life.

The following advertisement appeared in the *London Daily Post*, April 2, 1743: 'Mr. Hogarth intends to publish by subscription, Six Prints from Copper-plates engrav'd by the best masters in Paris, after his own paintings, representing a variety of Modern Occurrences in High - Life, and called *Marriage-à-la-Mode*. Particular care will be taken, that there may not be the least objection to the Decency or Elegancy of the whole work, and that none of the characters represented shall be personal.'[1] The engravings were issued at the end of May 1745.

Plates 1 and 6 were engraved by Scotin; Plates 2 and 3 by Baron; Plates 4 and 5 by Ravenet. 'Characters and Caricatures,' 'W. Hogarth Fecit 1743,' was the subscription ticket for the 'Marriage.'

---

[1] To the advertisement of April 4 and subsequent issues was added. 'The Heads for the better Preservation of the Characters and Expressions to be done by the Author.'

Under the design is inscribed: 'For a farthar (*sic*) Explanation of the difference betwixt Character & Caricatura See ye Preface to Jo^h Andrews.' This is a reference to that delightful passage where Fielding repudiates for Hogarth the charge of his being a Burlesque Painter, and claims that his figures not only seem to breathe but appear to think.

The prints soon became popular, and the subject formed the groundwork of a novel called *The Marriage Act*, by Dr. John Shebbeare. In 1746 was published a tract of 59 pages entitled '*Marriage a la Mode*: an Humourous Tale in six Cantos, in Hudibrastic Verse, being an Explanation of the six prints lately published by the ingenious Mr. Hogarth. London. . . .'

In the second quarter of the nineteenth century, the story was dramatised and a broadside comprising five woodcuts of the scenes was prepared as a playbill: 'Davidge's Royal Surrey Theatre. On Easter Monday, April 1st, and during the week will be presented an Original Pictorial Drama in five Tableaux entitled the Curse of Mammon! or the Earl's son and the Citizen's daughter! Forming a facsimile embodiment of Hogarth's justly celebrated Pictures: Marriage-a-la-Mode.'

Plate 1.—The Contract.
This picture contains a representation of an ostentatiously grand saloon, the walls of which are covered with paintings. Here the beginnings of the

sad drama are at work. The unfinished building seen from the window with no workmen about shows that expensive tastes have exhausted the Earl's treasury. The attentions of Councillor Silvertongue to the bride already appear to be pronounced, and the young Viscount Squanderfield is too much engaged with his own thoughts to pay any attention to the merchant's daughter soon to be his wife. Hazlitt says of him: 'He is the Narcissus of the reign of George II.; whose powdered peruke, ruffles, gold lace, and patches divide his self-love unequally with his own person,—the true *Sir Plume* of his day.' The prominent personage is the Earl, who appears no more in the drama after this. Racked with the gout, he is still grand in his manner, and he presents a wonderful picture of a haughty aristocrat. There is a tradition, although I have not seen it referred to in any of the books on Hogarth, that this striking character was drawn from a man with great pride in his ancestry, which he traced farther back than the William Duke of Normandy of the Earl's pedigree. John Wallop, Baron Wallop of Farleigh Wallop and Viscount Lymington, had been created Earl of Portsmouth in 1743, just about the time Hogarth was engaged upon these pictures, and his well-known pride of birth might cause Hogarth to take him as a model. The family of Wallop is said in Burke's *Peerage* to have been settled at Wallop, Hants, at a period antecedent to the Conquest. The building operations of the Earl

"The Marriage à la Mode." No. 1. 1745.

From the original painting in the National Gallery.

in the painting may bear some reference to the fact that the manor-house of Farley, destroyed by fire in 1667, was rebuilt by Lord Lymington in 1733. If there is truth in this tradition, it shows forcibly the spirit of Hogarth's work. When he used a particular person as a representative in his pictures of a special characteristic, he took care that nothing else in the picture should bear in any way upon his family history. Lord Portsmouth's son, Lord Lymington, married Catherine Conduit, great-niece of Sir Isaac Newton, the daughter of Mrs. Barton (afterwards Mrs. Conduit). His son became the second Earl of Portsmouth, and by this connection the Portsmouth family became the representatives of the great philosopher. The fourth Earl was named Newton Fellowes, and the fifth Earl, Isaac Newton Wallop.

> ' While the proud Earl of Rollo's race
> Points to the peers his pompous parchment grace,
> Builds all his honours on a noble name,
> And on his father's deeds depends for fame ;
> The wary citizen, with heedful eye,
> Inspects what 's settled on posterity ;
> Pours out the pelf by rigid avarice pil'd
> To gain an empty title for his child.'

It has been said by some that Lord Tylney was the original of the Earl, but this seems improbable. The person delivering the mortgage to the Earl is supposed to be one Peter Walter, the ' Peter Pounce ' of Fielding's *Joseph Andrews.*

Plate 2.—The Breakfast Scene.

We have here a very handsome room finely furnished in the style of the day, although with signs of confusion left from the rout of the previous night, and with the lights guttering in their candlesticks. The apartment is said to be copied from the drawing-room of No. 5 Arlington Street, where Horace Walpole was living at this time, and where he remained until 1779.

Of this Hazlitt wrote : ' The airy splendour of the view of the inner room in this picture is probably not exceeded by any of the productions of the Flemish School.' The husband appears to have just come home after a night of debauch, for which he left his wife to attend to her company. Of the latter Hazlitt writes : ' The expression of the Bride in the Morning Scene is the most highly seasoned, and at the same time the most vulgar of the series,' but adds, ' the figure, face, and attitude of the Husband, are inimitable.' Francis Hayman, Hogarth's friend and copyist, is said to have been the model for the dissipated husband, whose money has evidently almost come to an end. The poor steward, who can get no attention to his appeal and has to leave the room with his unpaid bills, is a prominent figure in the scene. There is considerable difference of opinion among the critics as to this man. The majority speak of the honesty and simplicity of the old faithful servant, and others think he is intended for a hypocritical fellow.

'Behold how Vice her votary rewards,
After a night of folly, frolic, cards,
The phantom pleasure flies—and in its place,
Comes deep remorse, and torturing disgrace,
Corroding care, and self-accusing fame!'

Plate 3.—The Scene with the Quack.

The subject of this picture need not detain us long, as it has rather to do with low life than with high life, with which it has only an incidental connection. The explanations of the commentators are very conflicting, and therefore nothing can be said with certainty as to the meaning of the particular action although the general idea of the scene is apparent enough.

Hazlitt's remarks on the painting of the girl are as usual most discriminating: 'The young girl in the third picture, who is represented as the victim of fashionable profligacy, is unquestionably one of the artist's *chefs-d'œuvre*. The exquisite delicacy of the painting is only surpassed by the felicity and subtlety of the conception. Nothing can be more striking than the contrast between the extreme softness of her person, and the hardened indifference of her character. The vacant stillness, the docility to vice, the premature suppression of youthful sensibility, the doll-like mechanism of the whole figure, which seems to have no other feeling but a sickly sense of pain—show the deepest insight into human nature.'

The interest of the picture for us is almost con-

fined to its local character. John Ireland, in alluding
to the miscellaneous contents of the Quack's
Museum, quotes a passage from Garth's *Dispensary*,
which with justice he thinks might have given
Hogarth some hints for the scene :

> 'Here mummies lie, most reverently stale,
> And there, the tortoise hung her coat of mail :
> Not far from some huge shark's devouring head,
> The flying fish their finny pinions spread ;
> Aloft, in rows, large poppy-heads were strung,
> And near, a scaly alligator hung ;
> In this place, drugs in musty heaps decay'd,
> In that, dry'd bladders and drawn teeth were laid '

J. T. Smith, in an interesting account of St.
Martin's Lane contained in the second volume of
his *Nollekens and his Times*, says that the large
room behind No. 96 was the original of the scene
of this picture, although he incorrectly describes it
as a part of the ' Rake's Progress.' ' The house has
a large staircase, curiously painted, of figures
viewing a procession, which was executed for the
famous Dr. Misaubin, about the year 1732 by a
painter of the name of Clermont, a Frenchman,
who boldly charged one thousand guineas for his
labour, which charge, however, was contested, and
the artist was obliged to take five hundred.'

Whether the quack and the big woman in the
picture were taken from Misaubin and his wife may
be doubted, although probably Hogarth took that
doctor as a type.

Bramston, in his 'Man of Taste,' contrasts him
with the respectable practitioners :—

> 'Should I perchance be fashionably ill,
> I'd send for Misaubin, and take his pill.
> I should abhor, though in the utmost need,
> Arbuthnot, Hollins, Wigan, Lee or Mead,
> But if I found that I grew worse and worse,
> I'd turn off Misaubin and take a nurse.'

Misaubin's father was a Huguenot clergyman who
preached at the Spitalfields French Church, and
was a well-known preacher. Fielding says in *Tom
Jones*, bk. xiii. chap. ii., that the Doctor boasted
that the proper direction for him was 'Dr. Misaubin
in the World.' He is one of four medical men
mentioned in that novel, the others being Syden-
ham, John Freke and John Ranby. There is a
miniature of the Doctor and his family by Joseph
Goupy which Smith mentions as being in the possession of Mr. Henry Moyley.

John Misaubin, M.D., licentiate of the College
of Physicians, 25th June 1719, brought a famous
pill into England, by which he made a fortune by
questionable means.

Misaubin died in 1734, but in August 1749 Martha
Misaubin advertised in the *London Evening Post*
that she continued the making and selling of Dr.
Misaubin's Pills at her house in St. Martin's Lane.
She affirms 'I am the only person that prepared
them during the Doctor's life and since his death,
nobody else having the secret but myself.' Mr.

Stephens thinks it probable that this was the same woman as the coarse virago in this picture.[1]

Plate 4.—The Toilette Scene.

A lady's boudoir and bedroom is represented in this picture, which is filled with a company of friends assembled at the Countess's levee. The Earl's coronet, seen on the bedstead, may indicate that the old Earl is now dead. We are not informed what was the Earl's title, and it could not well be Squanderfield, as some commentators seem to suppose it was, because that was the title of his son, Viscount Squanderfield. Probably Hogarth was himself confused in this matter, for the invitations on the floor are directed to Lady Squander.

The new Countess and Silvertongue (who is pointing to representations of a masquerade on the screen), are arranging an appointment at a masquerade. On the couch where the Counsellor reclines is a book inscribed *Sopha*, referring to the licentious novel by Crébillon *fils* which was much read at this time. Hogarth took the opportunity of expressing his burning indignation against the infatuation of the upper classes for the Italian Opera. The singer at this reception is said to be Giovanni Carestini,[2] the famous counter-tenor, who

---

[1] See *British Museum Catalogue*, vol. iii. p. 733.

[2] Carestini made his *début* in London on December 4, 1733, and with his support Handel was able to withstand the opposition of Farinelli. Handel was very indignant with him on one occasion when he sent back to the composer the song 'Verdi prati' in the Italian opera *Alcina* (1735) as not

according to Burney was one of the finest Italian singers ever heard; he was also a good actor, tall, handsome, and commanding. He died about 1758. Some have supposed the figure to be intended for Farinelli. Behind him is the famous flute-player Weidemann, who is also the principal figure in the print of 'The Modern Orpheus,' published in 1807, from an original sketch by Hogarth in the possession of the Marquis of Bute (*circa* 1745).

Below the engraving is printed in letterpress the following announcement: 'Speedily will be Published, Inscribed to all Lovers of Tweedledum Tweedle, the Art of Playing upon People, or, Memoirs of the German Flute, interspersed with the Character of Baron Steeple; in which the effect of Harmony will be shown in instances of a more surprizing Nature than any related of Amphion, Linus, Musæus or the most celebrated Flutists of Antiquity.

> "Music hath charms to wheedle Guineas forth;
> To draw, like Loadstone, Vituals, Drink and Clothes;
> Shirts, Stockings, Hats, Wigs, Rapiers, Shoes and Boots.
> I've read that Misers (griping Sons of Mammon!)
> Have, out of Idol Gold, been oft cajol'd,
> By Magic Numbers and persuasive Sound."'

Weidemann was, soon after the accession of George III., appointed Assistant-Master of Music to the King under Dr. Boyce, and afterwards Composer

suited to him Handel ran to the singer's house and addressed him thus: 'You tog! don't I know petter as yourseluf vaat es pest for you to sing? If you vill not sing all de song vaat I give you, I vill not pay you ein stiver'

of Minuets at the Court of St. James, and one of the band of musicians.   He died May 24, 1782.[1]

Mrs. Fox Lane (afterwards Lady Bingley), is the striking lady in a state of excited admiration of Carestini's singing.   She was the daughter of Robert Benson, Baron Bingley, and wife of George Fox Lane, who was created Lord Bingley of Bingley in 1762.   Mrs. Fox Lane had a perfect passion for Italian music, and was a zealous friend and patroness of Madame Regina Mingotti,[2] siding with her in her disputes with Vaneschi.   On one occasion she was earnestly declaiming to the Hon. General Crewe on the claims of her favourite to universal admiration, when her listener astonished her by asking, 'And pray, ma'am, who is Madame Mingotti?'   'Get out of my house,' cried the lady, 'you shall never hear her sing another song at my concerts, as long as you live.' Mingotti performed exclusively at Mrs. Lane's concerts, so there was no hope for the General.   This anecdote is given on the authority of Dr. Burney.

The gentleman in curl-papers who sits next to Carestini is said to be Herr Michel, Prussian Envoy. It is to be hoped that he was a better diplomatist than his vacant countenance would lead us to expect.

The argument of the fourth canto of the poem on the 'Marriage à la Mode,' thus sums up this scene:—

[1] *British Museum Catalogue* (F G. Stephens), vol III p 591

[2] This famous singer, born 1728 (*née* Valentini), married Mingotti, impresario of the Dresden Opera, and when she came to England retrieved the fortunes of the Opera.

'Fresh honours on the Lady wait,
A Countess now she shines in state,
The toilette is at large display'd
Where, whilst the morning concert's play'd,
She listens to her lover's call,
Who courts her to the midnight ball.'

Plate 5.—The Death of the Earl.

The end of the great tragedy is now arrived, and it takes two pictures to tell the story. The dying Earl is seen in the centre of the bedroom of the Turk's Head Bagnio killed by Silvertongue, who is escaping through the window. This scene is too serious in itself to allow of many external references, and although there are several of these the consideration of them need not detain us here. Hazlitt is not at his best in his criticism of this scene. He says it is inferior to the rest of the series. 'The attitude of the husband who is just killed, is one in which it would be impossible for him to stand or even to fall. It resembles the loose paste-board figures they make for children.' Few will agree with this, and it is well that we have a brilliant passage, written with wonderful insight, to set against it. 'Look on that dying man—his body dissolving, falling not like his sword, firm and entire, but as nothing but a dying thing could fall, his eyes dim with the shadow of death, in his ears the waters of that tremendous river, all its billows going over him, the life of his comely body flowing out like water, the life of his soul—who knows what it is doing? Fleeing through the open window,

principles; and to the fine example of passive obedience and non-resistance in the servant whom he is taking to task, and whose coat of green and yellow livery is as long and melancholy as his face. . . . The harmony and gradations of colour in this picture are uniformly preserved with the greatest nicety, and are well worthy the attention of the artist.' The point of greatest interest in this picture in relation to London topography is the view of the old tumble-down houses on London Bridge, seen through the window of the room. This is one of the latest representations of these houses, as they were all cleared away about a dozen years after Hogarth painted this scene.

It is fortunate for the world that these splendid pictures are in the possession of the nation, so that every one who wishes can see them at all times. They bear repeated study, and the tragedy is so vividly and truly painted that it is impossible not to feel you are in the presence of a great genius, who lives again in his great works. John Ireland very truly says: 'It will not be easy, perhaps not possible, to find six pictures painted by any artist, in any age or country, in which such variety of superlative merit is united.'

'The Rake's Progress' does not, as a whole, represent High Life as the 'Marriage' does, but as Tom Rakewell attempts to obtain an entrance into the 'inner circle' it is necessary to take notice of some of the scenes.

The eight pictures are to be seen at the Soane Museum, they having been bought by Sir John Soane in 1802 for £598, 10s. Hogarth originally sold them in February 1745 to Alderman Beckford for £184, 16s. They were sold at the Fonthill sale to Colonel Fullarton for £682, 10s. The engravings were published in June 1735.

Plate 2, where the Rake is surrounded by artists and professors at his levee, may be taken as a sort of pendant to Plate 4 of the 'Marriage' where the Countess is surrounded by her friends. The Rake is well attended by his instructors, some of whom are identified as characters of the day, while others remain anonymous. The bravo captain behind the Rake comes provided with a letter of recommendation from William Stab; a jockey in front holds on his knee a large silver bowl on which are engraved a racing horse and its rider and the inscription 'Won at Epsom, Silly Tom.' The dancing-master, holding his kit and bow, capers on the Rake's right; apparently he is a Frenchman, but it has been affirmed that he was intended to represent a man named Essex. The fencing-master displaying his skill in making a thrust towards the front of the design was Dubois, a Frenchman, who was killed in a duel fought in Marylebone Fields on May 10, 1734, by an Irishman also named Dubois. The man with staves standing between the fencing- and dancing-masters was Figg the prize-fighter who died 1734. At the back between the Rake and

the dancing-master is Bridgeman, the well-known
landscape gardener, who holds in his hand a design
which John Ireland does not consider to be worthy
of the man who attempted to 'create landscape,
to realise painting and improve nature.' Hogarth
takes the opportunity of satirising the presenters
of Italian Opera, so here is another instance of
likeness to Plate 4 of the 'Marriage.'

At the extreme left of the picture is a harpsichord
inscribed 'I. Mahoan fecit,' at which a man is seen
seated; his back only is presented to the spectator,
but it has been supposed by some to represent
Handel. This, however, is unlikely. Over the back
of the chair on which the musician sits a long scroll
of paper extends on the floor, which is inscribed:
'A list of the rich Presents Signor Farinello the
Italian Singer condescended to accept of ye English
Nobility and Gentry for one Night's performance in
the opera of *Artaxerxes*.' The last of the presents on
the list is 'A Gold Snuffbox chac'd with the Story of
Orpheus charming ye Brutes, by T. Rake-well Esq.'

On the floor near the end of the scroll is an
engraving representing Farinelli seated on a
pedestal, and with an altar between his feet on
which two hearts are burning; many ladies are offering burning hearts to the popular idol. In Plate 4
we see the Rake arrested on his way to Court, and
the picture contains an admirable view of St. James's
Street with the Palace at the foot. This street
was the very centre of High Life in London, and it

still remains its most distinguished street. Its position is unrivalled, and even now it has a little of the air of the eighteenth century left, although some tall new houses at the Piccadilly end have completely ruined the restful sense of proportion that once existed.

Plate 4, and Plate 6, representing the gaming at White's Chocolate House, and the commencement of the fire that destroyed the building, are more fully dealt with in Chapter IX. on Tavern Life. The other pictures have little to do with High Life, and a notice of Plate 5, the Marriage in Marylebone Church, will be found in Chapter XIII. (Suburbs); one on Plate 7, the Fleet Prison, in Chapter XII. (Prisons and Crime), and on Plate 8, Bedlam, in Chapter XI. (Hospitals).

Hogarth made three satirical designs on what he considered (often truly), the perverted taste in High Life. The first in 1724, called 'Masquerades and Operas,' also styled 'Taste of the Town,' which contains the gate of Burlington House, Piccadilly (described in Chapter X., Theatrical Life). The second in 1731, 'The Man of Taste,' or, 'Burlington House'; and the third in 1742, 'Taste in High Life.'

'The Man of Taste' (also called 'Taste à la Mode') contains the best view in existence of the old wall and gate of Burlington House cleared away in 1866. It is a sort of three-sided satire on Burlington, Kent, and Pope. Against Lord Burlington because he patronised Kent, and against Pope because he

"The Man of Taste." 1731. (Burlington Gate.)

satirised the Duke of Chandos under the name of
Timon in his Moral Epistle (IV.) to Burlington on
the false taste of magnificence.

On the engraving is the following explanation :

A P. a Plasterer white-washing and bespattering [Pope].
B Any body that comes in his way.
C Not a Dukes Coach as appears by ye crescent of one
      corner [Duke of Chandos's coach].
D Taste [The pediment so marked].
E A standing proof [statue of Kent between recum-
      bent figures of ' Raphael Urb.' and ' M^l Angelo '].
F A Labourer [Earl of Burlington].

The plate is said to have been suppressed, but it
was reproduced as a frontispiece to a pirated edition
of the first issue of the poem ' Of Taste,' which was
described as ' A Miscellany on Taste.'

Pope never referred to Hogarth publicly, but he
complained to friends, and he was evidently afraid
of the satirist.

Nichols, however, in *Biographical Anecdotes*, refers
to a copy of this piratical edition having the following
inscription written inside the book : ' Bo'^t this
book of Mr. Wayte, at The Fountain Tavern, in the
Strand, in the presence of Mr. Draper, who told me
he had it of the Printer, Mr. W. Rayner.—J. Cosins.'

He says Cosins was an attorney, and as Pope was
desirous on all occasions to make the law the engine
of his revenge, he supposes this attested memorandum was intended for the purposes of a prosecution.

' Taste in High Life ' was painted in ridicule of

the craze of the day for *outré* costumes and the collection of gimcracks of all kinds. Miss Edwardes of Kensington, an unmarried lady of great fortune, had been sharply satirised in Society for her oddities, and she thought that by employing Hogarth to perpetuate the absurdities of the dress worn by the most exalted personages of her time she would have ample revenge.

The picture represents a room furnished in the extreme of fashion, the chief figures being a lady and gentleman extravagantly dressed and ' gushing ' over the beauties of some old china. The man has a saucer in his hand, and the woman a cup. The beau represents the Earl of Portmore in the dress he wore at the Birthday Drawing-Room of 1742. A monkey in the front of the picture is dressed like a gentleman of the period. The little black boy is said to be taken from Ignatius Sancho whose portrait in later life was painted by Gainsborough.

The woman who is playing with the black boy is said to represent a courtesan of the day. On the wall, among a large collection of pictures, Desnoyers the great opera dancer is seen pirouetting.

Hogarth received sixty guineas from Miss Edwardes for the picture, which was bought by Mr. Birch at the sale of her effects for five guineas. It belonged to Mr. John Birch, surgeon, of Essex Street, Strand, son of the former proprietor, when it was engraved by Samuel Phillips in 1798. He exhibited it in 1814. The picture was sold at the

"Taste in High Life." 1746.

M'Murdo sale in July 1889 for £225, 15s., and is now in the possession of Mr. Fairfax Murray.

As this picture was painted to the order of another, the painter took little interest in it and would not allow it to be engraved. An engraver managed surreptitiously to obtain sight of the picture and published a print of it at the price of sixpence.

The publication was advertised in *The General Advertiser* of May 24, 1746. 'On Monday next will be published an entertaining new Print, called " Taste in High Life " (a companion to Taste à la Mode), from an incomparable Picture of Mr. Hogarth's (designed by a lady lately deceased) proving beyond contradiction, that the present polite assemblies of Drums, Routs, etc., are mere exotics and the supporters of such and other *Divertissemens modernes* a parcel of Insects. To be had at Mr. Jarvis's Print-shop in Bedford Court, Covent Garden, and the Printsellers of London and Westminster.'

CHAPTER IV

LOW LIFE

Low Life is exhibited in its many phases in a large number of Hogarth's pictures, and so universally has the public opinion been directed to this side of the artist's art that we find an anonymous writer dedicating to Hogarth his work on 'Low Life,' which we have Mr. Dobson's authority for saying was first published in May 1752 (a second edition in November 1754, and a third in 1764),[1] and attributing the idea of its publication to his pictures of 'The Four Times of the Day,' painted and engraved in 1738.

[1] 'Low-Life: or One half the World, knows not how the Other half lives, being a critical account of what is transacted by People of almost all Religions, Nations, and Circumstances, in the Twenty-four hours between Saturday Night and Monday Morning In a true description of a Sunday, as it is usually spent within the Bills of Mortality. Calculated for the Tenth [Twenty-first] of June With an Address to the ingenious Mr. Hogarth

'—— Let Fancy guess the rest.'—*Buckingham.*

'London : Printed for the Author, and sold by T. Legg, at the Parrot and Crown in Green Arbour Court in the Little Old Baily,' etc. [n.d.] [Price one shilling.]

The third edition. 'London : Printed for John Lever, at Little Moorgate, next London Wall near Moorfields, 1764' [Price one shilling and sixpence]. 8vo, pp. viii., 103.

The change of the date on the title-page of the third edition from the tenth to the twenty-first is of interest on account of the change in the calendar which took place between the publication of the two editions.

This remarkable book attracted the attention of Thackeray, Dickens, Sala (*Twice Round the Clock*, 1859), and others, and it requires some special notice here, as it contains a curious illustration of the habits of the Londoners of Hogarth's day. Sir Walter Besant in his *London in the Eighteenth Century*, has a chapter on Low Life entitled 'Twice Round the Clock.' He wisely remarks that the revelations of the book must be accepted with caution, as the frequent is usually made to appear to be the universal. Moreover, the author assumes the garb, which he wears somewhat awkwardly, 'of the moralist that deplores and the Christian who exhorts.' With this caution we can proceed to consider the author's revelations as they occur.

In the dedication to Hogarth we read : 'I say that this essay owes its existence partly to your works. And who will not believe me, when I direct them to those four pieces of yours, called "Morning," "Noon," "Evening," "Night" ? and where are many things made visible to the eye in the most elegant colours, which are here only recorded. But these I must leave the judicious Reader to compare.'

We are told that in the first hour from 12 to 1 A.M. 'The Salop man in Fleet Street shuts up his Beggar's Coffee-house,' and hackney coachmen are full of employment about Charing Cross, Covent Garden, and the Inns of Court, carrying to their respective habitations such people as are either too drunk or

1

too lazy to walk. Later on, the watchman cries
''Past four o'clock' at half an hour after three.
About this time the beggars go to the parish nurses
to borrow poor helpless children at fourpence a day
each. The keepers of she-asses about Brompton,
Knightsbridge, Hoxton and Stepney are getting
ready to run with their cattle all over the town to
be milked for the benefit of sick and infirm persons.
From seven to eight people are seen 'wishing the
compliments of the season, it being Whit Sunday.'
About this time 'the whole cities of London,
Westminster and the Borough of Southwark are
covered by a cloud of smoak, most people being
employed in lighting fires.'

The account of the doings during the dark hours
is full, and shows how dangerous the streets of
London were at night, and sometimes in the
day-time, owing to the incompetence and, in
many cases, to the corruptibility of the old watchmen.

Being Sunday morning, some of the early risers
were off to the suburbs to breakfast at Sadler's Wells,
but the larger number of the people waited till the
afternoon and walked to the fields of Islington which
were then filling with oxen and calves, sheep and
lambs, placed there to be ready for Monday morning
market at Smithfield. More will be found about
these suburban resorts in the chapter on Suburbs.
At the end of *Low Life*, there is an advertisement
of 'The Secret History of Betty Ireland, 6th edition,

price 6d.,' with these laudatory lines on this
woman :

'Read Flanders Moll, the German Princess scan,
Then match our Irish Betty if you can ;
In Wit and Vice she did them both excel
And may be justly called, a Nonpareil '

In the *Newgate Calendar* a print called 'Betty
Ireland's Dexterity' is borrowed from the woman
stealing the watch in Plate 3 of the 'Rake's Progress.'

Turning from the follower to the originator, we
can now consider the particular points of 'The Four
Times of the Day,' which series is of the greatest
interest for our present purpose as it illustrates
London streets in three of the pictures and the
suburbs in 'Evening.' Although the engravings
from the original paintings were published in 1738,
the pictures remained on Hogarth's hands until 1745,
when they were sold by the artist's ill-advised system
of auction for ridiculously low prices.

'The Four Times of the Day' were exhibited in
1814, and Mr. Dobson tells us that 'Night' and
'Morning' (shown in the Winter Exhibition of the
Royal Academy in 1885), belong to the Hursley
Park Trustees, and were originally purchased by Sir
William Heathcote for £27, 6s. and £21. 'Noon'
and 'Evening' belonged to the Duke of Ancaster,
who bought them for £38, 17s. and £39, 18s.
respectively ; they are now in the possession of the
Earl of Ancaster at Grimsthorpe Castle, Lincolnshire.

In the advertisement of the sale of pictures

lately exhibited by that gentleman in his print of a Winter's Morning, of which she was no improper emblem and may be seen walking (for walk she doth in the print) to Covent Garden Church, with a starved footboy behind, carrying a prayer-book.' [1]

Another story told by John Nichols is that this figure was taken either from an acquaintance or relation of Hogarth. 'At first she was well enough satisfied with her resemblance ; but some designing people teaching her to be angry, she struck the painter out of her will, which had been made considerably in his favour.' Such are the troubles of the Satirist.

Cowper was struck by this figure, and faithfully expounded it in eighteen lines of *Truth* commencing :

> 'Yon ancient prude, whose wither'd features show
> She might be young some forty years ago,
> Her elbows pinion'd close upon her hips,
> Her head erect, her fan upon her lips,
> Her eyebrows arch'd, her eyes both gone astray
> To watch yon am'rous couple in their play.'

The church, which forms the principal object in the east end of the picture, represents Inigo Jones's original church. This building was entirely destroyed by fire on September 15, 1795, and was rebuilt by Thomas Hardwick, architect, on the plan and in the proportions of the original.

'Tom King's Coffee-House,' a notorious resort of the most unruly of the London rakes, forms a

[1] *Tom Jones*, book 1. chap. xi

prominent feature in the picture. Tom King was
a native of West Ashton in Wiltshire and a scholar
at Eton, who early began his ignoble career. In
the account of the boys elected from Eton to King's
College, Cambridge, given by Harwood (*Alumni
Etonensis*), he writes : King 'went away (1713)
scholar in apprehension that his fellowship would
be denied him, and afterwards kept that coffee-
house in Covent Garden which was called by his
own name.' At the date of this picture Tom King
probably had been succeeded in the possession
of this place of entertainment by his widow, Moll
King, who became notorious. In October 1737 was
published a print entitled ' A Monument for Tom
K—g.'

Fielding frequently referred to King's Coffee-
House. J. T. Smith places the shed, for it was
little more, opposite to Tavistock Row, now cleared
away for new market buildings with one side in
Tavistock Street, and not in front of the church
where, as Mr. Dobson says, Hogarth has by artistic
licence placed it. Smith's localisation is corroborated by the view in ' *Tom K—g's* : or the
Paphian Grove, with the various Humours of
Covent Garden &c., the second edition to which is
added, a Dedication to Mrs. K—g . . . London
1738.'

In this little book there is a portrait of Mrs. Mary
K—g opposite to the dedication. In the author's
apology we are told : ' I have no private antipathy

to any person who may suppose himself to be here
satyriz'd ; my sole design being to expose a place
that has flourish'd for some years, either to the
shame of our laws or the scandal of our Magistrates.'
It is not clear whether this low place of entertainment, which must have been a scandal even in a
scandalous neighbourhood, was ever changed in
its position. The author of this 'Mock Heroic
Poem' thus describes the Market :

> 'Where a wide area opens to the sight
> A spacious Plain quadrangularly right,
> Whose large Frontiers with Pallisado's bound,
> From Trivia's filth inshrines the hallow'd ground:
> In which Pomona keeps her fruitful court,
> And youthful Flora with her Nymphs resort.'

Stacie wrote : ' Noblemen and the first beaux after
leaving court would go to her house in full dress
with swords and in rich brocaded silk coats, and
walked and conversed with persons of every description. She would serve chimney-sweepers,
gardeners and market people in common with her
lords of the knighted rank.'

Moll King was not allowed much longer to continue in her evil courses, and as we read in a newspaper cutting of May 24, 1739, ' Yesterday Mary
King, mistress of King's Coffee House, Covent
Garden, was brought to the King's Bench Bar to
receive judgment, when the Court committed her
to the King's Bench prison, Southwark, till they took
time to consider of a punishment adequate to the

offence.' We read further in the *Weekly Miscellany*,
June 9, 1739: 'Monday, Mrs. Mary King of Covent
Garden was brought up to the King's Bench bar
at Westminster, and received the following sentence,
for keeping a disorderly house; viz. to pay a fine of
two hundred pounds, to suffer three months imprison-
ment, to find security for her good behaviour for
three years, and to remain in prison till the fine be
paid.' This punishment may be said to have
finished her career. She retired to Haverstock
Hill and built three houses, in one of which she died
on the 17th of September 1747. Nancy Dawson,
the hornpipe dancer, lived here for a time.[1] The
three houses remained until a few years ago and
were known as Moll King's Row.

After this woman's death a book was published
entitled '*Covent Garden in Mourning*, a Mock
Heroick Poem, containing some Memoirs of the late
Celebrated Moll King.'

There was at Strawberry Hill a large drawing
of the interior of Tom King's by Captain Laroon
which Walpole bought from the artist. Another
interior will be found in an engraving by Bickham
jun. entitled 'The Rake's Rendez-vous, or the
Midnight Revels. Wherein are delineated the
Various Humours of Tom King's Coffee House in

[1] Nancy Dawson made her first appearance at Drury Lane Theatre on
Sept 23, 1760. She died May 27, 1767, and is buried in the burial-
ground of St George's, Bloomsbury, at the back of the Foundling Hospital.
A portrait of her, attributed to Hogarth, was sold at the Johnson sale in
1898 for £13, 13s.

Covent Garden,' which is a plagiarism of the Tavern Scene in the ' Rake's Progress.'

In Boitard's 'Morning Frolic in Covent Garden' Laroon is seen brandishing an artichoke, Captain Montague seated on the top of Bet Careless's sedan, which is preceded by Little Casey. Justice Welsh said that Captain Laroon, his friend Montague, and their constant companion, Little Casey, were the three most troublesome of all his visitors at Bow Street.

In the distance to the left of the picture is seen the quack Dr. Rock exhibiting his medicines for sale and expatiating on their virtues. John Ireland says that this was considered to be a striking likeness of the man, who made a practice of attending the market every morning.

'Noon.'—This picture does not properly come under the heading of Low Life, as it represents in vivid colours the issuing out of the congregation from the French Church in Hog Lane, afterwards Crown Street and now a part of Charing Cross Road. This district was the centre of a foreign quarter, and the church was well attended. It had previously been occupied as a Greek church, and there is still a Greek inscription over the west door, to the effect that the temple was created by the Greeks in 1677. An Independent chapel succeeded the French chapel, and the building is now the Anglican Church of St. Mary. The church is set back from the road, but additions have been made which front Charing Cross Road.

St. Giles's Church is seen in the distance; and on the whole this is one of the best of Hogarth's pictures of the London streets and full of humorous incidents, especially the despair of the poor boy who has just broken his dish, containing the Sunday's dinner from the baker's, by setting it down too smartly on a post.

'Evening' will be found referred to in the chapter on the Suburbs (XIII.)

'Night.'—This, the last of the four pictures, represents the congested condition of the narrow part of Charing Cross, at a time of rejoicing, before it was opened out to Whitehall, and the neighbourhood of St. Martin's Church. This is the night of the 29th of May, as will be seen by the oaken bough on the barber's pole and the oak leaves fixed in some of the hats of the passers-by. The principal window is fully illuminated with tallow candles, and there is a bonfire in the middle of the road.

The overturned coach, with its frightened passengers, occupies a prominent position in the picture. There is a tradition that the cause of the disaster was the Earl of Salisbury (James, fourth Earl: 1713-1780), whose hobby it was to drive coaches. Walpole describes him as driving the Hatfield stage, but this may only be a figure of speech. The conveyance is generally referred to as the Salisbury Flying Coach, but this may merely be some confusion with the name of the noble

driver. Pope alludes to him in the *Dunciad* (book
IV. ll. 587-8):

'From stage to stage the licens'd Earl may run,
  Pair'd with his fellow-charioteer, the sun.'

On either side of the road are the Rummer Tavern
and the Cardigan's Head. The former was an old-
established place of entertainment, and was kept
in 1685 by Samuel Prior, the uncle of Matthew
Prior. (It was at the Rhenish Wine Office in Canon
Row that the Earl of Dorset found the young poet
reading Horace.) In the distance is seen the statue
of Charles I.

The intoxicated freemason in the front of the
picture who is being led to his home by the tyler
of his lodge has been identified as Sir Thomas
De Veil, the magistrate. This incident was fully
discussed at a meeting of the Lodge Quatuor Coronati
on the 3rd May and 8th November, 1889. Brother
G. W. Speth alluded to it in a paper on the Foundation of Modern Freemasonry, and Brother W.
Harry Rylands read a paper on Hogarth's Picture
'Night' at the latter date.[1] Both writers are willing
to agree to the popular ascription to Sir Thomas
De Veil. Mr. Speth writes: 'The badge [of the
freemason] was a huge plain white apron, such as the
drunken W.M. and the tavern waiter or Tyler are
begirt with in Hogarth's well-known picture.' He
cannot find that any lodge met at the Cardigan's

[1] *Transactions of the Lodge Quatuor Coronati*, vol. ii. 1889, pp. 90, 116, 146.

Head previous to the date of the engraving, but from 1739 to 1742 a lodge, which was constituted 15th April 1728 and erased in 1743, held its meetings at the 'Earl of Cardigan's Head,' Charing Cross. Mr. Speth gives excellent reasons for believing that the figure with the lantern was intended for a tyler and not, as most commentators suppose, a waiter. 'The dress and wig are not those of a menial, and the masonic apron rather points also to a contrary conclusion. The sword under the arm at once suggests a Tyler, and distinct resemblance may be traced between Hogarth's picture and an engraved portrait dated 1738 of "Montgomerie, garder to yᵉ Grand Lodge," or as we should say, Grand Tyler. The cut of the coat sleeve and arrangement of the linen are also identical in both plates. What more consonant with all we know of Hogarth than the supposition that the Grand Tyler having issued an engraving of himself in 1738, the very year of Hogarth's plate, he should seize the first opportunity of caricaturing it ?'

Mr. Rylands enters very fully into the various points of the picture, more especially of the topography, but it is difficult to come to any definite conclusion as to the matter. He satisfactorily disproves Mr. Speth's suggestion that the scene was laid in Hartshorn Lane (afterwards Northumberland Street). It probably looks towards Charing Cross from the opening to Whitehall. Hogarth was not very particular as to these details.

"THE COCKPIT." 1759.

The remarkable engraving of 'The Cockpit' is one of Hogarth's most vivid illustrations of the manners of his time. It was published in 1759, and is therefore one of his latest works. In 1747 he was invited by a writer of verses in the *Gentleman's Magazine* of that year to take the Cockpit as a subject for his art:

'Come, Hogarth, thou whose art can best declare
What forms, what features, human passions wear,
Come with a painter's philosophic sight,
Survey the circling judges of the fight.
Touch'd with the sport of death, while every heart
Springs to the changing face, exert thy art;
Mix with the smiles of Cruelty at pain,
Whate'er looks anxious in the lust of gain,
And say, can aught that's generous, just, or kind,
Beneath this aspect, lurk within the mind.'[1]

Cock-fighting is a very ancient game, and as 'the sport of kings' cockpits have been attached to palaces, the one at Whitehall gave its name to the Council Chamber in St. James's Park. In the seventeenth century London was filled with cockpits, but the most famous was the Royal Cockpit, which stood in Dartmouth Street near the top of Queen Street. The winding stone steps leading from Birdcage Walk to the site of the building still exist, and continue the name as Cockpit Steps. Mr. W. B. Boulton in his *Amusements of Old London* gives an advertisement of this place from one of the news sheets of 1700.

'At the Royal Cockpit, on the south side of St.

[1] John Nichols, *Biographical Anecdotes* (1785), p 368.

James's Park, on Tuesday the 11th of this instant February, will begin a very great cock match, and will continue all the week, wherein most of the considerablest cockers of England are concerned. There will be a battle down upon the pit every day precisely at three o'clock, in order to have done by daylight. Monday the 9th instant March will begin a great match of cock-fighting between the gentlemen of the city of Westminster and the gentlemen of the city of London, for six guineas a battle and one hundred guineas the odd battle, and the match continues all the week in Red Lion Fields.'

It is the Royal Cockpit which is supposed to be the scene of Hogarth's engraving. The building was taken down in 1816, as a renewal of the lease for the old purpose was refused. The cock-fighters removed to the Cockpit Royal in Tufton Street, Westminster, which remained until the year 1828. A few years afterwards the game was prohibited by Act of Parliament (5 and 6 Wm. iv. cap. 59).

Mr. Boulton, who gives a learned account of cock-fighting, highly praises Pepys's word-picture of his single visit to a cockpit (Dec. 21, 1663). He writes : ' We think this wonderful plate [by Hogarth] may be placed by the side of Mr. Pepys's vivid description of his visit to Shoe Lane as one of the best presentments of the humours of the cockpit existing. The same "celestial spirit of anarchy" animates the other classic representation of a cock match by Thomas Rowlandson which appeared in the *Microcosm of London* some sixty years later.'

The expression ' celestial spirit ' used above is a quotation from Dr. Martin Sherlock's *Letters to a Friend at Paris* referred to by John Ireland : ' It is worth your while to come to England, were it only to see an Election and a Cock-match. There is a celestial spirit of anarchy and confusion, in these two scenes that words cannot paint, and of which no countryman of yours can form even an idea.'

Ireland adds to this : ' Mr. Sherlock is perfectly right in his assertion, that neither of these scenes can be described by *words* ; but where the writer must have failed, the artist has succeeded, and the Parisian who has never visited England may, from Mr. Hogarth's prints, form a tolerably correct idea of the anarchy of an election, and the confusion of a Cockpit.' We have seen in the case of Samuel Pepys that it is not necessary for the writer to fail in the description of a cock-fight. It is a curious coincidence in Sherlock's remarks that, though he means two things when he speaks of an Election and a Cock-match, the word election was a recognised term in ' cocking.' Election is the act of choosing, and ' in the election of a fighting cock, there are four things principally to be considered, and they are shape, colour, courage, and sharp heel.'

The number of known characters, most of them taken from the life, in this picture gives great value to this representation of a scene full of the wildest

excitement.   The worst qualities of human nature
are discovered in the company consisting of all
classes, and on every man's face is seen the exhibition
of the greed of gain.

An ornamentation at the foot of the design
represents an oval medallion containing the figure
of a crowing cock ; on the ground of the medallion
is inscribed 'Royal Sport.'   This medallion is
named 'Pit ticket,' and represents a token of
admission to witness a cock-fight.

The engraving represents a cockpit, as seen by
artificial light during a combat between two fowls.
This is interesting, as the advertisement quoted
above speaks of the fight as taking place by daylight.
The central figure is that of a blind man who occupies
the central position.   This was intended for Lord
Albemarle Bertie, second son of Peregrine, second
Duke of Ancaster.   This gambler is also seen in the
'March to Finchley' as an attendant at a boxing
match.   The figure of the stout nobleman with the
star and riband has not been recognised, but is
evidently a portrait.   The reflection on the table is
the shadow of a man who has been drawn up to the
ceiling as a punishment for having made bets for
more money than he can pay.   John Ireland
quotes from the second canto of a poem entitled
'The Gamblers' the following illustrative notes :
' By the Cockpit laws, the man who cannot, or will
not pay his debts of honour, is liable to exaltation
in a basket.'—'Stephen's exaltation in a basket,

and his there continuing to bet, though unable to
pay, is taken from a scene in one of Hogarth's
prints, humorously setting forth, that there are
men whom a passion for gaming does not forsake,
even in the very hour that they stand proclaimed
insolvents.'

Mr. Dobson gives a further illustrative quotation
from 'Another Occasional Letter from Mr. Cibber
to Mr. Pope' (1744)—'As the merry mob at a Cock-
match hoist up a cheat into the basket, for having
lost a bet he was not able to pay.'

John Ireland says the scene is probably laid at
Newmarket, but adds : 'This is mere conjecture,
but from Jackson the hump-backed jockey, and some
other *sedate* personages who are present, I think
it is more likely to be designed for that place than
any other.' On the wall hung the royal arms,
and a full-length portrait of Nan Rawlings, a famous
cock-feeder, well known at Newmarket, also known
as Deptford Nan and Duchess of Deptford.

The prominence of the royal arms is a strong
argument in favour of the supposition that the
scene was taken from the Royal Cockpit, which is
reported to have been founded by Charles II.
Hogarth was interested in pugilism and the Art
of Self-Defence, which, however brutal it may be
considered, was found by many in the eighteenth
century to be a very useful accomplishment at a
time when little protection could be expected from
the watchmen in any possible street frays. Some

who remember how well Samuel Johnson could use his fists when occasion called may think it unfair to place prize-fighters in a chapter on Low Life, but at all events the exhibitions of pugilism come fairly under that heading, even if they were generally supported by those who are usually supposed to belong to High Life. James Figg, who died on the 7th December 1734, was much appreciated as a model by Hogarth, who introduced him into the Rake's Levée (Plate 2) and the 'Midnight Modern Conversation.' The most important is the figure in the corner of the picture of Southwark Fair, where Figg, bald-headed, seated on a pony, is seen starting to ride through the Fair. It was the practice of a great Master of Defence to ride through the City preceded by trumpets and drums and colours flying. Figg kept a great tiled booth on the Bowling Green, Southwark, during the time of the Fair. There was a performance daily at noon, which closed at four. He established himself at the corner of Wells Street and Castle Street near the Oxford Road, and built a wooden structure on a piece of waste ground there.

Samuel Ireland published in his *Graphic Illustrations* (vol. i. p. 89) a copy by A. M. Ireland of an etching by Simpson of Hogarth's drawing for Figg's business card. Mr. Dobson notes that an original impression in the possession of Mr. Fairfax-Murray is from the Bessborough Collection. The inscription below figures on a stage preparing for

an encounter, and spectators around, reads as
follows :

'JAMES FIGG

Master of yᵉ Noble Science of Defence
on yᵉ right hand in Oxford Road
near Adam and Eve Court teaches Gentlemen yᵉ use of yᵉ small back sword &
Quarterstaff at home & abroad '

This was the first London School of Arms, and Figg
is called the ' Atlas of the Sword ' in Captain John
Godfrey's *Useful Art of Defence*, 1747.

Dr. Byrom wrote 'Extempore Verses upon a Trial
of Skill between the two great Masters of Defence,
Messieurs Figg and Sutton,' which are printed in
Dodsley's *Collection of Poems* (vol. vi. p. 286). They
commence thus :

'Long was the great Figg by the prize-fighting swains,
Sole monarch acknowledg'd of Mary-bone plains,
To the towns, far and near, did his valour extend,
And swam down the river from Thames to Gravesend ,
Where liv'd Mr. Sutton, pipe-maker by trade,
Who, hearing that Figg was thought such a stout blade,
Resolv'd to put in for a share of his fame,
And so sent to challenge the Champion of Thame '

The end is a complete victory for Figg.

'Though Sutton, disabled as soon as he hit him,
Would still have fought on, but Jove would not permit him,
'Twas his fate, not his fault, that constrain'd him to yield,
And thus the great Figg became lord of the field.'

Samuel Ireland says that Ellis, an artist who
imitated the style of Hogarth in small conversations,
painted a portrait of Figg which was engraved by

Faber in mezzotint, and published by Overton in 1731. Mr. Dobson mentions a painting of Figg by Hogarth which belonged to S. Ireland, and was bought in 1801 by Mr. Vernon for eleven shillings, from which small sum it may be guessed that it is not a genuine work. J. P. Malcolm publishes an advertisement containing a challenge of Matthew Masterson and Rowland Bennet to James Figg, and Figg's acceptance of the challenge. He also notes that ' in December 1731 Figg and Sparks contended with the broadsword at the French or Little Theatre in the Haymarket before the Duke of Lorrain, Count Kinski, and many persons of distinction.' In one of the papers of the day we are told that ' the beauty and judgement of the sword was delineated in a very extraordinary manner by those two champions, and with very little bloodshed.'[1]

Samuel Ireland prints an advertisement of an encounter ' At Mr. Figg's Great Room at his house, the sign of the City of Oxford in Oxford Road . . . the Nobility and Gentry will be entertained (for the last time this season) in a most extraordinary manner with a select trial of skill in the Science of Defence, by the four following masters,' viz. William Holmes and Felix MacGuire against Figg and Edward Sutton.

Chetwood in his *History of the Stage* relates the ingenious way in which Figg supplied himself with

---

[1] Malcolm's *Anecdotes of the Manners and Customs of London during the Eighteenth Century* (1810), vol. ii. p. 176.

shirts at the expense of others. He told Chetwood
that he had not bought a shirt for years. It was
his practice when he fought in his Amphitheatre,
to send round to some of his scholars to borrow a
shirt for the ensuing combat. As most of the young
nobility and gentry were in his train, he obtained a
good many fine shirts from his admirers, the return
of which was not accepted by the lenders, as they
saw the cuts in the one Figg wore, and each man
supposed this to be what he lent. Among Figg's
chief pupils was George Taylor, or George the
Barber, as he was called, who succeeded his master in
the occupation of the amphitheatre in the Oxford
Road. Captain Godfrey treats Taylor as a link
between Figg, who was mainly a swordsman, and
John Broughton, whose fame rested on his eminence
as a pugilist.

Taylor was very successful and opened an
additional amphitheatre—the Great Booth, Tottenham Court.

There are two plates engraved by Richard Livesay
from the original sketches of Hogarth 'in the
Collection of Mr. Morrison.' They are entitled:
'George Taylor the Pugilist wrestling with Death'
(1) In which Taylor who was celebrated for his
skill in giving 'a back fall' has overthrown Death
and kneels on the chest of the skeleton. (2) 'George
Taylor the Pugilist overcome by Death' is here
seen lying on his back and still grasping the wrists
of his conqueror, who stoops over him. The two

sketches were afterwards sold to the Marquis of Exeter. Taylor died on February 21, 1750, and was buried in Deptford churchyard. These prints were published on March 1, 1782, by R. Livesay, ' at Mrs. Hogarth's, Leicester Fields, London.'

John Broughton (1705-1789), was apprenticed to a Thames waterman, and when at work on his own account generally plied at Hungerford Stairs. A quarrel and successful fight with a brother waterman is said to have settled his future employment as a pugilist. He attached himself to George Taylor's booth in Tottenham Court Road and remained there until 1742, when he quarrelled with Taylor. He set up a new amphitheatre in Hanway Yard on the 10th March 1743, and was acknowledged as the founder of the Prize-ring, and the head of his profession. He formed a code of rules which were accepted and remained without verbal alteration until 1838. Taylor acknowledged himself to be beaten by Broughton, and joined his rival's establishment in Hanway Yard.

Broughton opened an Academy of Boxing in the Haymarket and invented boxing-gloves, or ' mufflers ' as he called them. His advertisement of these novelties is quoted by Mr. Boulton from the *Advertiser* of February 1747.

' Mr. Broughton proposes with proper assistance to open an academy at his house in the Haymarket for the instruction of those who are willing to be initiated in the mystery of boxing, where the whole theory and practice of that truly British Art, with all the various blows, stops, cross buttocks, etc., incidental to combatants will be fully taught and explained ; and that persons of quality and distinction may not be debarred from entering into a course of these lectures, they will be given with the utmost tenderness and regard to the delicacy of the frame and constitution of the pupil, for which reason mufflers will be provided that will effectually secure them from the inconveniency of black eyes, broken jaws and bloody noses.'

This school was attached to a public-house kept by Broughton, the sign of which was a portrait of himself. The house was opposite the Haymarket Theatre. Mr. Dobson mentions a portrait of Broughton by Hogarth which was exhibited in 1817 by Lord Camden. It afterwards belonged to Mr. H. R. Willett, at whose sale in 1869 it was sold for £75, 12s. There is a version at Lowther Castle (Earl of Lonsdale).

Less than two months after Taylor's death, Broughton was defeated and his career ended. He met a Norwich butcher named Slack, who was a pugilist of some note although he treated him with disdain, and when a meeting was arranged for 11th April 1750, he had every confidence in his own success. Broughton started well, but suddenly Slack made a jump and dealt his opponent a prodigious blow between the eyes which blinded him. Broughton's patron the Duke of Cumberland, who had backed him to the amount of ten thousand pounds, was mad with excitement and called out: 'What are you about, Broughton? You can't fight; you're beat.' Broughton replied: 'I can't see my man, your Highness; I'm blind, not beat. Let me see my man, and he shall not gain the day.' Slack pursued his advantage and pummelled the blinded man into submission 'under fourteen minutes.'[1]

After this unfortunate occurrence Broughton retired on a small competence to Walcot Place, Lambeth. He died on the 21st January 1789, and was buried at Lambeth Church; the pall-bearers by his own request consisted of certain noted pugilists.

In the second volume of his *Graphic Illustrations* Samuel Ireland includes a sketch of Broughton and Slack fighting, which he says was intended 'as a card of admission to a great contest of skill,' but he gives no information as to its being the work of Hogarth; and although there is no improbability in the artist doing something for Broughton, it is rather unlikely that so late as 1750 he should compose a ticket of this kind. Mr. Dobson merely mentions it, and does not say anything further respecting it. The description of the fight is not very good, and as Slack was only a common-place boxer with a provincial reputation it is rather absurd to speak of the ' two immortal heroes of the pugilistic art.'

[1] W B Boulton's *Amusements of Old London*, 1901, vol. ii. p. 91.

In the years 1750-51 Hogarth must have been very busy with his remarkable series of prints specially illustrating some of the most flagrant evils in the Low Life of his time. Gin Lane and Beer Street are of the utmost importance as exhibiting the appearance of the streets of London. The Four Stages of Cruelty are almost too horrible for representation, and they belong more properly to a later chapter on Prisons and Crimes (XII.).

The announcement of the publication of these prints was made in the *General Advertiser* for February 13, 1750-51, as follows: 'On Friday next will be publish'd. Price 1ˢ. each. Two large prints design'd and etch'd by Mr. Hogarth, call'd Beer-Street and Gin-Lane. A number will be printed in a better manner for the curious at 1s. 6d. each. And on Thursday following will be published, Four Prints on the subject of Cruelty. Price and size the same. *N.B.*—As the subjects of these Prints are calculated to reform some reigning vices peculiar to the lower class of people in hopes to render them of more extensive use, the Author has published them in the cheapest manner possible. To be had at the Golden Head in Leicester-fields, where may be had all his other works.'

Beer Street is usually put before Gin Lane, as in this advertisement, but elsewhere Hogarth himself gives the following account of their origin: 'When these two prints were designed and engraved, the dreadful consequences of gin drinking appeared in every street. In *Gin Lane* every circumstance of its horrid effects is brought to view *in terrorem.* Idleness, poverty, misery and distress, which drives even to madness and death, are the only objects that are to be seen : and not a house in tolerable condition but the Pawnbroker's and Gin shop. *Beer Street,* its companion, was given as a contrast, where that invigorating liquor is recommended, in order to drive the other out of vogue. Here all is joyous and thriving. Industry and jollity go hand in hand. In this happy place the Pawnbroker's is the only house going to ruin ; and even the small quantity of porter that he can procure is taken in at the wicket, for fear of farther distress.'

G. Steevens supposes that Hogarth received his first idea for these prints from a pair by Peter Breughel, commonly called Breughel *d'Enfer* to distinguish him from his brother John, known as Breughel *de velours.* Of the two pictures referred to, ' the one is entitled *La Grasse,* the other *La Maigre Cuisine.* In the first all the personages are well-fed and plump ; in the second they are starved and slender. The latter of them also exhibits the figures of an emaciated mother and child, sitting on a straw mat upon the ground, whom I never saw without thinking on the female, etc., in Gin Lane. In Hogarth the fat English blacksmith is insulting the gaunt Frenchman, and in Breughel the plump cook is kicking the lean one out of doors. Our artist was not unacquainted with the works of this master.' If this be true, it shows the remarkable power Hogarth possessed of imbuing any idea he took from others with his own special character.

Gin Lane consists of Hogarth's representation of a street in that part of St. Giles's known as the Rookery, and cleared away in the middle of the nineteenth century for the new junction of Oxford Street with Holborn, known as New Oxford Street. The foremost figure is too horrible for pictorial art. It represents a miserable diseased woman, in tattered and scanty clothing, who sits at the top of a flight of stone steps, and, drunk with gin, lets the child she is suckling fall from her arms over the rail in the area. On the steps below her is an emaciated being, little more than a skeleton, who retails gin and ballads, but now is in a dying condition. This miserable creature is said to have been painted from nature after one whose cry was 'Buy my ballads, and I'll give you a glass of gin for nothing.'

The steps lead to a gin-cellar, over the doorway of which a large sign like a gin measure and inscribed 'Gin Royal' is suspended. Over the doorway is written :

> 'Drunk for a Penny,
> Dead drunk for two pence,
> Clean straw for nothing.'

Mr. Stephens refers to *The Old Whig* of February 26, 1736, for the statement that a strong-water shop had lately been opened in Southwark with the inscription on the sign which Hogarth fifteen years afterwards used on his print.

The Rev. James Townley's verses are engraved below the design :

'Gin, cursed fiend ! with fury fraught,
　Makes human race a prey :
It enters by a deadly draught,
　And steals our life away.

Virtue and Truth, driven to despair,
　Its rage compels to fly,
But cherishes, with hellish care,
　Theft, murder, perjury.

Damn'd cup ! that on the vital preys,
　That liquid fire contains !
Which madness to the heart conveys
　And rolls it thro' the veins.'

Gin or 'Hollands' is said to have been brought to England by William III. It was cheap and was sold in the streets, so that the demoralisation caused by this facility of purchase was grievous and widespread. The Middlesex magistrates insisted on the necessity for legislation, and the first Gin Act was passed in 1729. By this Act a new and additional excise duty of five shillings per gallon was put upon gin and other compounded spirits, and the retailer was to pay £20 a year for a licence, hawking about the streets being prohibited. The Act was quite ineffectual, and led to the invention of new forms of spirit, one being called in derision 'Parliament Brandy.' A satire on gin-drinking designed by Heemskirck and engraved by Toms was published about 1730. The Act was repealed in 1733 on the plea that, while doing no good, it checked the sale of barley to the distillers. This repeal was disastrous in its effects, and the almost universal orgy was terrible.

Another attempt to mitigate the evil was made by Sir Joseph Jekyll, Master of the Rolls, and the second Gin Act was passed in 1736. The prohibition led to riots, and it was found that the law could not be put in force.[1] As the 29th September 1736, the day on which the 'act for suppressing Geneva' was to come into operation approached, the retailers in gin put their signs in mourning, and made a parade of mock ceremonies for Madame Geneva's lying in state and her funeral.

Mr. Stephens quotes from the *Grub Street Journal*, the *London Daily Post*, the *Daily Advertiser*, and the *Daily Journal* particulars of the tumults that resulted.[2] The following are specimens : '*Mother Gin* lay in state yesterday at a distiller's shop in Swallow Street near St. James's Church ; but to prevent the ill consequences from such a funeral, a neighbouring justice took the undertaker, his men and all the mourners into custody.'—'Yesterday morning double guard mounted at Kensington ; at noon the guards at St. James's, the Horse Guards and Whitehall were reinforced, and last night about

[1] Sidney and Beatrice Webb, *History of Liquor Licensing in England from 1700 to 1830.* 1903.

[2] *British Museum Catalogue of Satires,* vol. iii p. 192.

300 life guards and horse-granidier guards paraded in Covent Garden, in order to suppress any tumult that might arise at the going down of Gin.'—' A party of foot-guards was posted at the house of Sir Joseph Jekyll, Master of the Rolls.'—' Two soldiers with their bayonets fixed were planted at the little door next Chancery Lane in case any persons should offer to attack the house . . . which the mob had tumultuously surrounded.'—' Several persons were committed, some to prison and some to hard labour, for publickly and riotously publishing, No Gin, No King.'

In the year 1736 a large number of pamphlets on the subject were published, far too numerous to record here. Two of them may be mentioned— ' *The Life of Mother Gin* . . . by an Impartial Hand,' and ' *The Deposing and Death of Queen Gin* . . . an Heroic Comi-Tragical Farce written by Jack Juniper a Distiller's Apprentice, just turn'd Poet, as it is acted at the New Theatre in the Haymarket.' The Act of 1736 was repealed in 1743, largely owing to the action of Lord Sandys. Lord Hervey made three orations against the repeal.

Sir Charles Hanbury Williams wrote two poems to ridicule both Lord Sandys and Lord Hervey. One of these is printed in *The Foundling Hospital for Wit* :

' Deep, deep in S——'s blund'ring Head,
   The new Gin Project sunk:
O happy Project ! sage, he cry'd,
   Let all the Realm be drunk.'

On June 25, 1751, the royal assent was given to another Bill for restricting the sale of spirituous liquor, and in the following September an engraving, ' The Funeral Procession of Madam Geneva, Sept[r] 29, 1751,' was published.[1] Hogarth's 'Gin Lane' was not published until February 1, 1751-2, but a drawing in Indian ink in the British Museum (' The Gin Drinkers, or the Gin Fiend ') is supposed to be a tracing from a scarce print ascribed to Hogarth and dated 1736. This statement, however, must be taken on the authority of Mr. Stephens.[2]

It is interesting to remember that Fielding published his most valuable *Enquiry into the Causes of the late Increase of Robbers*, etc., in January 1751, shortly before the appearance of ' Gin Lane,' and in the second section of this book ('Of Drunkenness, a second consequence of Luxury among the Vulgar '), although he does not specially refer to Gin Acts, he strongly argues that nothing but complete prohibition of poisonous spirits ' will extirpate so stubborn an evil.' He concludes the chapter thus : ' But if the difficulty be really insuperable, or if there be any political reason against the total demolition of this poison, so strong as to countervail the preservation of the morals, health and beings, of such numbers of his Majesty's subjects, let us however in some measure, palliate the evil, and lessen its immediate ill consequences, by a more

[1] *British Museum Catalogue of Satires*, vol. iii. p. 808.
[2] *Ibid.*, vol. iii. p. 217.

effectual provision against drunkenness than any we have at present, in which the method of conviction is too tedious and dilatory. Some little care on this head is surely necessary; for though the increase of thieves, and the destruction of morality, though the loss of our labourers, our sailors and our soldiers, should not be sufficient reasons, there is one which seems to be unanswerable, and that is the loss of our gin-drinkers; since should the drinking this poison be continued in its present height during the next twenty years, there will, by that time, be very few of the common people left to drink it.'

Another Act relative to the distilleries was in contemplation in 1759, and an anonymous letter to Hogarth was found among his papers in which he was urged again to take part in the fray :

'*December* 12, 1759.

' Sir,—When genius is made subservient to public good, it does honour to the possessor, as it is expressive of gratitude to his Creator by exerting itself to further the happiness of his creatures. The poignancy and delicacy of your ridicule has been productive of more reformation than more elaborate pieces would have effected. On the apprehension of opening the distillery, methinks I hear all good men cry Fire !—it is therefore the duty of every citizen to try to extinguish it. Rub up then Gin Lane and Beer Street, that you may have the honour and advantage of bringing the two first engines to the fire; and work them manfully at each corner of the building, and instead of the paltry reward of thirty shillings allowed by Act of Parliament, receive the glorious satisfaction of having extinguished those fierce flames which threaten a general conflagration to human nature, by pouring liquid fire into the veins of the now brave Britons, whose robust fabrics will soon fall in, when these dreadful flames have consumed the inside timbers and supporters.—I am, Sir, yours, etc.,

'AN ENGLISHMAN.'[1]

There is still the companion picture, 'Beer Street,' to be considered. The sentiment of this is the popular one of the glorifying our national drink, which when pure is well worthy of its great fame, for porter has been called the 'British Burgundy.'

Townley's lines on this print are as follows :

'Beer, happy product of our isle,
    Can sinewy strength impart,
And wearied with fatigue and toil,
    Can cheer each manly heart.

Labour and art, upheld by thee,
    Successfully advance;
We quaff the balmy juice with glee,
    And water leave to France.

---

[1] J. Ireland's *Hogarth Illustrated*, vol. iii. p. 353 (note). This letter or other suggestions seem to have caused Hogarth to draw attention to his prints, as *The Public Advertiser*, December 13, 1759, has the following announcement: 'By Desire This day are republished Price 1s. each, Two prints drawn and engraved by Mr. Hogarth call'd BEER STREET and GIN LANE' (*British Museum Catalogue*, vol. iii. p 818).

Genius of health, thy grateful taste,
  Rivals the cup of Jove;
And warms each English generous breast,
  With liberty and love'

As in Gin Lane the pawnbroker's house is the handsome building, so in Beer Street it is the only one falling to decay.

The scene is thus described by Mr. Stephens: ' A street in London, with the steeple of a church visible over the tops of some of the houses, and near the middle of the design; this structure being decorated with a flag, and formed in a peculiar manner, was probably intended for the steeple of St. Martin's in the Fields, Westminster. The day was an anniversary of the birth of George II. [October 30], the flag-hoisting being a practice in the so-called " royal parish " of St. Martin's, a practice familiar to Hogarth as a resident in Leicester Square.'

The sign-painter is said to have been intended for John Stephen Liotard, a portrait-painter of merit, but there is little likeness in face, as Liotard grew a long beard when he travelled in the Levant and was in consequence known as ' The Turk.' He lived at the ' Two Yellow Lamps ' in Golden Square. Two fishwomen are seated on the pavement in the front of the picture; one reads from a broadsheet on which is printed ' A New Ballad on the Herring Fishery by Mr. Lockman.' John Lockman, known as ' The Herring Poet,' was a friend of Hogarth, who

designed for him the frontispiece to the first volume
of his *Travels of Mr. John Gulliver* (1731). This
plate is entitled 'Gulliver presented to the Queen
of Babilary.' Lockman was secretary to the British
White Herring Fishery Company.

At the right-hand corner of the engraving is a
porter drinking his beer, who has just set down
his load, a large basket directed 'For Mr. Pastem
the Trunk Maker in Pauls C^h Y^d,' which is filled
with books the artist had a dislike for, such as
Hill on Royal Societies, Turnbul on Ant[ient]
Painting, Lauder on Milton. The mountebank Hill
and the forger Lauder deserved their position. Dr.
George Turnbull had been too laudatory of the
Black Masters to please the artist.

Fielding's *Causes of the late Increase of Robbers*
contains so much information and is so full of
valuable suggestions for the correction of the
rampant evils of Low Life that it may be recommended as a useful help to the intelligent study of
Hogarth's works.

CHAPTER V

POLITICAL LIFE

HOGARTH was in no sense a politician, and all his interests in the political life of his time were centred in the remarkable scenes which were acted in periods of excitement continually occurring, and the incidents which he introduced in his pictures as illustrations of the manners of eighteenth-century men and women. Whatever private opinions he may have had, he was unable to resist the representation of striking humours even when they were exhibited by his own friends. He was a friend of demagogues, as well as of those whose opinions were of a diametrically opposite character. At no time in our history were party politics so thoroughly unsatisfactory as they were in the middle of the eighteenth century. Walpole with his strong hand had passed away, and parties had divided into personal cliques. The division of Whigs and Tories was of little meaning, because the former had become so triumphant during the reigns of George I. and George II. that the condition of the Tories was almost hopeless unless they joined with some of the discontented Whigs. There were plenty of

Tories in the country, but they had little political interest on account of their possible connection with Jacobites.

Bribery and corruption had eaten into the hearts of all parties, and in consequence a man like William Pitt stood out as a name to conjure with because it stood for political purity.

Hogarth's picture of ' The Politician,' who represented one Tibson, a lace dealer in the Strand, reading with absorbed attention a copy of the *Gazetteer*, a paper which supported Sir Robert Walpole, was painted about the year 1730. An etching by J. K. Sherwin from the picture was not published until 1775, when Mrs. Hogarth issued it.

The painter gave the picture to Theodosius Forrest, son of one of his companions of the Five Days' Tour of 1732. It belonged successively to Peter Coxe, W. Davies, bookseller, and George Watson Taylor. At the sale of the latter's property in 1832 it was bought by Count Woronzow for thirty guineas.

The picture represents a man seated in a chair and wearing a broad-brimmed hat, who has taken a lighted candle from the candlestick on the table before him. Holding the candle in his right hand, he does not notice that the flame had set light to the projecting brim of his hat.

There is an anecdote of Bishop Burnet, who took precautions to prevent a similar accident which Hogarth may have known. The Bishop is said to

have advice that Lord Lovat was actually taken in a little Cabbin, dress'd in an old woman's habit a spining, and three Lords with him ; and that he was taken by an officer who had received intelligence of his lodging and habit at a little distance from where he was found.'

Mr. Stephens describes two engravings of this incident entitled respectively 'The Beautiful Simone' and 'Lord Lovat a spinning.'[1]

Lovat was carried in a litter to Fort William, and from thence by easy stages to London. When he reached St. Albans he was attended by Dr. Webster, a physician of the town, for an alleged sickness. Webster invited Hogarth to St. Albans to take a likeness of the prisoner at the White Hart Inn. It is stated that when, on August 14, Hogarth was introduced to Lovat the latter was being shaved, and he rose to welcome the painter, kissing him in the French manner. Owing to this embrace Hogarth received some of the soap-suds on his face, and he did not accept the salute with much satisfaction.

There is some doubt as to the original sketch from which the etching was made. There is one at the National Portrait Gallery which was purchased by the Trustees in June 1866, and another was, in 1879, in the possession of Mr. Henry Graves of Pall Mall, and purchased by him for £31. The original drawing was said, in the *Illustrated London News* of

[1] *British Museum Catalogue*, vol. iii. p. 601.

April 30, 1859, to be then in the possession of Lord Saltoun.

Lovat was not executed until 9th April 1747. Four small prints of Lord Lovat's trial were published by W. Birch, Hampstead Heath, August 1, 1791. These were from sketches belonging to Horace Walpole. One of these, in Indian ink and vermilion, is in the Print Room of the British Museum, having been purchased in August 1842 (Dobson). A mezzotint entitled 'Lovat's Ghost on Pilgrimage' was published on June 15, 1747, but it is doubtful as a work of Hogarth. Samuel Ireland affirmed that this was given to him by Dr. J. Webster, who had it from Hogarth with an assurance that it was his own design.[1]

'The Stage Coach, or Country Inn Yard' (1747) must be mentioned here on account of its connection with the general parliamentary election of that year, and its interest as the precursor of the famous series of the 'Election' (1754). It can also be compared with the first scene of the tragedy of the 'Harlot's Progress' (1731-2), which takes place in a London inn yard. The engraving of the inn yard shows, in the foreground, the coach ready to start on its journey, with the travellers seated and grouped around. The fat woman entering requires to be pushed in order to pass through the door. The two men on the roof look as if they might easily roll off on the occurrence of a sudden jolt. They are

[1] *British Museum Catalogue of Satires*, vol iii. p. 636

an English sailor and a French lackey, not very congenial companions. In the 'basket' is an old woman smoking a pipe and completing the picture of the preparations for what is likely to be a very uncomfortable journey, such as we read of in the realistic novels of the time. The fat hostess in the bow window of the bar of the house, which projects into the yard, adds to the general uproar by vociferating and vigorously ringing a bell. The sailor's bundle is labelled '——— of the *Centurion*.' This was the name of the ship in which the famous Anson sailed from Portsmouth on September 18, 1740, with four other vessels of war, and gained many successes in his attacks upon the Spaniards. He was made Rear-Admiral of the Blue and took command of a fleet which left Plymouth April 9, 1747, and included the *Centurion*, a fifty-gun ship with three hundred men on board, then under the command of Captain Denis. In the action off Cape Finisterre on May 3 the *Centurion* began the battle, but in the course of the fight its maintopmast was shot away. Captain Denis dropped out of the fight for a time in order to refit, and having done so returned to action and took part in the capture of the enemy's vessels. He brought news of the victory to England, and in consequence the Admiral was raised to the peerage as Baron Anson.[1]

Commander Charles Robinson, R.N., in his interesting volume on *The British Tar in Fact and Fiction*,

[1] *British Museum Catalogue*, vol. iii. p. 669.

1909, writes respecting this : ' The best example of the sailor of his period to be found in Hogarth's moral dramas in pictorial form is the figure seen on the top of a coach in " The Stage Coach in a Country Inn Yard." This sailor has just returned to England in the *Centurion*. He has been round the world with Anson, and is on his way home.'

At the back of the engraving (which was published on June 26) is seen a procession of men armed with sticks, some of the men carry a large effigy of a baby holding in one hand a child's rattle and in the other a hornbook. A flag is carried behind the chair in which the figure sits and is inscribed ' No Old Baby.' This refers to the cry used by the opponents of the Hon. John Child Tylney, Viscount Castlemaine, and afterwards Earl Tylney, who stood as candidate for the county of Essex as the opponent of Sir Robert Abdy and Mr. Bramstone. At the election a man was placed on a bulk with an infant in his arms and exclaimed as he whipped it, ' What, you little child, must you be a member ? ' Child Tylney was at this time only twenty years of age. There are three states of the plate : (1) in which the flag afterwards occupied by ' No Old Baby ' has no inscription ; (2) in which those words appear ; (3) in which they have been obliterated. On the wall of the house is the sign, a picture of an angel at full length, under which is inscribed ' The Old Angle In. Tom Bates from Lundun.' The galleries in the inn yard are filled with spectators.

Before dealing somewhat fully with the splendid series of four pictures of 'The Election' (1754), a slight reference must be made to the election of 1734, which was largely fought on the opposition party's cry of 'No Excise.' An etching was published in this year entitled 'Sir Robert Fagg bribing a Woman,' which has been attributed to Hogarth. It shows an old man sitting on horseback holding a purse in one hand offering a piece to a young woman, who stands at his horse's head with a basket of eggs on her arm and laughs at him. Fagg was a well-known man in his day and interested in horse-racing. He was member for Steyning, Sussex, and is stated to be one of the audience in Hogarth's picture of the 'Beggar's Opera.' There is a reference to him in Bramston's 'Art of Politicks':

> 'Leave you of mighty interest to brag,
> And poll two voices like Sir Robert Fagg.'

The baronet died on September 14, 1740.

In 1734 was also published a print in three divisions entitled 'The Humours of a Country Election,' and John Nichols hints that Hogarth may have borrowed the idea of illustrating the election of 1754 from this outcome of the election of 1734. Mr. Stephens gives a full account of the old print, which certainly contains some points of resemblance in idea, if not in expression.[1]

Hogarth's four pictures are of the greatest interest

---

[1] *British Museum Catalogue*, vol. iii. p. 23.

and illustrate the manners of the time in a very
remarkable degree.   They are fine examples of the
artist's best manner of painting, and are to be seen
in an excellent state of preservation at Sir John
Soane's Museum in Lincoln's Inn Fields.   The
incidents of all the scenes are in low comedy, but
Hogarth has raised his treatment of these incidents
with such distinction that they become instances
of high comedy, with perhaps the exception of the
first picture.   In passing, it may be remarked that
the pictures contain beauties of which the engravings
give but little idea.

Garrick with great judgment bought the pictures
for the ridiculously small price of two hundred
guineas.   At Mrs. Garrick's sale in 1823, Soane
bought them for £1732, 10s.

In justice to Garrick it is necessary to give the
particulars of the purchase.   Mr. Dobson, quoting
from Galt's *Life and Works of West*, 1820, pt. ii. 17,
gives an account of the disposal of the pictures.
Hogarth arranged that they should be raffled for,
with two hundred chances at two guineas the stake.
Among a few subscribers, Garrick was the only one
who appeared.   Much mortified, Hogarth insisted
that Garrick 'should go through the formality of
throwing the dice,' but for himself only.   The
actor for some time opposed the irritated artist,
but at last consented.   On returning home he
despatched a note to Hogarth stating that he could
not persuade himself to remove works so valuable

and admired without acquitting his conscience of an obligation to the painter, and to his own good fortune in obtaining them, and knowing the humour of the person he addressed, and that if he sent a cheque for the money it would in all probability be returned, he informed Hogarth that he had placed to his credit at his banker's two hundred guineas, which would remain there at his disposal or that of his heirs, if it were not accepted by himself.[1]

Garrick was very proud of these pictures and preserved them with care. When he was in Italy with his wife, he wrote to his man conjuring him to take care of them, and to keep them out of the sun.[2]

The parliamentary election following the dissolution of April 8, 1754, was a noteworthy one. The Jews Naturalisation Bill, passed in June 1753, greatly increased the unpopularity of Henry Pelham, and after his death, in order that his successors might the better be able to face the election, the Act was repealed. There were, however, many other cries against the administration, and its members fought at a great disadvantage, while the opposition—the True Blue Interest— were more than ever jubilant and hopeful of success.

The election for Oxfordshire was marked by a more animated conflict than what took place elsewhere. Some of the incidents in that contest

---

[1] Dobson's *William Hogarth*, 1907, p. 120
[2] J. Knight's *David Garrick*, 1894, p. 203.

survive in Hogarth's pictures. Although London is not the scene of these election incidents they are true to the manners of the eighteenth century both in country and town, so that we may be allowed to consider the pictures as representing what also occurred in London.

The engraving of these elaborate pictures occupied a considerable time. Plate 1, dedicated to the Right Hon. Henry Fox, was published on February 24, 1755; Plate 2, to Sir Charles Hanbury Williams, on February 20, 1757; Plate 3, to Sir Edward Walpole, on February 20, 1758; and Plate 4, to Sir George Hay, Judge of the Prerogative Court and the High Court of Admiralty, on January 1, 1758-9. Hay was an intimate friend of Hogarth, and possessed several of his paintings. He was a highly esteemed judge, praised for his enlightened judgment by Thurlow. The first plate was engraved entirely by Hogarth, the second entirely by C. Grignion, the third by Hogarth and Le Cave, and the fourth by Hogarth and F. Aviline.

There is a folio volume, lettered 'Subscribers' names for Four Prints of Election, March 19, 1754,' in the British Museum (Add. MSS. 22,394). The list is headed by the names of H.R.H. the Prince of Wales and H.R.H. the Princess Dowager of Wales. We can now deal more particularly with the incidents of the different pictures.

Plate 1, 'An Election Entertainment,' discovers a large room in a country inn in which members of one of the political parties[1] are holding a lively debauch not unlike in general effect that represented in the 'Midnight Modern Conversation' (1733). One of the candidates, a young man, sits at the head of the table (Richard Slim), and on his left is an elderly man, his fellow candidate (Sir Commodity Taxem). A flag on which is inscribed 'Liberty and Loyalty,' is fixed at the back of the latter's chair.

The younger candidate was said to be taken from Thomas Potter, the very clever but worthless son of Archbishop Potter, although this has been denied by others, probably with truth. Hogarth told George Steevens that there was only one portrait in the picture; this was Sir John Parnell, nephew of the poet Thomas Parnell, who desired to be put in because he was so generally known that the introduction of his face would be of service to the artist in the sale of prints in Dublin. He is seen diverting the company by showing a face drawn with a burnt cork upon the back of his hand, while he sings the song entitled 'An old woman clothed in grey.' Mr. Dobson refers to *Angelo's Reminiscences* (1830, ii. 425) to show that this was the way in which the song was usually sung.

---

[1] It shows how impartial Hogarth is in his satire on the humours of the election that there is a difference of opinion among authorities as to which party is represented in this picture. John Ireland says that the company consists of the friends of the Court party, while Dr Trusler expresses no doubt that 'the present are tories under false pretences.' The 'Poetical Description' said to be written under 'Mr. Hogarth's sanction and inspection' contains no hint either way. The painter was content to direct impartial attention to the humours of both parties.

John Nichols refers to a pamphlet in which another of the characters is identified.[1] This is the portly clergyman sitting at the table who, having taken off his wig with one hand, is rubbing his bald head with the other. The writer of the pamphlet says this was the Rev. Dr. Cosserat, and he deals not over tenderly with ' the Doctor represented sitting among the freeholders and zealously eating and drinking for the sake of the New Interest.'

The incidents in this riotous scene are so numerous and appeal so vividly to the eye that it is only necessary to refer to a few of them. Stones and brickbats are supposed to be thrown in at the open window by the opponents outside; one of these stones strikes the lawyer, counting up the votes, on the forehead so that he falls back over his chair, but the compliment is vigorously returned by those inside. In the tobacco tray is a paper of Kirton's best, and a slip from the Act against bribery and corruption has been torn to light pipes with. Kirton was a tobacconist who kept a shop near St. Dunstan's Church, Fleet Street, and impaired his circumstances as well as ruined his constitution by wasting his time on the Oxfordshire election of 1754. On the butcher with *pro patria* on his cap and his wounded companion in the front of the picture, John Ireland found among his papers the following note by

---

[1] ' The Last Blow, or an unanswerable Vindication of the Society of Exeter College, in reply to the Vice-Chancellor, Dr. King, and the Writers of the *London Evening Post*, 1755,' 4to, p. 21.

Hogarth: 'These two patriots, who, let what party will prevail, can be no gainers, yet spend their time, which is their fortune, for what they suppose right, and for a glass of gin lose their blood, and sometimes their lives, in support of the cause, are, as far as I can see, entitled to an equal portion of fame with many of the emblazoned heroes of ancient Rome: but such is the effect of prejudice, that though the picture of an antique wrestler is admired as a grand character, we necessarily annex an idea of vulgarity to the portrait of a modern boxer. An old blacksmith in his tattered garb is a coarse and low being; strip him naked, tie his leathern apron round his loins, chisel out his figure in freestone or marble, precisely as it appears, he becomes elevated,—and may pass for a philosopher, or a Deity.' [1]

The one of these two men who is having gin poured upon his head is said to have been painted from Teague Carter of Oxford, a fighting man or 'bruiser.' Another well-known character was the blind violinist who represents a woman called 'Fiddling Nan,' who frequented the neighbourhood of Oxford.

The elector's arms on the wall, 'A chevron, sable between three guineas, or,' with the crest of a gaping mouth and motto 'Speak and Have,' are quite appropriate to the evident sentiments of most of those present at this entertainment. The various election cries are curious, like the inscription on the flag

---

[1] *Hogarth Illustrated*, vol. iii. p. 361.

M

thrown down on the floor, ' Give us our eleven days '
—a shocking appeal to the ignorance of the populace
against the valuable Act passed 1752 for the alteration of the Style in accordance with the Gregorian
Calendar.

> ' When the country folk first heard of this Act,
>   That old father Style was condemned to be rack'd,
>   And robb'd of his time, which appears to be fact,
>   Which nobody can deny ;
>   It puzzl'd their brains, their senses perplex'd,
>   And all the old ladies were very much vex'd,
>   Not dreaming that Levites would alter our text ,
>   Which nobody can deny.'

Outside the window is seen a cavalcade in the
street following an effigy of the Duke of Newcastle,
on the breast of which is inscribed ' No Jews.' The
flags have these mottoes—' Liberty and Property
and No Excise,' ' Marry and Multiply in spite of
the Devil and the [Court],' alluding to the Marriage
Act of 1753.

Plate 2.—Canvassing for Votes.

In the village street of Guzzledown are seen in the
foreground two places of entertainment : on the left
hand an inn of some importance with the sign of the
Royal Oak, and on the right hand the Porto Bello
alehouse.   At a table in front of the latter house
the village cobbler and the barber are engaged in a
discussion as to the taking of Portobello by Admiral
Vernon in the year 1739 with six ships only.   The
barber is distinguished by the implements of his
trade on the ground, and the cobbler by a pair of

shoes on the table by his side. The barber, to illustrate his argument, has broken from the stem of his
pipe six pieces which he has arranged crescent-wise on
the table, and points to this arrangement with the
stump of his pipe. The cobbler appears to have
won the bet, as he draws the stakes to himself.
Over the doorway is a signboard with a painting of
ships at sea and the name [Por]tobello. On the
barber's pot of beer is inscribed the owner's name,
'John Hill at the Porto Bello.' Admiral Vernon
became so popular owing to his great victory that his
head was painted on a large number of the signposts
of the country, and at the next general election in
1741 was elected for three different constituencies.
In front of the bow window of the bar of the Royal
Oak is seen the candidate talking to two ladies in
the balcony. A kneeling porter offers him a letter
addressed to Tim Partitool, Esq.

Part of the sign of the inn is obscured by a large
show cloth, at the foot of which is 'Punch, Candidate
for Guzzledown.' On the cloth two subjects are
painted, which are divided horizontally near the
middle. On the upper picture the Horse Guards
and the Old Treasury building are represented.
The lower picture displays the destiny of the money
taken from the Treasury; in the upper picture
Punch is seen trundling a wheelbarrow with one
hand, while with the other he ladles out coins. In
the barrow are two bags of money, respectively
labelled 9000 and 7000. Two men with hats in

their hands eagerly meet Punch and catch the coin he scatters. An old hunchbacked woman holds out her hand for a bribe. These pictures were intended to advertise the puppet show to be seen later in the inn yard. On one of the boxes set down by the porter previously mentioned is inscribed 'Punch's Theatre, Royal Oak Yard.'

In describing the upper picture of the show cloth the commentators seem to have gone too far in their guesses as to Hogarth's meaning. J. Nichols writes: 'The height of *The Treasury* is contrasted with the squat solidity of *The Horse Guards,* where the arch is so low, that the State Coachman cannot pass through it with his head on ; and the turret on the top is so drawn as to resemble a beer-barrel. Ware the architect very gravely remarked, on this occasion, that the chief defect would have been sufficiently pointed out by making the coachman only stoop. He was hurt by Hogarth's stroke of satire.' John Ireland repeats this story, but Dr. Trusler, who wrote earlier, says nothing about Ware or the contrast between the Horse Guards and the Treasury. Both these buildings were really designed by Hogarth's enemy Kent. The Horse Guards was built in 1751-53 by John Vardy, after a design furnished by William Kent. The Old Treasury, a stone building still fronting the Horse Guards Parade, was erected in 1733 from Kent's design for a much more extensive front. The explanation of the intrusion of Isaac Ware's name by Nichols and

Ireland under the impression that he was the architect of the Horse Guards is to be found in the life of Ware in the *Dictionary of National Biography.* ' In 1751-2 and again in 1757-8 he was employed as draughtsman at a salary of £100 on the building of the Horse Guards from Kent's designs.'

There is still to be mentioned the Crown Inn, which is inscribed 'The Excise Office.' Trusler notes that in country places the excise office was generally held at public-houses. A crowd of men are assembled before this building with the intention of sacking it. Stones are thrown at the windows, and the landlord fires a blunderbuss which wounds one of the crowd. Another man, determined to destroy the sign of the Crown, has bestridden the beam which supports it, and saws the beam, forgetting that he must fall with it. At the back of the picture there is a rising ground with trees and fields, and on the ridge is a village with a church.

We leave for the last a notice of the group of three men (a countryman between the hosts of the rival inns who both put coins into his hands) in the centre of the picture, which, without demanding the special attention of the spectator, forms the very pivot of the scene and gives a harmony to the whole, which presents a perfect marvel of pictorial composition. It has been said that the idea of Reynolds's picture of 'Garrick between Tragedy and Comedy' was taken from this elegant group, but this seems to be a rather far-fetched suggestion. John Ireland writes :

'I am tasteless enough to prefer this to "Garrick between Tragedy and Comedy." From Hogarth the hint was indisputably taken, but exquisite as is the face of Thalia (and it is perhaps not to be paralleled in any other picture) the countenance of the actor from the contention of two passions has assumed a kind of idiotic stare of which our honest farmer has not an iota. In the true spirit of Falstaff he says, or seems to say : " D'ye think I do not know ye ? Ha ! ha ! ha ! he ! he ! he ! " ' [1]

The remarkable circumstance about this is that the charm of this group is entirely due to the artist's innate conception of beauty as the persons themselves, although true to life, are commonplace, with no pretence to charm.

Plate 3.—Polling at the Hustings.

We have here the election polling-booth set up in a meadow near the bank of a river which is crossed by a substantial bridge. The platform of the booth is approached by a flight of wooden steps. In the front is a voter, imbecile in body and mind. A man in a laced cocked hat is eagerly whispering into the voter's ear. It will be seen that on one of the man's legs there is a manacle. In his pocket is seen ' The 6th Letter to the [People of England],' which proves that the man was the notorious Dr. Shebbeare, who was condemned by Lord Mansfield to the pillory for this treasonable letter. It was reported that he

---

[1] *Hogarth Illustrated*, vol. ii p. 113.

frequently said in the public coffee-house that he would have a pillory or a pension. He had both, for Lord Bute gave him the latter. The reserve voters, consisting of the blind and the halt, are being brought to the booth, and on the top of the steps a dying man wrapped in a blanket is carried by two porters. None of these horrors appear to be exaggerated, for any dangers would be risked to get a vote. John Ireland relates that Dr. Barrowby persuaded a dying man that, being much better, he might venture with him in his chariot to the hustings in Covent Garden, to poll for Sir George Vandeput. The unhappy voter took his physician's advice, and in less than an hour after his return, expired. In the midst of all these realistic incidents a bit of allegory seems somewhat out of place—in the right corner of the picture Britannia's state coach is seen in a dangerous condition, while the coachman dropping his reins plays cards with the footman on the box. Britannia's attempts to attract their attention by pulling the check-string are quite unheeded.

Plate 4.—Chairing the Members.

We have here a street in a country town where the road passes between a brook and the wall of a church. At the back of the picture is a building with a belfry on the roof, the pediment of which contains the royal arms. On the right are two houses; the one at the back apparently has been wrecked by the mob :

the front one is full of life; it is supposed to be the committee room of the defeated candidate at his lawyer's house. Many persons are at the window, and three cooks bearing dishes are seen entering the door.

A blind and bearded fiddler leads the mob, followed by a bear carrying a monkey with a carbine over its shoulder which is accidentally discharged, to the imminent danger of the chimney-sweeps on the churchyard wall. This is said to allude to an incident which actually occurred at the Oxfordshire election of 1754. A mob attempted to throw a post-chaise into the river, when Captain T——, who was in the carriage, shot a chimney-sweeper who was a ringleader in the assault, and his followers dispersed. The captain was tried and acquitted. Now comes the new member borne aloft on a chair by four strong men. A countryman in charge of a sow and her litter strikes the head of one of the bearers at his back with his flail. The bearer staggers and the member, terrified and in danger of falling, clutches the arms of the chair as his hat flies from his head. A young lady on the wall of the churchyard, one of the spectators of the procession, faints at the suddenness of the accident. A crowd follows the first member, amongst which is the second member, whose shadow only is seen on the side of the building at the back.

The goose hovering over the chaired member is said to be intended as a parody of the eagle above the laurelled helmet of Alexander in Le Brun's picture of the 'Battle of the Granicus.' The little fat member previously dubbed Punch is generally supposed to be a vivid representation of the intriguing manager of the Leicester House party—Bubb Dodington (afterwards Lord Melcombe), although he does not seem to have had anything to do with this election. This is another instance of the generality of Hogarth's satire, which was never allowed to be completely personal. Dodington's figure was too grotesque to be passed by, and his head was used as the first in the second row of the 'Five Orders of Periwigs.' Hogarth does not appear to have had any prejudice against the man himself—in fact, he may have felt some interest in him on account of his connection with Sir James Thornhill. George Bubb Dodington (1691-1762) spent £140,000 in completing a magnificent mansion begun by his uncle, George Dodington, at Eastbury in Dorsetshire, of which Vanbrugh was architect. Thornhill painted a ceiling there in 1719, and subsequently represented Weymouth in Parliament as Dodington's nominee. Dodington's name does not stand high in political history ; he has been taken as the representative jobber of his day, partly owing to the full particulars of corruption given in his Diary. There is therefore all the more reason why any incident in his career that does him credit should be recorded. He showed great courage when, on the 22nd of February, 1757, he made a strong speech in the House of Commons against the execution (or rather judicial murder) of Admiral Byng. The milestone at the extreme right of the picture is inscribed 'xix miles from London'—another attempt to confuse the locality of the Election.

The inscription on the sun-dial fixed on the church contains an atrocious pun. There are two words, 'We must,' and 'die all' (dial) is inferred.

Special reference is made in the second chapter of this book to the deadly quarrel between Hogarth and Wilkes near the end of the artist's life, but its political character must be more fully described in the present chapter.

Hogarth was the aggressor by reason of his publication of 'The Times, Plate 1,' which was a satire strongly in favour of Lord Bute and against Pitt, Temple and Wilkes. One cannot be surprised at Wilkes's anger, but the way he exhibited this anger was quite inexcusable, and is difficult to understand, as Wilkes was naturally a placable man. These are some of the vitriolic words in No. 17 of the *North Briton* published on Saturday, September 25, 1762, which is entirely devoted to Hogarth: 'We all titter the instant he takes up a pen, but we tremble when we see the pencil in his hand.' 'I need only make my appeal to any one of his historical or portrait pieces which are now considered as almost beneath criticism.' Then follows a ridiculous and unkind condemnation of 'Sigismunda.' 'He never caught a single idea of beauty, grace or elegance, but on the other hand he never missed the least flaw in almost any production of nature or of art. This is his true character. He has succeeded very happily in the way of humour, and has miscarried in every other attempt. This has arose in some measure from his head, but much more from his heart. After "Marriage à la Mode," the public wished for a series of prints of a happy marriage. Hogarth made the attempt, but the rancour and malevolence of his mind made him very soon turn with envy and disgust from objects of so pleasing contemplation, to dwell and feast a bad heart on others of a hateful cast, which he pursued, for he found them congenial, with the most unabating zeal and unrelenting gall.'

Wilkes must have been ashamed of what he had written, as Hogarth said he was, and he wrote no more abuse. In his preliminary note for a reprint of the 'Epistle to William Hogarth' in the collected edition of Churchill's Poems, he writes with a certain amenity, although he does not express regret for what Churchill wrote: 'Mr. Hogarth had for several years lived on terms of friendship if not intimacy with Mr. Wilkes. . . . A friend wrote to him, that Mr. Hogarth intended soon to publish a political print of the Times, in which Mr. Pitt, Lord Temple, Mr. Churchill and himself were held out to the public as objects of ridicule. Mr. Wilkes on this notice remonstrated by two of their common friends to Mr. Hogarth that such a proceeding

would not only be unfriendly in the highest degree,
but extremely injudicious ; for such a pencil ought
to be universal and moral, to speak to all ages and
all nations, not to be dipped in the dirt of the
faction of a day, of an insignificant part of the
country, when it might command the admiration
of the whole.   An answer was sent, that neither
Mr. Wilkes nor Mr. Churchill was attacked in the
Times, though Lord Temple and Mr. Pitt were, and
that the print would soon appear.   A second
message soon after told Mr. Hogarth that Mr.
Wilkes would never think it worth his while to take
notice of any reflections on himself ; but when his
friends were attacked he found himself wounded
in the most sensible part, and would as well as he
could revenge their cause ; adding that if he thought
the *North Briton* would insert what he should send,
he would make an appeal to the public on the very
Saturday following the publication of the print.'

Churchill's poem is full of unjust and ill-bred
abuse.   The earlier part is poor stuff till we come
to line 309, where the direct attack upon Hogarth
commences, and then it becomes strong.   Here is
a bitter line :

'He had desert, and Hogarth was his foe.'

The vituperation now is in full swing :

'When Wilkes, our countryman, or common friend,
Arose his king, his country to defend :

.   .   .   .   .   .

What could induce thee, at a time and place,
Where manly foes had blush'd to shew their face,

To make that effort which must damn thy name
And sink thee deep, deep in thy grave with shame ?
Did virtue move thee ? No, 'twas pride, rank pride,
And if thou hadst not done it, thou hadst died.'

Again :

'Oft have I known thee, Hogarth, weak and vain,
Thyself the idol of thy awkward strain,
Through the dull measure of a summer's day,
In phrase most vile, prate long, long hours away,
Whilst friends with friends all gaping sit, and gaze
To hear a Hogarth babble Hogarth's praise.
But if athwart thee interruption came
And mention'd with respect some ancient's name,
Some ancient's name who in the days of yore,
The crown of art with greatest honour wore.
How have I seen thy coward cheek turn pale,
And black confusion seize thy mangled tale !
How hath thy jealousy to madness grown,
And deemed his praise injurious to thy own !
Then without mercy did thy wrath make way
And arts and artists all became thy prey.'

Churchill returned to his abuse in his last poem, *Independence* (published late in September 1764), where he parries the attack in Hogarth's caricature of him as the Bruiser and, accepting the figure of a Bear, draws a spirited description of himself ending thus :

'A subject met with only now and then,
Much fitter for the pencil than the pen ;
Hogarth would draw him (Envy must allow)
E'en to the life, was Hogarth living now.'

In spite of Churchill taking the painter's death for granted, he did not die till four weeks later, and the poet only survived him nine days. It is very distressing that these unfortunate circumstances

as he never saw a cheese with a hole bored through the middle, he ventures to pronounce it a millstone, which, by the way, the doggerel writer quoted by Nichols also does.

The Highlander (Lord Bute) who helps to supply water in buckets from the spring to the fire is driven into by a man with a wheelbarrow loaded with waste paper described as *Monitors* and *North Britons*. These are to help increase the fire, and the man is trying to destroy the waterpipe with his wheel-barrow. The man is said to be intended for the Duke of Newcastle. One of the signs to the left of the picture is the Newcastle Arms; this is to be superseded by the sign of the Patriot's Arms dated 1762, which is being hoisted up a ladder. The arms consist of four clenched fists in direct opposition to each other. These are introduced here in contrast with the double hand-in-hand of the Union Office. John Ireland notes that Hogarth seems to have had a strong antipathy to the politics of this year. In later impressions of Plate 8 of the 'Rake's Progress' will be found a halfpenny with the same date, 'in which Britannia is represented in the character of a maniac, with dishevelled hair.'

As the year is specially distinguished on the Patriot's Arms, so the month of August is marked by the introduction of the treasure wagon marked Hermione. This treasure contained in twenty wagons passed through the streets of London in its way to the Tower on the 12th of that month. It was seen entering St. James's Street by the King and his Court from the windows of St. James's Palace, a large company being present, as George Prince of Wales was born on that day.

The *Hermione*, a Spanish register ship, which left Lima on the 6th January bound for Cadiz, was taken on the 21st May off Cape St. Vincent by three English frigates and carried into Gibraltar. The introduction of this treasure of immense value into the picture is a heavy asset for Pitt's party against all that is figured against it. There are many more points that might be added to this description, for the incidents included are innumerable.

The two figures in the garret of the Temple Coffee-House were intended to represent Hogarth's former friends and present enemies, Wilkes and Churchill. Ireland says that previous to publication the faces were altered and adds: ' If Hogarth must be so unmercifully abused for what he inserted, he is entitled to some credit for what he erased. I hope this blot in his original design will not be considered as an additional blot on his escutcheon.' In considering this plate of ' The Times,' which presents so many points open to severe criticism, one cannot but feel astonishment that two such men as Wilkes and Churchill should so thoroughly have mismanaged their attack upon Hogarth. They neither touch the question at issue nor attempt to show where he is wrong. Instead of this, they merely abuse, and abuse in a particularly truculent and

objectionable manner, which must have disgusted
any respectable person who read their prose and verse.
They exaggerate some of his faults, but the greater
portion of their words are not only untrue but the
exact opposite of the truth. When Churchill saw
the portraits of himself and Wilkes he most certainly
must have known how untrue were these words :

> ' Thy feeble age ! in which, as in a glass,
> We see how men to dissolution pass.
> Thou wretched being, whom, on reason's plan
> So changed, so lost, I cannot call a man,
> What could persuade thee, at this time of life,
> To launch afresh into the sea of strife ?
> Better for thee scarce crawling on the earth,
> Almost as much a child as at thy birth,
> To have resign'd in peace thy parting breath,
> And sunk unnoticed in the arms of Death.'

Hogarth's triumphant answers to Wilkes and
Churchill were his portraits of them, which show
the painter at his best in all his original vigour and
versatility. The portrait of ' John Wilkes, Esq.,
drawn from the Life, and Etch'd in Aquafortis by
Willm Hogarth,' was published on May 16, 1763.
It can scarcely be considered as a caricature, and
Wilkes himself acknowledged that he was daily
becoming more like it. The etching was very
rapidly made, for Hogarth did not draw the portrait
until May 6th, when Wilkes was brought before
Lord Chief-Justice Pratt (afterwards Lord Camden)
at Westminster. Churchill was very indignant at
the artist skulking behind a screen, as he expressed it.

N

'The Bruiser, C. Churchill (once the Rev^d !)
in the character of a Russian Hercules, regaling
himself after having kill'd the Monster Caricatura
that so sorely call'd his Virtuous friend, the Heaven
born Wilkes,' was published on August 1. For this
caricature Hogarth took the copper-plate on which
was engraved (1749) his own portrait from the picture
now in the National Gallery, and erasing nearly all
the work, leaving the dog and part of the curtain
and palette, he drew the poet as a bear with a staff
marked N.B. for *North Briton*, and covered with
knots inscribed Lye 1, 2, 3, etc. In the fourth
state of the plate a framed picture representing
a tomb similar to that of Newton in Westminster
Abbey, with Pitt reclining in place of Newton,
concealed part of the palette.

The production of these plates was an act of
revenge, and instances of revenge are not pleasant
to contemplate, but it certainly was just. The two
men made their mark in the history of the eighteenth
century and are not likely to be forgotten, but it
may truly be said that they will be remembered
more owing to Hogarth's caricatures than by their
own writings. Sandby renewed his attacks upon
Hogarth, and other caricaturists of less ability
made fun of 'The Times' and its designer, but it is
scarcely worth while to deal with these here because
their very existence was lost sight of by Hogarth in
his indignation against the two writers.

Soon after 'The Times, Plate 1' was published

' The Times, Plate 2' was prepared, probably in the same year 1762, but the sky and some parts of the plate were never finished. It is not easy to understand the intended object of the design. The general idea seems to be to represent a state of peace as Plate 1 showed a state of tumult and disorder. Mr. Stephens describes the plate fully and writes, ' It is certain that whatever might have been the direction of the satire in " The Times, Plate 1," it was opposed in more than one direction by the sequel to that design.' [1] Hogarth was wisely dissuaded by his friends from publishing the print, and Mrs. Hogarth, knowing the reasons urged to her husband, adhered to the same resolution. At her death only one impression had been taken, and that had been sold to Lord Exeter for ten guineas. All the property was left to Mrs. Lewis, Hogarth's cousin, and she sold the plate to Alderman Boydell, who struck off prints from it in 1790: ' Designed & engraved by W. Hogarth. Published May 29, 1790, by J. & J. Boydell, Cheapside, & at the Shakespeare Gallery, Pall Mall, London.'

John Ireland writes of Mrs. Hogarth's decision: ' In withholding this print from the public she acted prudently, in attempting to describe it, I may be thought to act otherwise.' In a large open space among buildings, the centre of which is a platform surrounded by a trench, the sides of which are supported by a brick wall, is a statue of George III.

[1] *British Museum Catalogue*, vol. iv. p. 197.

in his coronation robes.   The base of the statue is inscribed A. Ramsay del^t, and as the plummet may be taken as a guide to the squareness of the drapery, we may believe this to be a satirical reference to the portrait painter.   The pedestal occupies the centre of the platform to indicate that here is the fountain of honour.   A Scotch gardener, supposed to be Lord Bute, controls the passage of water in the pipe that supplies the fountain and nourishes the roses and oranges.   The other gardener, supposed to be Henry Fox, afterwards Lord Holland, casts away the old-fashioned plants.

On the left of the plate is a representation of the House of Commons, with Sir John Cust, the Speaker, in the chair.   Various members of the House of Lords are also present.   On the right of the plate are two figures in the pillory. 'Conspiracy,' 'M^s Fanny' refers to the fraud of the Cock Lane Ghost.   The other figure is marked as Wilkes and the word ' Defamation ' is inscribed on the top of the pillory. On the roof of a building which stands prominently forward are many workmen hoisting a huge palette marked ' Premium,' and having a sheaf of painters' brushes stuck in the thumbhole.   This is intended to represent the Society of Arts, but the building is entirely imaginary, as the Society did not occupy a building of importance until they removed to the Adelphi in 1774.   At this time they had apartments in Beaufort Buildings.   In the distance is seen the steeple of the new church of St. Mary le Strand.

Still further back is the Chinese pagoda in Kew Gardens, designed by Sir William Chambers, and to the left Somerset House, then in course of construction, and also the work of Chambers.

On 27th September 1762 was published an etching intended as a sequel and rejoinder to 'The Times, Plate 1.' It is entitled 'The Times, Plate 2,' and must not be confused with Hogarth's Plate 2, which was not published until 1790, and therefore unknown to the public in 1762. In the middle of a large open space among houses Hogarth is seen standing in a pillory. There are allusions to the incidents brought into Hogarth's Plate 1, but one of the best is the Patriot Arms, shown to be two hands clasped and enclosing a sword and an olive branch.

In this chapter we have obtained a fair insight into the political life of the eighteenth century, but it is to be feared that most of the methods of politicians are seen to be coarse and revolting.

CHAPTER VI

CHURCH AND DISSENT

HOGARTH was keenly alive to the existence of a widespread immorality throughout the country during his lifetime, and set himself to reform the world by satire of some of the worst evils which were open to the day. (He also realised the want of earnestness in religious life, but he was equally opposed to a religious revival, and could only see evil in the great movement of Wesley and Whitefield which helped to reform the world as the Coming of the Friars did, for a time at least, in a former age.

The main cause of the evils of the day was a want of earnestness in Church and State, or in other words the universal dread of enthusiasm—a feeling which overlooked the fact that enthusiasm, tempered it is true by judgment, is the moving spirit of the world. Many of the great men of the eighteenth century were moved to do their fine work by enthusiasm, but they called the moving force by another name. Talleyrand's constant cry *Pas de zèle* may sometimes be a useful caution, but naturally it has a deadening effect upon the soul.

In the middle of the eighteenth century Dr.

Edward Young, the well-known author of *Night Thoughts*, wrote a book on the manners of his time which was long a popular work. It was entitled '*The Centaur not Fabulous*, in six Letters to a Friend on the Life in vogue.' He found 'as in the fabled centaur the Brute runs away with the Man,' and reviewing the Life then lived showed how Infidelity and Pleasure degraded the men and women. He then by preaching the dignity of man paints the centaur's restoration to humanity. No characteristic of at least a portion of the eighteenth century was more marked than the deadness or somnolence of the Church. The stability of the Hanoverian dynasty during a dangerous time made it necessary for the Ministry to choose the governors of the Church from men of the same political opinions as themselves. The High Church party were supposed to be too intimately connected with nonjurors and Jacobites to be treated as safe men for office, and the field was thus limited so that it was often difficult to discover proper persons to fill the office of Bishop. The Broad Churchmen or Latitudinarians were mostly lifeless in their beliefs, while highflyers such as Sacheverell were equally unspiritual. However, it is unwise to condemn the clergy generally, for such names as those of Tillotson, Stillingfleet, and Tenison must not be forgotten on the other side.

It is interesting to mark the difference between the government of the Church in the seventeenth

and eighteenth centuries respectively. In spite of
the dissoluteness of the Court, the appointments to
bishoprics in the reign of Charles II. seem to have
been carried out conscientiously, and many very
distinguished men sat upon the episcopal bench,
who were the superiors of such men as Gibson and
Hoadly, who both find a place in the Hogarth
gallery. (In the eighteenth century many of the
Bishops were haughty and inactive, although there
were a few exceptions as Thomas Herring, Archbishop of Canterbury, whose portrait was painted
by Hogarth. He was a strong Whig and zealous for
the Hanoverian dynasty. He was colourless as a
theologian, but the practical side of religion appealed
to him, and he did his utmost to improve the
religious feeling of his age. He was certainly more
popular than Gibson and Hoadly, who were constantly caricatured in the pictorial satires of the
day. Herring was Bishop of Bangor in 1737, and
Archbishop of York in 1743. In the northern
archbishopric he took a prominent part in preparations against the rebellion of 1745. As Arch-
deacon Coxe writes in his Life of Horatio Lord
Walpole: ' He exerted himself with great zeal in
favour of government; having convened a public
meeting in his diocese, he made a sensible and
animated speech, obtained a subscription to a
considerable amount, and contributed to raise and
embody volunteers and other corps of troops, who
performed essential services against the rebels.'

The younger Horace Walpole writing to Sir Horace Mann (Oct. 4, 1745) was even more laudatory. He said: 'Dr. Herring has set an example that would rouse the most indifferent; in two days after the news arrived at York of Cope's defeat (at Preston Pans), and when they every moment expected the victorious rebels at their gates, the Bishop made a speech to the assembled county, that had as much true spirit, honesty and bravery in it as ever was penned by an historian for an ancient hero.'

A pictorial satire was published entitled 'The Mitred Champion; or the Church Militant,' which consists of a full-length portrait of the Archbishop in a half-clerical, half-military costume, armed with a drawn sword, and wearing an officer's cocked and laced hat instead of his own mitre, which lies on the ground at his feet. He is marching at the head of a company of armed clergymen, who carry the royal standard of England. The Archbishop cries, 'Religion! Liberty! my Country!' His lieutenant, who marches on the right of the company, says, 'King George and ye Church of England for ever.' [1]

This may be called a satire, but it is really little more than a representation of what actually occurred by putting words into action. The artist who designed the satire evidently approved of the action, and the lines engraved on the print are distinctly laudatory and end thus:

[1] F. G. Stephens, *British Museum Catalogue of Satires*, vol. iii p. 508.

'Our Civil Rights, and Sacred Worship shall
Never a sacrifice to Bigots fall,
But as our Birthright we'll secure enjoy
While Herring can his Sword and Eloquence employ.'

Hogarth's portrait of Herring is dated in this same
year 1745, and was engraved as a heading to the
Archbishop's published speech at York, 24th Sept.
1745. The portrait was engraved subsequently by
B. Baron and was published in 1750.

It is said that Herring did not admire the portrait,
and an uncomplimentary epigram was made at the
time :

'Lovat's hard features Hogarth might command,
A Herring's sweetness asks a Reynolds' hand.'

Herring became Archbishop of Canterbury in 1747,
and a copy of Hogarth's picture at York is included
in the gallery of Lambeth Palace.

Bishops Gibson and Hoadly were leaders of two
different parties, and were both objects at which
numerous satires were aimed. The latter was the
leader of the Low Church party, and the former
of a new High Church party dissociated from the
Jacobites and equally loyal to the Hanoverian
dynasty as the other party. Gibson is ridiculed
in an engraving published in 1736 and entitled
'Tartuff's Banquet (or Codex's Entertainment),'
the design of which is ascribed to Hogarth, but the
ascription is doubtful. The engraving by G. Vandergucht is described by Mr. Stephens as showing the
interior of a dining-room where a sleek divine is

seated at table with three lean clergymen. The only person provided with a knife and fork is the sleek divine. Mr. Stephens says that this figure was previously supposed to be intended for Orator Henley, until he showed that it was aimed at Dr. Edmund Gibson, well known as 'Codex' from his great work entitled *Codex Juris Ecclesiastici Anglicani* (1713). In another satirical print entitled 'The Parallel; or Laud & C[o]d[e]x compared,' published also in 1736, Britannia is shown seated and holding her spear; she rests her hand upon the British royal shield, and by pointing to medallion portraits of Archbishop Laud and Bishop Gibson, indicates their characters to be equally autocratic and overbearing. Two years before he had been satirised in an engraving entitled 'The State Weathercocks,' and here he possesses a fellow-sufferer in Bishop Hoadly. Gibson was supposed to be ambitious of succeeding Archbishop Wake in the Primacy, but he died Bishop of London. In the verses attached to the engraving we read:

> 'For gold Pastorius will exchange his soul,
> See how to La[mbe]th he does turn his face;
> And views the Pa[la]ce with a sly grimace,
> 'Tis true, indeed, Pastorius pants for grace,
> This right-hand Man of Sidrophel's [1] first troop,
> This party-tool to anything will stoop;
> Say black is white and white does black appear.'

The writer attacks both sides with equal injustice; and later on Hoadly, who had been Rector of St.

[1] Sir Robert Walpole.

Peter le Poer, Bread Street, from 1704 to 1720, is satirised for tergiversation.

> ' Whate'er the R——r of St. P——r P——r
> By dint of Argument maintained before,
> The B[isho]p to reform the sinful age
> Mounted with intrepidity the stage,
> Benhada did with Benhada engage.
> In publick, but yet mildly, he disputes,
> And all his former Arguments refutes.
> If he no Kingdom in this World can have,
> Close to the Steeple's pinnacle he 'll cleave.'

The last two lines refer to the text of the Bishop's sermon at Court, ' My kingdom is not of this world.' It was this sermon which occasioned the famous Bangorian Controversy. In 1709 the House of Commons voted an Address to Queen Anne ' that she would be graciously pleased to confer some dignity in the Church upon him [Hoadly] for his eminent services to the Church and State.' This unusual appeal had no effect, but Mrs. Howland, a rich widow, presented him to the rectory of Streatham, ' to show that she was neither afraid nor ashamed to give him that mark of regard at that critical time.' Promotion came with the next reign, but Hoadly continued to hold both these livings after he became Bishop of Bangor, which diocese he never visited. He was successively Bishop of Hereford, Salisbury, and Winchester, and died at the latter city April 17, 1761.

Hoadly and his family were great friends of Hogarth, who painted the Bishop's portrait in

THE SLEEPING CONGREGATION. 1736.

collaboration with the first Mrs. Hoadly (*née* Sarah Curtis). This is now in the National Portrait Gallery.

Hogarth has left a sad picture of the deadness of public services in the eighteenth century in his 'Sleeping Congregation' (1736). If common sense was so predominant that enthusiasm and zeal were treated as objectionable, how was the preacher to attract his congregation without the exhibition of some vivid interest in his theme? The preacher in Hogarth's picture looks as if he would have been dull in any age, but Churchill the poet was full of life and vigour, yet even he could not fix the attention of his audience.

> 'I kept those sheep,
> Which for my curse, I was ordain'd to keep.
> Ordain'd alas! to keep through need, not choice,
> Whilst sacred dulness ever in my view
> Sleep at my bidding crept from pew to pew.'

We are told that Sir Roger de Coverley would suffer none to sleep in church but himself. 'The Sleeping Congregation' is referred to in Vincent Bourne's *Conspicillum*. The droning preacher has been supposed to represent the Rev. John Theophilus Desaguliers, F.R.S. (1683-1744), but there is reason to doubt this assumption as the head of the preacher does not resemble the portrait of Desaguliers by Hyssing. He was extremely short-sighted and his personal appearance unattractive, by reason of being short and thickset, with irregular features, so the general appearance of the man may have been copied.

Desaguliers was a man of science of some distinction and held in high esteem by Newton. He received the Copley medal of the Royal Society in 1742, and his lectures on physics were popular. In theology he only printed a thanksgiving sermon preached before George I. at Hampton Court in 1716.

In the advertisement of the print it is stated that it represents the interior of a church in the country —' A print representing a sleepy congregation in a country church '; but Mr. Stephens points out that in ' one of the windows is emblazoned in stained glass an escutcheon resembling that of the City of London, thus suggesting it is a city church.'[1]

Desaguliers was Rector of Whitchurch or Little Stanmore, Middlesex, from 1715 until his death in 1744. He initiated Frederick Prince of Wales into Freemasonry at a special lodge held at Kew on the 5th October 1737. Hogarth painted a portrait of a Mrs. Desaguliers, wife of General Thomas Desaguliers, which Mr. Dobson says is a beautiful head.

It is possible to be too critical of the methods of the men of the eighteenth century, and Sir Walter Besant, after taking a careful survey of the Church of that time in London, wrote that ' the chief reason for calling the time of George II. a dead time for the Church seems to be, so far as London is concerned, that its clergy were not like our own.' He analysed

[1] *British Museum Catalogue*, vol. iii. p. 204.

the services in every London church in 1732, and
found that daily services were general. He also considered that there was no more immorality among
the middle classes than at any other time.

The names of several London churches represented
in Hogarth's pictures may be set down here. St.
Paul's, Covent Garden, occupies a prominent position
in ' Morning,' and the French Church, Hog Lane, in
' Noon,' with St. Giles's in the background. St.
George's, Bloomsbury, in ' Gin Lane,' and the interior of old Marylebone Church in the fifth plate of
the ' Rake's Progress,' and St. Martin's in ' Industry
and Idleness,' Plate 2. This last is only a suggestion, but it is a probable one.

Mr. Stephens writes : ' The church represented . . .
is probably that of St. Martin's in the Fields, Westminster, in respect to the architecture of which, and
that of the print, there are several resemblances.
The probability of this being the case is strengthened
by the fact that a royal crown surmounts the chandelier, which is pendant from the roof in the design.
St. Martin's in the Fields is the so-called royal parish
of Westminster. The design and the church differ,
however, in many respects; the architectural characteristics of the former are seemingly due to a rough
sketch of the features of the latter, not to an intention on the part of Hogarth to represent this, or any
particular church.' [1]

It is but fair to refer to this as a very complete

[1] *British Museum Catalogue*, vol. iii. p. 678.

contrast to the 'Sleeping Congregation,' showing a service in which the congregation is thoroughly interested.

Plate 3 of the same series shows the exterior of another church and 'the Idle 'Prentice at play in the churchyard, during Divine Service.' Respecting this Mr. Stephens writes : ' The churchyard has not been identified, but it must have been in or near the City of London, as appears by the escutcheon over the door. There are points of resemblance between Hogarth's picture and the churches of St. Michael, Crooked Lane, and St. Paul, Shadwell.' [1]

Boswell supplies us with a delightful anecdote of the audacity of Topham Beauclerk, which must ever associate Samuel Johnson with the Idle Apprentice in the mind of all readers.

' Johnson was some time with Beauclerk at his house at Windsor. . . . One Sunday, when the weather was very fine, Beauclerk enticed him, insensibly, to saunter about all the morning. They went into a churchyard in the time of divine service, and Johnson laid himself down at his ease upon one of the tomb-stones. Now, sir, (said Beauclerk), you are like Hogarth's Idle Apprentice.'

The Church of St. Clement Danes, in the Strand, must be added to this list. It is not, however, on account of a representation of the church, but of a scathing satire on the altar-piece by Kent which once stood in this church. Hogarth's contempt for

[1] *British Museum Catalogue*, p 682.

Kent as a painter is well known, and he seldom lost an opportunity of publishing it.

It has sometimes been supposed that Hogarth's engraving caused the removal of the original picture; but this is a mistake, as the popular feeling against the altar-piece seems to have been caused partly by political feelings and partly from the strong dislike to the admission of pictures in churches. Hogarth took the opportunity of showing the absurdity of the drawing itself, and he declared that he neither 'parodied' nor 'burlesqued,' but produced a fair and honest representation of a contemptible performance.

The explanation of the plate is as follows: ' This Print is exactly engraiv'd after yᵉ Celebrated Altar-peice in St. Clement's Church, which has been taken down by order of yᵉ Lord Bishop of London (as 'tis thought) to prevent disputes and laying of wagers among yᵉ Parrishioners about yᵉ artists meaning in it. For publick satisfaction here is a particular explanation of it humbly offerd to be writ under yᵉ Original that it may be put up again, by which means yᵉ Parish'es 60 pounds, which they wisely gave for it, may not be entirely lost.

> 1st. 'Tis not the Pretender's wife and children, as our weak brethren imagin.
> 2ly. Nor St. Cecilia, as the Connoisseurs think, but a choir of angells singing in Consort.'

[Below are letters from A to K as references to the points of the picture.]

o

A violently-written pamphlet on Kent's picture, entitled ' A Letter from a Parishioner of St. Clement Danes, to the Right Reverend Father in God Edmund [Gibson], Lord Bishop of London, occasion'd by his Lordship's causing the picture over the altar to be taken down. With some observations on the use and abuse of Church Paintings in general, and of that picture in Particular,' was published on September 10, 1725.

The author writes: ' And of *all* the abuses your Lordship has redress'd, *none* more timely, *none* more acceptable to all *true* Protestants than your last injunction to remove that *ridiculous, superstitious* piece of *Popish foppery* from our *Communion table*: this has gain'd you the *applause* and good-*will* of all *honest men*, who were *scandalized* to see that *holy Place* defiled with so *vile and impertinent a representation*. To what end or purpose was it put there, but to *affront* our *most gracious Sovereign* by placing at our *very altar*, the *known resemblance* of a Person, who is wife of his *utter enemy* and *Pensioner* to the *Whore* of Babylon ? When I say the *known resemblance* I speak not only according to my *own knowledge*, but appeal to *all mankind* who have seen the *Princess Sobieski* or any picture or resemblance of her.' The author further refers to ' a continual *hurly burly of loiterers* from *all* parts of the *Town* to see our *popish Raree Show*.'

When the picture was removed from the church it was placed in the old vestry-room of the parish, and was occasionally taken to the Crown and Anchor Tavern in the Strand for exhibition at the music meetings of the churchwardens of the parish.

Of the regular dissenting ministers Hogarth has taken little or no note. Some of these were men of repute, but as a rule the worship in the Chapel was as dull as that in the Church and a 'revival' was required equally in both.

John Henley, of St. John's College, Cambridge, known as Orator Henley (1692-1756), was a dissenter in that he broke off his connection with the Church because he considered that he was not appreciated, but he had nothing in common with any of the Nonconformist bodies.

He was pompous, but with a ready wit and an effective elocution, and about 1726 he rented a large room over the market-house in Newport Market, and registered it as a place for religious worship. He then, by advertisements in the papers, invited all persons to come and take seats for twopence apiece, promising them diversion under the titles of Voluntaries, Chimes of the Times, Roundelays, College Bobs, etc. Great numbers of people flocked to witness his buffooneries, until at last these were put an end to by a Presentment of the Grand Jury of Middlesex in January 1729.

Henley then removed to Portsmouth Street, Clare Market, where he was more careful in the entertainment he provided. He called his chapel the Oratory, and every Sunday he preached a sermon in the morning and delivered an oration in the evening on some special theological theme, and lectured on weekdays, sometimes Tuesdays, Wednesdays and Fridays, on other subjects.

The crowd of persons of all classes who flocked to his lectures was so great that he had to obtain more commodious quarters, which he found in the old Lincoln's Inn Fields Theatre in Bear Yard, Vere Street.

Pope has pictured for us the Orator in his 'gilt tub':

'Embrown'd with native bronze, lo ! Henley stands,
Turning his voice, and balancing his hands,
How fluent nonsense trickles from his tongue !
How sweet the periods, neither said, nor sung !
Still break the benches, Henley ! with thy strain,
While Sherlock, Hare, and Gibson preach in vain '

Samuel Ireland gave two engravings of Orator Henley in the first volume of his *Graphic Illustrations*. One, Henley christening a child, he says is from a sketch in oil which he bought from Mrs. Hogarth, and supposes to have been painted by Hogarth about the year 1745. At Ireland's sale, May 6, 1797, it was sold or bought in for three guineas. It afterwards came into the possession of Payne Knight, and with the whole of his collection was bequeathed to the British Museum. Mr. Stephens says of the sketch, 'It is in perfect condition, painted with Hogarth's characteristic skill and fine sense of female beauty, and on a piece of canvas which was originally of a slightly greenish brown.' [1]

[1] *British Museum Catalogue*, vol. III. p. 630.

Orator HENLEY christening a Child.

Etched by Sam.l Ireland from an Original Sketch in Oil...o his possession...by HOGARTH.

To Francis Grose Esq.r.S.A.S an Encourager & promoter of the Arts this Etching from his favorite Hogarth is inscribed by his oblig'd friend & Servant Sam.l Ireland.

ORATOR HENLEY CHRISTENING A CHILD.

The other is the 'Oratory Chappel,' which Ireland says 'exhibits a true portrait of that place of which no other has come within our knowledge.' There is no doubt that this was not the work of Hogarth, although it is interesting in itself. Stephens says of the original that it is supposed to be a forgery by Powell, although it has 'W. Hogarth fec^t' at one corner of the print.

Stephens thus describes the print: 'This etching shows Orator Henley preaching in a chapel; his clerk is armed with a club. One side of the pulpit is decorated with a medallion of an imp resembling an owl. On the top of the sounding board is a dancing dog, in Scotch plaid, holding a board inscribed "Politicks and Divinity." The floor is covered with men standing or sitting, and more or less attentively listening to the Orator; one man reads from a newspaper, another addresses Henley, although the latter is in the heat of his discourse. The gallery is filled with men who are shouting and brandishing clubs. Over them is written, "It is written my house shall be called ye house of prayer, but ye have made it a den of thieves." In a pew marked "Pens for ye Doctors Friends, etc," is a very rough-looking group, described thus on the pew:

"Butcher Frenchman Scot and Tory,
Join to rob Britain of its glory." ' [1]

Another engraving of 'The Oratory,' showing 'Henley in full canonicals addressing a few persons

[1] *British Museum Catalogue*, vol iii. p. 621.

who are standing below,' by George Bickham, has been attributed falsely to Hogarth.[1]

Ireland says that Henley frequently made Pope the object of his satire, which caused the poet to gibbet him in the *Dunciad*. George Alexander Stevens of the *Lecture upon Heads* was a perpetual nuisance to the Orator, who prosecuted him for breeding riots in the chapel.

Henley was continually at loggerheads with the ministry, and on one occasion he parodied the text of Dr. Croxall with some effect.

This Doctor preached a sermon on the 30th June 1730 before the House of Commons from the text, 'Take away the wicked from before the King, and his throne shall be established in righteousness.' This gave so much offence to Sir Robert Walpole that he prevented the thanks of the House being presented to the preacher. Henley was so pleased with this that he posted the following lines as a subject for his next address :

> 'Away with the wicked before the King,
> And away with the wicked behind him ;
>   His throne it will bless
>   With righteousness,
> And we shall know where to find him.'

This chapter may be concluded with a short notice of Hogarth's two prints, 'Enthusiasm Delineated' (n.d., published 1795), and 'Credulity, Superstition, and Fanaticism: a Medley' (March 15, 1762).

[1] *British Museum Catalogue*, vol. ii. p. 746.

'Enthusiasm Delineated' appears to be intended as a general satire upon the evils of superstition. Its object is explained in an advertisement on the plate: 'The intention of this Print is to give a lineal representation of the strange effects of literal and low conceptions of Sacred Beings, as also of the Idolatrous tendency of Pictures in Churches and Prints in Religious Books, etc.' The plate was dedicated to the Archbishop of Canterbury, but was never published. Only two impressions are in existence: both belonged to John Ireland, and now one is in the British Museum and the other in the possession of Mr. Fairfax Murray.

At the end of his life Hogarth took the copper-plate which had been discarded and altered the whole scheme of the design completely, so as to satirise the Methodist and Evangelical revival and the popular follies of his own day. Almost every figure was altered, some more and some less. The result was the print entitled 'Credulity, Superstition, and Fanaticism.' The most unintelligible alteration is the introduction of Mary Tofts in the later plate to replace the figure of Mother Douglas in the original one. The Tofts imposture took place in 1726 before the date of the original plate, and was almost forgotten in 1762. The two prints are reproduced in John Ireland's *Hogarth Illustrated*, and are placed opposite each other for purposes of comparison,

CHAPTER VII

PROFESSIONAL LIFE

ONE of the Professions—the Clerical—is dealt with in the previous chapter.   In this we have to consider the Law, Medicine, and the Army, as well as later additions to the Professions—Art and Literature. Physic is fully represented in Hogarth's works, so also is the Law.   Soldiers find little place there, and Art and Literature can hardly claim much distinction, as exhibited in the 'Enraged Musician' of the first or the 'Distressed Poet' of the second class.

Law.—The engraving of 'The Bench' was first published on the 4th September 1758.   In the first state above the heads of the four judges is seen a wall on which is painted the Royal arms of England with the motto 'Semper eadem,' the escutcheon being partly obliterated by the shaft of a column at the left of the picture. In the second state the escutcheon has been obliterated and replaced by a row of heads, eight in number, as examples of caricature.   The shaft remains, and causes a curious effect to the caricature of an apostle which is partly in front and partly behind the column.

The four judges are supposed to be sitting on the

Bench of the Court of Common Pleas. The chief figure, a portly personage who is seen reading through his eyeglasses from notes made in a book held in his left hand. This was intended to represent Sir John Willes (born 1685), Chief Justice of the Court of Common Pleas, a man of great learning and ability, but little esteemed on account of the grossness of his manners and morals. He hoped to be Lord Chancellor in succession to Lord Hardwicke, but he had to content himself with being the first of three Commissioners for the Great Seal (1756-7). He was offered the Chancellorship in the Duke of Newcastle's and Pitt's administration, but he stipulated for a peerage which was refused, and Sir Robert Henley was appointed Lord Keeper instead. Horace Walpole tells an anecdote of Willes, which shows the kind of man he was. A grave person came to reprove the judge for the scandal he gave, observing that the world talked of one of his maidservants being with child. Willes said: 'What is that to me?' The monitor answered: 'Oh! but they say it is by your lordship.' 'And what is that to you?' was the reply.

The next figure is Henry Bathurst (son of Sir Allan Apsley, first Earl Bathurst), born 1714, Justice of the Common Pleas 1754, and Lord Chancellor in 1771. He succeeded his father as Earl Bathurst in 1775, and died in 1794. He was an amiable man, but not so companionable as his father. It is reported on one occasion when the

son retired from a convivial party that Lord
Bathurst said, 'Now, my good friends, since the old
gentleman is off, I think we may venture to crush
another bottle.' The third figure is the Hon.
William Noel, born 1695, who is called by Horace
Walpole 'a pompous man of little solidity.' On
the trial of Lord Lovat in 1746, he was one of the
managers for the House of Commons. He became
a Justice of the Common Pleas in March 1757, and
continued in that Court till his death on December
8, 1762. Both Bathurst and Noel are pictured
asleep.

The fourth judge who is shown in profile to the
left of Willes is Sir Edward Clive, born 1704. He
was made a Baron of the Exchequer in 1745, and
remained in that Court nearly eight years. He was
removed to the Common Pleas in January 1753.
He resigned in 1770, and died in 1771. Sir
Edward Clive's brother George was the husband of
Kitty Clive, the famous actress.

The row of caricature heads added in the second
state of the plate, already referred to, strengthen
the portrayal of the difference between 'Character,
Caricature and Outré,' which Hogarth had
previously indicated in 1743, when he published
'Characters and Caricaturas' as the subscription
ticket for the 'Marriage à la Mode.' The neglect
of this distinction by others was a constant source
of annoyance to him, as he hated to be treated as a
caricaturist. He himself said with regard to this

print of ' The Bench '—' I have ever considered the knowledge of character, either high or low, to be the most sublime part of the art of painting or sculpture ; and caricature, as the lowest ; indeed as much so as the wild attempts of children, when they first try to draw : yet so it is, that the two words, from being similar in sound, are often confounded. When I was at the house of a foreign face-painter, and looking over a legion of his portraits, Monsieur, with a low bow, told me that he infinitely admired my caricatures ! I returned his *congé* and informed him that I equally admired his.'

The original picture differed from the print somewhat. It was the property at one time of Sir George Hay, and afterwards of Mr. Edwards. It was exhibited by Mr. Fairfax Murray at the Winter Exhibition of the Royal Academy, 1908.

The representation by Hogarth of the Lawyer in Butler's *Hudibras* must be mentioned here, as his character is so differently treated in Hogarth's two sets of illustrations :

> ' To this brave man, the Knight repairs
> For counsel in his Law affairs,
> And found him mounted in his Pew,
> With Books and Money plac'd, for shew,
> Like Nest-eggs to make Clients lay,
> And for his false opinion pay :
> To whom the Knight, with comely grace
> Put off his hat, to put his case.'

In the duodecimo edition of *Hudibras* (1726) the Lawyer is represented as sitting on a settle and writing at a desk in a corner of a room in front of a window, and with three shelves of books above his head. In the large series of engravings published by Hogarth without a text, the Lawyer is seen sitting in state on a sort of throne in a handsome apartment. In front of the Lawyer's desk sit two clerks busily engaged in writing. At the side of the room is a large bookcase filled with important-looking books. In front of the bookcase, and at the right-hand side of the picture, is a handsomely carved figure of Justice holding her scales.

The picture of 'Paul before Felix,' which Hogarth painted for the decoration of the old Lincoln's Inn Hall in 1748, is still to be seen in the new buildings of Lincoln's Inn Hall. Thomas, Lord Wyndham, Lord Chancellor of Ireland, 1726-39, who died in 1745, left a legacy of £200 for the decoration of the Hall, and Hogarth obtained the commission through the instrumentality of Lord Mansfield. Mr. Dobson gives in his book a facsimile of Hogarth's letter respecting the proposed position of the picture in the hall, with his sketch of the design of the frame. This letter was found among the archives of the Society of Lincoln's Inn. The receipt is as follows :

'*July the 8th*, 1748.

' Reced of Jn° Wood Esq. Treasurer of the Honble Society of Lincoln's Inn by the hands of Richd Farshall Chief Butler to the Said Society the sum of two hundred pounds being the Legacy given by the late Lord Wyndham to the Said Society laid out in a picture drawn by Mr. Hogarth. According to order of Council Dated the 27th day of June last.

WILLIAM HOGARTH.'

'£200.

This picture was engraved and published in 1752, and in the previous year was prepared 'Paul before Felix Burlesqued.' 'Design'd and scratch'd in the true Dutch taste, by Wm. Hogarth,' to serve as a receipt for subscriptions to two prints to be published at the same time, viz. 'Paul before Felix,' and 'Moses brought before Pharaoh's Daughter.' These receipts were not originally intended for sale, but they were given to subscribers and to Hogarth's friends, who begged them. The beggars became so numerous that the designer after a time resolved to part with none except at the price of five shillings each.

What could have induced Hogarth to burlesque his own picture, which was already too much of a caricature, it is almost impossible to understand. The orator Tertullus who was retained against St. Paul is said to represent Dr. King, Principal of St. Mary Hall, Oxford.

Leigh Hunt, in 'The Town,' described the serious 'Paul before Felix' as 'Hogarth's celebrated failure.'

Medicine.—Hogarth painted the portraits of several well-known physicians and surgeons, or

introduced them into his works. The portrait of
Thomas Pellett, M.D., President of the Royal College
of Physicians, 1735-39, was exhibited at Whitechapel
(Georgian England) in 1906 by Mr. W. C. Alexander.
The painting was engraved by Charles Hall and
published June 1, 1781, by J. Thane. Pellett and
Martin Folkes (whose portrait was also painted by
Hogarth), were joint editors of Sir Isaac Newton's
Chronology of Ancient Kingdoms (1728). The
College possesses a portrait of Pellett by Dahl.

The portrait of Sir Cæsar Hawkins, Bart., by
Hogarth belongs to the Royal College of Surgeons,
and was exhibited by the College at Whitechapel
(Georgian England) in 1906.

Cromwell Mortimer, M.D., was a man of considerable importance in his day, a friend of Sir Hans
Sloane, and Secretary of the Royal Society from
1730 until his death in 1752. He was very unpopular with members of his own profession. In
the *Gentleman's Magazine*, 1780, p. 510, he is styled
' an impertinent assuming empiric.' The portrait of
Mortimer, engraved by Rigou, from a sketch by
Hogarth, is a severe satire, and probably some of the
artist's professional friends suggested the need of
some such satire. Mr. F. G. Stephens says that the
date and immediate occasion of this print is not
apparent, but he supposes that the circulation of
Mortimer's letter, 1744, caused its publication. The
letter was subsequently published in the *Gentleman's
Magazine*, November 1779, and is described as ' the

A CONSULTATION OF PHYSICIANS. 1736.

plan of Dr. Mortimer's present method of practice.'
In it specifics for every disease are recommended.[1]

The original drawing in bistre was in the Standly
Collection.

Hogarth seems to have been in doubt as to the
exact object of his biting satire on some of the
healers of men when he gave his gallery of medical
heads the double title of ' The Company of Undertakers, or a Consultation of Physicians.' The title
of the etching was originally intended to be ' Quacks
in Consultation,' and it was so advertised. This
was first published on March 3, 1736, and the following burlesque heraldic description is engraved below
the design :

' The Company of Undertakers
Beareth Sable, an Urinal *proper between* 12 Quack-
Heads *of the Second* and 12 Cane Heads *or* consultant.
On a chief Nebula, Ermine, one compleat Doctor
*issuant, chekie, sustaining in his Right Hand a Baton
of the Second. On his Dexter and Sinister sides two*
Demi-Doctors, *issuant of the second and two Cane
Heads issuant of the third ; The first having one eye
couchant, towards the Dexter Side of the Escocheon ;
the second faced per pale proper and gules, guardent.
With this motto—*Et Plurima Mortis Imago.'

The three half-length figures in the upper portion
of the shield are intended to represent Mrs. Mapp
in the centre, Chevalier Taylor on her right, and Dr.
Joshua Ward, or ' Spot ' Ward, on the left.

[1] *British Museum Catalogue,* vol. iii. p. 541.

Sarah Mapp, the bone-setter or shape mistress, was a woman of masculine habits who distinguished herself by some extraordinary cures. Her father, a man named Wallin, was also a bone-setter settled at Hindon in Wiltshire, but his daughter quarrelled with him and wandered about the country calling herself Crazy Sally. She married Hill Mapp, a servant of Mr. Ibbetson, mercer, Ludgate Hill, on August 11, 1736, but the husband ran away soon after the marriage, taking with him one hundred and two guineas.

Mrs. Mapp set up a carriage and four, and the newspapers were full of her doings in this year 1736. A mare was named after her, and Mrs. Mapp's plate for ten guineas was run for at Epsom; but her career was a short one, for she died in Seven Dials in December 1737 in great poverty.

John Taylor (1703-1772) appears to have been an oculist of distinction who exhibited great skill as an operator, but he chose to advertise himself and act generally as a charlatan. Dr. Johnson said of him that he was ' an instance of how far impudence would carry ignorance.' He studied surgery under the great William Cheselden at St. Thomas's Hospital, and practised for some time at Norwich. He then travelled through the country and abroad, and was known as Chevalier Taylor. He early obtained a recognised position by his appointment as oculist to George II. in 1736. He published a vain-glorious account of himself and his adventures in 1761, and died in a convent at Prague in 1772.

John Ireland says that he saw Taylor once at Shrewsbury, and he recognised the likeness in Hogarth's drawing. He also tells some good anecdotes of him which show his ready wit. On one occasion when he was enumerating the honours he had received from the different princes of Europe, and the orders with which he had been dignified by innumerable sovereigns, it was remarked that he had not named the King of Prussia. 'I suppose, sir, he never gave you an order?' 'You are mistaken, sir,' replied the Chevalier; 'he gave me a very peremptory *order to quit his dominions.*'

On his return from a tour on the Continent he met a working man who, addressing him with great familiarity, was repulsed with a frown, and 'Sir, I really don't remember you.' 'Not remember me! Why, my goodness, doctor, we once lodged in Round Court' [out of Bow Street, Covent Garden]. 'Round Court, Round Court! Sir, I have been in every court in Europe, but of such a court as Round Court I have no recollection.'[1]

Joshua Ward (1685-1761) was a quack doctor, but it is said that he was a quack of genius. In 1717 he was returned Member of Parliament for Marlborough, but by a vote of the House of Commons he was declared not duly elected. It is supposed that he was mixed up with his brother John Ward in the troubles connected with the South Sea Bubble, as he left England rather abruptly. During his exile he

---

[1] *Hogarth Illustrated,* vol. ii. p 285 (*note*).

P

acquired his knowledge of medicine and chemistry, and then he became a Roman Catholic.

About the year 1733 he began to practise medicine. Ward's famous drop was first made known in England, 1731-2, by Sir Thomas Robinson ('long Sir Thomas'), whose zeal was ridiculed in verse by Sir Charles Hanbury Williams:

> 'Say, knight, for learning most renown'd,
>   What is this wondrous drop?
> Which friend ne'er knew nor can be found,
>   In Grah'ms or Guerney's shop.'[1]

Horace Walpole affirms that 'the Duke of Newcastle dragged poor Sir Thomas into light and ridicule.' Ward when called in to attend on George II. for an affection of his hand, was successful in curing the disease. 'In lieu of a pecuniary compensation [he] was, *at his own request*, permitted to ride in his gaudy and heavy equipage through St. James's Park, an honour seldom granted to any but persons of rank; besides this, the King gave a commission to his nephew, the late General Gansel.'

In 1748 when the Apothecaries' Act was passed to restrain unqualified persons from compounding medicines, a special clause was inserted exempting Ward by name.

Fielding paid a high tribute to Ward's kindness and sagacity in his Introduction to the *Journal of a Voyage to Lisbon* (1755). He wrote: 'Obligations to Mr. Ward I shall always confess; for I am con-

[1] *Works,* 1822, vol. ii. p. 1.

vinced that he omitted no care in endeavouring to
serve me, without any expectation or desire of fee
or reward. The powers of Mr. Ward's remedies
want, indeed, no unfair puffs of mine to give them
credit ; and tho' this distemper of the dropsy stands,
I believe, first in the list of those over which he is
always certain of triumphing, yet possibly, there
might be something particular in my case, capable of
eluding that radical force which had healed so many
thousands.'

Ward was generous to poor patients, and was very
popular in consequence. He prided himself on the
sad loss his death would be to the poor. Pope made
an ill-natured reference to this: 'Ward try'd on
Puppies, and the Poor, his Drop.' Ward 'left the
receipts for compounding his medicines to Mr. Page,
member for Chichester, who bestowed them on two
charitable institutions which have derived considerable advantage from the profits attending their
sale.'[1] Ward made a fortune by his sulphuric acid
patent, 1749, and it is to his improvement in the
production of this important substance that he owes
the posthumous honour of having his truculent-look-
ing statue by Carlini preserved in the hall of the
Royal Society of Arts.

Of the dozen heads below the great trio there is
little to be said. John Ireland affirms that many of
them are unquestionably portraits, but there is no
advantage in trying to discover what must at least

[1] J. Ireland, *Hogarth Illustrated*, vol. ii. p. 288 (*note*).

be extremely doubtful. Mr. Stephens's remarks upon these are very much to the point: ' Of the other doctors represented below the nebulous dividing line, each wears a big wig and carries a cane with a large head. All but two of them hold their canes at or near their nostrils; some affect an air and expression of profoundity of thought; some smell at the heads of their canes, thus illustrating the original purpose of the gold heads, to hold a pomander or disinfectant. The urinal referred to in the engraved description is in the hands of the quack in the centre of the composition. He is a fat fellow and holds the vessel, which is filled with liquor, in the palm of his left hand . . . he has tucked his cane under his arm. Below this man, or in front of him, two other quacks are pretending to study the liquor through their eyeglasses. These heads are said to comprise portraits of Dr. Bamber and Dr. Pierce Dod. This is extremely improbable, as these were not considered to be quacks, and were eminent in their profession.' [1]

The notorious quack John Misaubin, M.D. (who died in 1734), has already been described in Chapter III. (High Life) in connection with the third plate of the 'Marriage à la Mode.' It has also been suggested that the two Doctors quarrelling in the fifth plate of the 'Harlot's Progress' represent Misaubin and Joshua Ward. Another quack in high places was Nathaniel St. André, who made a

---

[1] *British Museum Catalogue*, vol. iii. p. 209.

criminal blunder by supporting the gross imposture of Mary Tofts, the rabbit-breeder. In connection with this 'Cunicularii, or the Wise Men of Godliman in Consultation,' attributed to Hogarth, has already been mentioned. The reference-table below the design of this print describes the figure lettered A as 'The Dancing Master, or Præturnatural Anatomist.' This is St. André, who is shown with a fiddle under his arm in allusion to his having originally been a dancing-master. He was a native of Switzerland, who is supposed to have joined with this business that of teaching the French and German languages, in the knowledge of which he was a proficient. He afterwards studied under a surgeon of eminence, and was so fortunate as to be appointed in 1723 anatomist to the Royal household. He was also surgeon to Westminster Hospital (then a dispensary), and delivered public lectures on anatomy, although apparently he was an unqualified practitioner. He was living at this time in Northumberland Court, Strand.

Queen Caroline was determined that a thorough investigation should be made of the story that Mrs. Mary Tofts, an illiterate woman of Godalming, had produced rabbits instead of children. St. André went to Godalming and was deceived by what he saw. Sir Richard Manningham, Dr. Douglas, Dr. Mowbray and Mr. Howard, surgeon of Guildford, expressed themselves satisfied of the truth of the miracle. Tofts's imposture was so outrageous, that it could not have been carried out unless she had received considerable assistance. The nurse and Howard must, one would think, have been in collusion. The others may have only been foolish. The cheat was at length discovered by Sir Thomas Clarges, and the deluded medical men were overwhelmed with disgrace. St. André was particularly unfortunate, as he had been held in considerable favour by George I., but after this exposure, although he retained his office, he neither received a salary nor returned to Court again.

George Steevens wrote a very severe account of St. André in Nichols's *Biographical Anecdotes*, which was answered, but not very successfully. The answer with a reply by Steevens was added to the *Anecdotes*, and the remarks on St. André occupy a rather disproportionate part of the book. John Nichols seems to have considered that his colleague was rather too severe, but there can be no doubt St. André was a worthless character even if he did not murder his friend in order to marry the widow, a crime of which he was accused.

St. André married Lady Elizabeth Molyneux after the death of her husband, Samuel Molyneux, secretary to George Prince of Wales (afterwards George II.). She is said to have left the house with St. André on the night her husband died. In consequence she was dismissed from attendance upon Queen Caroline. St. André was well off during her lifetime, but he died poor in 1776 at the age of ninety-six. A portrait of Mary Tofts was painted by Laguerre and engraved by Faber. 'She has a rabbit in her lap, and displays a countenance expressive of the utmost vulgarity.' This woman died in January 1763 at Godalming.

Reference has already been made in the previous chapter to Hogarth's late introduction of Mary Tofts into his 'Credulity, Superstition and Fanaticism' (1762).

This monstrous imposture created some stir abroad, and a print was published entitled 'Mr. Petit, a French Surgeon sent from Paris to Dr. Meagre to take an exact account from him of ye Preternatural Delivery of Rabbits,' etc. Dr. Meagre is meant to represent St. André.[1]

There is little about the Army in Hogarth's works except in the case of the contrast of the English and French soldiers, and the rabble disorder of the 'March to Finchley' which, although it is one of his finest pictures, was rather unfortunate in that it excited the displeasure of the King.

Literature.—The one picture in illustration of Literature by Hogarth is the spirited and charming 'Distressed Poet,' which can scarcely be called a satire, as one's sympathy is entirely with the unfortunate poet and his pleasant and industrious wife.

This picture is the more interesting if it be true that it was intended to allude to the troubles of

[1] *British Museum Catalogue,* vol. ii. p. 640.

Lewis Theobald, the highly respected commentator
on Shakespeare, for one of whose plays, *Perseus
and Andromeda*, 1730, Hogarth designed two illustrations.   But this point will be again referred to
later on.   The picture is a vivid representation of a
garret in a Grub Street house, which we are told in
Johnson's *Dictionary* was 'much inhabited by
writers of small histories, dictionaries and small
poems.'   Pope made his *Dunciad* the standard
epic of this place.   However much we may admire
Pope as a poet, we cannot but feel disgust at his
rancorous attack upon his poorer brethren.   It is
therefore a satisfaction to find Hogarth continually
satirising the poet, who was too afraid of the artist
to reply to him.   'The Distrest Poet' was 'Invented
Painted Engraved and Publish'd by Wm Hogarth
March the 3^d, 1736.   According to Act of Parliament, Price 3 Shillings,' and was afterwards re-
issued with some alterations on 'Decem^{ber} the 15.
1740.'

The poet sits at a table by the window engaged in
writing 'Poverty, a Poem,' but disturbed by the
wrangling milkwoman.   In front of him is a book
inscribed   'Bysshe' (intended for Bysshe's *Art of
Poetry*, a once famous rhymers' manual).   On the
floor is the *Grub Street Journal* and the poet's sword.
Above his head is an engraving of Pope thrashing
Curll and crying out 'Veni, vidi, vici, 1735.'   On a
shelf below this are four books and three tobacco
pipes.   In the middle of the room sits the poet's

comely wife mending a pair of her husband's breeches, and at her feet the poet's coat on which a cat, with her kittens, has made herself comfortable.

Hartley Coleridge comments on the central figure and writes, ' The poet's wife is perhaps the most lovable figure that ever Hogarth drew ; while the milkwoman has as little milkiness about her as if she had been suckled on blue ruin [*i.e.* gin] and brimstone.' [1]   Mr. Dobson asks if Goldsmith was thinking of this engraving when in 1758 he described himself to his friend Robert Bryanton as ' in a garret writing for bread and expecting to be dunned for a milk-score ' ?

Mr. Stephens explains the curious object over the mantelpiece as ' a circular mirror surrounded by eight smaller ones,' which seems to be a complete explanation.[2]   John Ireland describes it as ' a dare for larks ! '

Below the design an extract from the *Dunciad* (1729) is engraved :

' Studious he sate, with all his books around,
Sinking, from thought to thought, a vast profound !
Plung'd for his sense, but found no bottom there ;
Then writ and flounder'd on, in mere despair.'

In the second state of the print (1740) the title of the poem is changed from Poverty to Riches, the engraving of Pope thrashing Curll replaced by a view of the gold mines of Peru, and the library on the shelf is reduced to two volumes.   Pope's lines are also

[1] *Essays and Marginalia*, 1851, vol. ii. p 217.
[2] *British Museum Catalogue*, vol. iii. p. 213.

omitted.   The original picture was given by Hogarth to Mrs. Draper, a midwife, at whose death it was sold to Mr. Ward for five guineas.   Lord Grosvenor gave fourteen guineas for it at Ward's sale, and it is now in the possession of the Duke of Westminster.

It was George Steevens who, being unable to find a portrait of Theobald to add to those of the chief Shakespearian commentators, copied the 'Distrest Poet' for one of these.   Although Steevens is a very doubtful authority, there is plausibility in this, and two reasons given for associating Theobald with Hogarth's picture have much force.

The quotation from the *Dunciad* just referred to is not from the final form of the poem, but is taken from the edition of 1729, where Theobald stands for the hero before he was pushed aside that Colley Cibber might take his place.   The passage commences :

> 'In each, she marks her image full exprest,
> But chief in Tibbald's monster-breeding breast.'

Afterwards 'Bayes's' replaced 'Tibbald's' in the second line.

Hogarth left out the most offensive of Pope's allusions, and only printed what suited his purpose in illustration of his design.

Another point is that the earliest of Theobald's productions was 'The Cave of Poverty, a Poem,' which bears a striking likeness to the title of what the 'Distrest Poet' is writing.   The alterations made in the second state are significant if we suppose that Hogarth was wishful to obliterate any hint of an allusion to a praiseworthy author who was no dunce, but an editor of far superior merit to Pope, and thus evoked the venomous poet's ire.[1]

Hogarth's severe satire on Pope has already been alluded to, and it was not likely ever to have been forgiven by the poet, but the latter had a wholesome fear of the painter, and did not venture to retaliate. But the chief literary portrait by Hogarth is that of Fielding, who was one of the artist's most ardent admirers. It is strange that we should have no first-rate portrait of so distinguished a man as the author of *Tom Jones* and the foremost magistrate of his time. It is satisfactory that what we have is due to his friend Hogarth. There is a curious history respecting this portrait which was engraved by James Basire from Hogarth's pen-and-ink sketch prepared as a frontispiece to the edition of Fielding's works published by Andrew Millar in 1762. Arthur Murphy gave an explanation of the origin of the portrait in the Life prefixed to the first volume. He wrote: ' After Mr. Hogarth had long laboured to try if he could bring out any likeness of him from images existing in his own fancy, and just as he was despairing of success, for want of some rules to go by in the dimensions and outlines of the face, fortune threw the grand desideratum in the way. A lady with a pair of scissors had cut a profile, which gave the

---

[1] A reprint of the original *Dunciad* (1729) which relates to Theobald will be found in Nichols's *Literary Illustrations* (vol. ii. pp 716-728) In the same volume, pp. 745-747, are remarks by W. Richardson on the connection of Theobald with the 'Distrest Poet.'

distances and proportions of his face sufficiently to restore his lost ideas of him.   Glad of an opportunity of paying his last tribute to the memory of an author whom he admired, Mr. Hogarth caught at this outline with pleasure, and worked, with all the attachment of friendship, till he finished that excellent drawing which stands at the head of this work, and recalls to all, who have seen the original, a corresponding image of the man.'   This is a high tribute to the likeness.   Mr. Dobson says that the lady mentioned by Murphy was Miss Margaret Collier, daughter of Arthur Collier the metaphysician, who accompanied Fielding and his wife to Lisbon in 1754.

Mr. Knight in his Life of Garrick writes that the story of Garrick making up his face as Fielding for Hogarth to paint was narrated in Paris, and caused some incredulity.   Garrick in order to convince the most sceptical once more personated Fielding, and his personation won instant recognition.   This story forms the basis of a comedy entitled *Le Portrait de Fielding* (1800), by M. de Ségur.

Neither George Steevens nor John Ireland would allow the truth of either of these stories.   Steevens says in Nichols's *Biographical Anecdotes*: ' Our Roscius, however, I can assert, interfered no farther in this business than by urging Hogarth to attempt the likeness, as a necessary adjunct to the edition of Fielding's works.   I am assured that our artist began and finished the head in the presence of his wife and another lady.   He had no assistance but from his own memory, which on such occasions was remarkably tenacious.'

John Ireland (*Hogarth Illustrated*, vol. iii. p. 291) says much the same. 'These are trifling tales to please children, and echoed from one to another, because the multitude love the marvellous. . . . Hogarth . . . sketched this from memory.'

These denials seem to be too sweeping. It is quite possible that the artist was helped by a silhouette—in fact a portrait entirely from memory is scarcely likely to be a profile, and the accentuation of the appearance of the nose reminds one of a silhouette. Moreover, it is scarcely likely that Murphy invented the story which he so particularly relates.

John Ireland says that the 'etching is so nearly a facsimile of the original, that when it was brought home Hogarth mistook it for his own drawing, which, considering of no value, he threw in the fire, whence it was snatched by Mrs. Lewis, though not before the paper was scorched.'

There is an engraving 'from a miniature in the possession of Miss Sophia Fielding' in Nichols's *Literary Anecdotes* (vol. iii. p. 356), but this is evidently taken from Hogarth's portrait.

Another great novelist, Laurence Sterne, was friendly with Hogarth, and praised the *Analysis of Beauty* in the second volume of *Tristram Shandy*. 'Such were the outlines of Dr. Slop's figure, which—if you have read Hogarth's *Analysis of Beauty*, and if you have not, I wish you would—you must know may as certainly be caricatured, and conveyed to the mind, by three strokes as three hundred.'

This compliment doubtless induced Hogarth to design the frontispiece to the novel, containing a portrait of Dr. Burton of York, the Jacobite physician and antiquary in the character of Dr. Slop, which appears in the second volume of *Tristram Shandy*. He designed another frontispiece for the fourth volume.

Mr. Dobson refers to a letter sold at Sotheby's in November 1891. 'It was addressed by Sterne to Mr. Berenger of Suffolk Street, and begged him to go to Leicester Fields, and persuade Hogarth ("Howgarth," he calls him) to make a drawing, to clap at the front of my next edition of *Shandy*.' . . . 'The loosest sketch in Nature of Trim's reading the sermon to my Father w^d do the business—and it w^d mutually illustrate his [Hogarth's] System and mine !'[1]

Hogarth painted or sketched portraits of his literary friends as T. Morell (engraved 1762), the Hoadlys, etc., which have already been alluded to. The portrait of William Huggins, a translator of Ariosto and Dante, was engraved by Major in 1760 for the *Dante*, but was not published, as Huggins died in July 1761. There is a pencil drawing of the translator with a bust of Ariosto in the Royal Collection. William Huggins of Headly Park,

[1] Dobson's *William Hogarth*, 1907, p. 258.

Hants, was the son of John Huggins, warden of the Fleet and a great friend of Hogarth, who employed him to draft the bill to vest in designers and engravers an exclusive right to their own works (Act 8, Geo. II. cap. 13), and Hogarth also designed the frontispiece to Huggins's oratorio of *Judith* (1733). In the official catalogue of the Art Treasures and Industrial Exhibition at Bradford, 1870, No. 109 is described as a portrait of Dr. Johnson painted by Hogarth and contributed by the late Marquess of Ripon (then Earl de Grey and Ripon). There is no other record of a portrait of Johnson by Hogarth, and it would be interesting to know more of this picture.

Art.—Pictorial art was a subject so near to Hogarth's heart that it naturally pervades the whole scheme of this book, and need not be mentioned in a division of it. He was chiefly interested in girding at connoisseurs for the neglect of British Art, and did not as a rule introduce his colleagues and rivals into his works. He painted Bonamy showing a picture, and portraits of James Gibbs the architect and Michael Rysbrach, sculptor.

One of the cleverest of his satires on the connoisseurs will be seen in the tailpiece which he produced for the Catalogue of the Exhibition of Pictures which was held in 1761. In the frontispiece to this same Catalogue he was not so succesful, as his humour is lost in the elaboration of the allegory.

Mention may be here made of three pictures which have nothing to do with London Topography, but need some notice as good examples of the variety and wide range of Hogarth's pictorial power. The first of these is the beautiful group of heads representing his six servants, which was added to the National Gallery quite recently. We have little information respecting this triumph of portraiture, and we are therefore unable to give the names of the individuals forming the group.

The marvellous oil sketch of the 'Shrimp-girl' was added as lately as 1884, and is a great addition to the National Gallery. The critic Richard Muther uses strong words of praise when he calls it 'a masterpiece to which the nineteenth century can hardly produce a rival.' This picture was engraved in 1781 by Bartolozzi.

The head of *Diana* here reproduced is of special interest as an illustration of Hogarth's sense of female beauty. We have no further information respecting the original than that it belonged to Samuel Ireland in 1794. The engraving was published by him in his *Graphic Illustrations* (i. 170), with the following interesting anecdote respecting it: 'Mr. Garrick chanced to visit Hogarth one morning, when the artist was engaged in his painting-room ; and being about to retire hastily from the door, Old Ben Ives, the servant, called out to him, to beg he would step back, as he had something to shew him, that he was sure would please ; and then

THE SHRIMP GIRL.

From the original painting in the National Gallery.

HEAD OF DIANA.

Reproduced from S. Ireland's etching from an original sketch in oil by Hogarth.

HOGARTH'S SIX SERVANTS.

From the original painting in the National Gallery.

taking him into the parlour, exclaimed in raptures,
"There, sir! there's a picture! they say my
master can't paint a portrait, and does not know
what true beauty is; there is a head, that I think
must confound and put all his enemies to the blush."'
One would be glad to know if Ben Ives was one of
those represented in the group of servants.

Hogarth advertised that the prints of the
'Distressed Poet' and the 'Enraged Musician'
would be followed by a third on Painting. It is not
known if this was really contemplated or was merely
the notification of a possibility. There is nothing
extant to guide us in forming an idea as to how the
subject would be treated.

An advertisement in the *London Daily Post*
(November 24, 1740) announces: 'Shortly will be
published, a new Print, call'd THE PROVOKED
MUSICIAN. Designed and Engraved by Mr. William
Hogarth; being a Companion to a Print, representing a Distressed Poet, published some time since,
to which will be added a Third on Painting, which
will compleat the set; but as the subject may
turn upon an affair depending between the L—d
M—r and the Author it may be retarded for some
time.'

'The Enraged Musician' is one of Hogarth's most
interesting prints. The arrangement of the miscellaneous collection of discordant noises which the
artist has collected together is perfect, dominated
as the whole picture is by the charming milkmaid in

the centre of the picture. At the same time the musician at the open window gives the key to the effect of the riot of confused sound that, as we have said, caused Fielding to write in his *Journal of a Voyage to Lisbon* that the picture is 'enough to make a man deaf to look at.'

As to the musician who was used as a model, a great amount of ingenuity has been expended, and the following names have been put forward: Signor Cervetto, a bass player at the theatres; and Mr. John Foster, a player on the German flute when a boy; and Castrucci, a violinist of repute; but there appears to be more authority for supposing the figure was taken from Michael Christian Festin, who was known to Hogarth and related the circumstances of the interruption of his studies which have been added to by the artist.

George Colman wrote a musical entertainment for the Haymarket Theatre founded on this picture, the music for which was composed by Dr. Arnold.

'The Modern Orpheus,' which was etched by D. Smith from an original sketch in the possession of the Marquis of Bute and published in 1807, is a satire on the performances of the celebrated flautist, C. Weidemann, who is introduced into the fourth plate of the 'Marriage à la Mode.' The engraving discovers a street where a man is walking and playing on a flute, while he is attended by an enraptured audience. An effect of his music is to compel legs of mutton and other objects to move towards him

"The Enraged Musician." 1741.

through the air. In the distance stand Sir Robert Walpole and George II., the latter speaking in delight to the former, while coins issue from his pocket and pass to that of Weidemann.

This engraving was reproduced in the *Genuine Works* (Nichols and Steevens, 1817, vol. iii.), but Mr. Dobson is doubtful as to the genuineness of 'The Modern Orpheus' as actually the edsign of Hogarth.

We know that Hogarth had a high opinion of Handel in spite of his connection with the hated Italian opera. Some one suggested that the player on the harpsichord in Plate 2 of the 'Rake's Progress' was intended for the great composer, but this is most improbable. Mr. Felix Cobbold, M.P., is in possession of an oil painting of Handel by Hogarth, which was engraved by Charles Turner in 1821. This engraving is dedicated 'To the Noblemen, Directors and Patrons of the Antient Music,' but it is not stated in whose possession the picture then was.

There are other portraits of Handel attributed to Hogarth, but there is no definite information respecting them.

CHAPTER VIII

BUSINESS LIFE

THE subject of Business Life is intimately associated with Hogarth's first start in business by himself, and we have his own card as an engraver (which has already been alluded to) to guide us as to the date of the various business cards which have been attributed to him. The charming card— ' W. Hogarth Engraver '—in an elegant border after the manner of Callot is dated 1720, and most of the other cards can probably be placed about the same date. It is a question difficult, or rather impossible, to settle whether Hogarth prepared the book-plate and shop-bill for Ellis Gamble before he left the service of that goldsmith, or after he had set up his own business, in the immediate neighbourhood of his old master's shop.

The shop-bill representing an angel with a very large palm branch in her left hand is a bold and spirited production. Beneath the figure is inscribed Gamble's name and description in English and French. The English inscription to the left is as follows :

HOGARTH'S BUSINESS CARD. 1720.

Ellis Gamble
Goldsmith,
at the Golden Angel in
Cranbourn-Street,
Leicester - Fields,
*Makes, Buys & Sells all
sorts of Plate, Rings, &
Jewells &c.*

Samuel Ireland says of this bill: 'Whether by accident or design we know not, but he [Hogarth] has given to the right hand of the angel a finger too much. A redundancy of the same kind, we observe in his print of The Sleeping Congregation, where he has intentionally added a joint more to the thigh of the Angel, than is usually found in the works of Nature. The original of this print is become extremely scarce, and although an early production, and without name or date, has yet established itself, in the minds of the most scrupulous connoisseur, as a genuine work of Hogarth.'[1]

Hogarth's book-plates have already been alluded to, but it seems necessary to mention again the delightful little book-plate which Hogarth made for Gamble. This goldsmith must have been a superior man if he possessed a sufficient number of books to require book-labels.

Respecting the Lambert (engraved Lambart) plate Samuel Ireland writes: 'Hogarth's great intimacy with George Lambert, the landscape-painter, for whom the annexed coat-of-arms was

[1] S. Ireland, *Graphic Illustrations*, vol. i. 1794, pp. 7-8.

engraved by him as a book-plate, is well known; the design is simple, and the execution masterly; yet the principal motive for introducing it here is, that the original is a unique print. This circumstance is the more extraordinary as I am informed by Mr. Richards, secretary to the Royal Academy, and who was a pupil of George Lambert, that it was stuck in all his books; and that his library consisted of seven or eight hundred volumes.'[1]

Samuel Ireland reproduces a shop-bill of William Hardy engraved in the manner of Callot from a unique copy with a corner torn off. He adds that the original was given to him 'as an early performance of Hogarth's by his friend the late Mr. Bonneau, who received it from him as a very early production.'[2] The inscription is as follows:

Will^n Hardy
GOLDSMITH
and Jeweller in Ratcliff highway
near Sun Tavern Fields
Sells all sorts of
Gold and Silver Plate &c.

In the *Genuine Works* (vol. iii.) is reproduced a shop-bill of a Soho goldsmith which presents the interior of a shop with figures and a furnace in the left-hand corner. The inscription is:

Peter De La Fontaine, GOLDSMITH
At the Golden Cup in Litchfield Street
Soho. Makes and Sells all sorts of Gold and Silver
Plate, Swords, Rings, Jewells, &c., at ye lowest prices.

---

[1] *Graphic Illustrations*, vol. i p. 115.   [2] *Ibid.*, vol. i. p. 3.

The shop-bill of Hogarth's two sisters is of great interest, but must be placed a few years later in date than those already described, as Mary and Ann Hogarth did not commence business until the year 1725. Samuel Ireland writes : ' The originality of this print has never yet been doubted, even by the most scrupulous ; its ornaments are bold and animated ; and the masterly though careless touch of the graver justly gives it a claim to approbation ' [1] Mr. Dobson notes that there is an impression of the original bill in the British Museum. The design of the interior of a shop of the period is of much value, and is of rather imposing proportions. The inscription is as follows :

Mary & Anne Hogarth

from the old Frock-shop the corner of the
Long Walk facing the Cloysters, Removed
to ye King's Arms joyning to ye Little Britain-
gate, near Long Walk. Sells ye best & most Fashi-
onable Ready Made Frocks, sutes of Fustian,
Ticken & Holland, stript Dimmity & Flañel
Wastcoats, blue and Canvas Frocks and bluecoat Boys Dra^{rs}.
Likewise Fustians, Tickens, Hollands, white
stript Dimĩtys, white & stript Flañels in ye piece,
by Wholesale or Retale, at Reasonable Rates.

Mrs. Holt's shop-bill, also reproduced by Samuel Ireland in his *Graphic Illustrations* (vol. i. p. 17) is of considerable interest, and the design shows much originality of invention although its ascription to Hogarth has been doubted.

[1] *Graphic Illustrations*, vol. i p. 16

Ireland writes thus of this shop-bill: 'The following print is selected as a farther specimen of the early talent of Hogarth in the line of his profession. . . . This print, though intended merely as a shop-bill, is put together with no small degree of knowledge in the ordinary affairs of commerce in our quarter of the globe. Mercury, the god of merchandize and gain, whether lawfully or unlawfully obtained, is here judiciously placed in the midst of the scene of action: he seems assiduous in executing the orders of the civic figure, who represents Florence the capital of Tuscany, and who is pointing to a jar of oil, one of the principal articles of Commerce of that country. This fair city seems pouring its richest treasures into the lap of Britain, as we may collect from the arms of England seen at the stern of the vessel, which they are busily loading. Nor has Hogarth forgot to introduce [at the four corners of the design] the other principal states of Italy, Naples, Venice, Leghorn and Genoa, as equally emulous to trade with our city of London, the great emporium of Europe.' The inscription is as follows :

AT MRS. HOLTS,

Italian Ware House

at yᵉ two Olive Posts in yᵉ Broad part of the Strand almost opposite to Exeter Change are sold all Sorts of Italian Silks as Lustrings, Sattins, Padesois, Velvets, Damasks, &c.

Fans, Legorne Hats, Flowers Lute & Violin Strings, Books of Essences, Venice Treacle, Balsomes, &c.

*And in a Back Warehouse all Sorts of Italian
Wines, Florence Cordials, Oyl, Olives, Anchovies,
Capers, Vermicelli, Bolognia Sausidges, Par-
mesan Cheeses, Maple Soap,
&c.*

This description is very instructive. A particular kind of grocer's shop was formerly styled an Italian warehouse, and the name is not entirely unused now. This shows that in the original Italian warehouse there were two departments—the silk mercer's and the wine merchant's and grocer's.

Samuel Ireland has reproduced something much more doubtful than anything already described, and that is what he calls a ' Design for a Shop-bill.' The picture represents a room with several persons in different positions; one, supposed to be Hogarth himself, is showing a portrait of St. Luke with his ox and book, inscribed ' W. Hogarth Painter.' Ireland gives Charles Catton, R.A., as his authority for supposing that Hogarth for a time worked as a sign-painter, and he reproduces the two sides of a sign for a Paviour which he attributes to Hogarth. These were painted on a thick piece of mahogany that had been divided by a saw before they came into the possession of Ireland. They are interesting illustrations of London streets with paviours at work mending the roads. In the background of one side is a rough sketch of the Dome of St. Paul's.

There is another shop-bill—that of ' Richard Lee at yᵉ Golden Tobacco Roll in Panton Street near

Leicester Fields '—which is entirely different from those which have been previously described.

It is reproduced by Samuel Ireland in his *Graphic Illustrations* from an original in his possession, which he supposed to be unique. There is one in the British Museum which is dated *circa* 1730, and described by Mr. Stephens as follows: 'It is an oblong enclosing an oval, the spandrels being occupied by leaves of the tobacco plant tied in bundles ; the above title is on a frame which encloses the oval. Within the latter the design represents the interior of a room, with ten gentlemen gathered near a round table on which is a bowl of punch ; several of the gentlemen are smoking tobacco in long pipes ; one of them stands up on our right and vomits ; another, who is intoxicated, lies on the floor by the side of a chair ; a fire of wood burns in the grate ; on the wall hang two pictures . . . three men's hats hang on pegs on the wall.' [1]

Ireland expresses the opinion that this engraving contains the germ of the idea which at a later period was developed by Hogarth in a ' Midnight Modern Conversation.'

Mr. Dobson, however, doubts the ' shop-bill' being the work of Hogarth, and he suggests that the design is based upon the ' Midnight Modern Conversation.' This is probable, but it is but fair to Ireland to quote what he says as to its authenticity. ' This little print is so very like the other early works of

[1] *British Museum Catalogue*, vol ii p. 728.

Hogarth both in the style and manner of engraving, as well as the ornaments and even the writing that is round it, as to place its authenticity out of all question.   A farther proof might be urged if necessary.   It is totally unlike the manner of his contemporaries ; amongst whom it stood in such a degree of repute as to induce them repeatedly to copy it : three of these copies are now before us, and so ill executed as to be deemed mere servile imitations.'[1]

Nearly allied to Shop-bills are Undertakers' Funeral Tickets, one of which was the work of Hogarth.

A reproduction from the scarce original will be found in Ireland's *Graphic Illustrations*.   It represents the front of a London church, where a funeral party is about to ascend the steps.   The pall over the coffin is surmounted by plumes and enriched by coats-of-arms.   The mourners (men and women) follow in pairs.   Below the design is the inscription :

'You are desired to accompany ye Corps of   from h   late Dwelling in   to on   next at   of the Clock in the Evening. Perform'd by Humphrey Drew, Undertaker, in King Street, Westminster.'

Samuel Ireland only knew of three copies of the original engraving, the one which he reproduced, one belonging to Horace Walpole on which he wrote ' W. Hogarth sc.'   This is now in the British

[1] *Graphic Illustrations*, vol i pp 12-13

Museum.[1] The third copy is in the Royal Collection.

This funeral ticket is a gloomy-looking thing as is natural, but is also, as might be expected, very superior to those then in general use. Mr. John Ashton, in a chapter on Death and Burial in his *Social Life in the Reign of Queen Anne*, reprints one of these Invitations to a Funeral, the ornaments round which are Time, skeletons, skulls, cross-bones, pick-axe and shovel, shroud, etc.

When the funeral was in the evening the mourners were usually supplied with wax tapers. These sometimes excited the cupidity of the roughs who were always to be found in case of public gatherings. An advertisement in the *Daily Courant* for September 30, 1713 (quoted by Mr. Ashton) shows what might be expected: 'Riots and Robberies. Committed in and about Stepney Churchyard, at a Funeral Solemnity, on Wednesday the 23rd day of September; and whereas many Persons, who being appointed to attend the Funeral with white Wax lights of a considerable value, were assaulted in a most violent manner, and the said white Wax lights, taken from them. Whoever shall discover any of the Persons, guilty of the said crimes, so as they may be convicted of the same, shall receive of Mr. William Prince, Wax Chandler in the Poultry, London, Ten shillings for each person so discovered,' etc. It may be mentioned that at this time it was the custom to make a

---

[1] *British Museum Catalogue*, vol. ii. p. 725.

distinction in the mourning for the married and the unmarried; thus white and black was used for maids and bachelors. In the fine engraving of the west front of Covent Garden Church (St. Paul's) drawn by Paul Sandby, R.A., and engraved by E. Rooker, will be noticed the funeral of an unmarried girl, where the women mourners are in white and the men wear white sashes.

The instructive series of twelve plates of ' Industry and Idleness,' illustrating the Adventures of an Industrious and an Idle Apprentice, is full of information respecting the progress of business life in London, and in this chapter we shall have to deal almost entirely with the Industrious Apprentice as the Idle one has little to do with business.

Hogarth's design in producing these plates is described by himself in a paper published by John Ireland in his *Hogarth Illustrated* (vol. i. p. 185). ' Industry and Idleness exemplified, in the conduct of two fellow 'prentices : where the one by taking good courses, and pursuing points for which he was put apprentice, becomes a valuable man, and an ornament to his country : the other by giving way to idleness, naturally falls into poverty, and ends fatally, as is expressed in the last print. As the prints were intended more for use than ornament, they were done in a way that might bring them within the purchase of whom they might most concern ; and lest any print should be mistaken, the description of each print is engraved at top.'

The *General Advertiser* for Saturday, October 17, 1747, contains the following announcement: 'This Day is publish'd, Price 12s. Design'd and Engrav'd by Mr. Hogarth. Twelve Prints call'd "Industry and Idleness," shewing the advantages attending the former and the miserable effects of the latter, in the different Fortunes of Two Apprentices. To be had at the Golden Head in Leicester Fields, and at the Print-shops. There are some printed on a better paper for the curious at 14s. each set, to be had only at the Author's in Leicester Fields. Where may be had all his other works.'

The moralists of the eighteenth century paid little attention to fine distinctions and drew the difference between good and evil with the clearest-cut contrast. It was this that induced Thackeray to express his sympathy with Tom Idle, who he thought never had a chance in life.

Commentators have found considerable likeness in the story of Hogarth's prints to the plot of the old play, *Eastward Hoe*, by Ben Jonson, Chapman and Marston (1605), and in the year 1751 it was revived at Drury Lane for Lord Mayor's Day. This alteration was not successful, but another made by Mrs. Lenox and called *Old City Manners* was favourably received.

There is sufficient justification for calling attention to the likeness, although there does not seem much probability that Hogarth should seek for so very evident a story in an old play. Golding (Goodchild) marries Touchstone's (West's) daughter and becomes a magistrate, when Quicksilver (Idle) is brought before him as a criminal.

The first plate shows the interior of a weaver's workshop in Spitalfields. Francis Goodchild is seen working busily while Tom Idle is sleeping. In front of the latter on the loom is a quart pot which has engraved upon it 'Spittle Fields.' The door of the room has been opened by the master of the apprentices, who calls to the sleeper and threatens him with his stick. In the fourth plate Goodchild has been transferred to the office, and his master is seen leaning affectionately upon his shoulder. The master extending his right hand points to the looms in the background 'as if he intended to give the apprentice control in his place.' John Ireland writes : ' A partnership, on the eve of taking place, is covertly intimated by a pair of gloves upon the writing-desk.' The position of the gloves indicates the clasping of hands, and the *London Almanac* on the side of the desk is headed by a design above the calendar of Industry taking Father Time by the forelock.

A city porter at the left of the plate is delivering stuffs from Backwell Hall, addressed to ' Mr. West.' These two plates give an excellent illustration of a business establishment in Spitalfields where the silk trade once flourished in London.

In Plate 6 the Industrious Apprentice out of his time obtains the fulness of his reward for good conduct by marrying the daughter of his master and becoming a partner in the firm. In the first state of the plate Hogarth made the mistake of placing the junior partner's name first on the sign, but ' Goodchild and West ' of the first state became ' West and Goodchild ' in the second state.

Mr. Stephens thus describes this plate: 'The engraving shows part of a street in London, near the Fire Monument, the Pedestal of which appears in the middle distance with part of an inscription thus: "*In remembrance —— of Burning y' Protestant City by the treachery of the Papish Faction In —— year —— of our —— Lo—d 1666.*" A band of musicians, including a butcher who performs on a cleaver with a bone, and his companion, another such performer, are assembled before a house to celebrate in their noisy way the wedding of the Industrious 'Prentice with the daughter of his Master, Mr. West. . . . The musicians appear to be making a great noise, their instruments are mostly drums . . . One of the drummers has approached a window of the house of Messrs. West and Goodchild ; the lower sash of this window is pushed up and the Industrious 'Prentice appears there, holding a teacup in one hand while with the other he gives a coin to the drummer, who bows obsequiously and has taken off his hat. Goodchild wears his dressing-gown and cap, having put aside his coat and wig on returning home from the church after his marriage to Miss West. The bride is seen in the interior of the room, with a patch on her forehead . . sipping her tea and looking very happy. The door of the house is open and a footman, wearing a shoulder-knot, stands on the threshold, pouring a plateful of broken victuals into the apron of a woman, who kneels on the step to receive the alms; a child's face appears at the shoulder of the woman.' [1]

John Ireland identifies the cripple to the left of the picture holding a broadside of the ballad of 'Jesse or the Happy Pair' as 'a man known by the name of Philip in the Tub, who had visited Ireland, and the United Provinces, and in the memory of many persons now living [1793] was a general attendant at weddings.' [2]

The abstract of the monstrous inscription on the Monument given above is not correct, in that the inscription occupied four sides of the plinth and therefore could not all be seen at one view. The offensive words were not the original inscription, but were added at the time of the terror caused by the so-called Popish plot. They were obliterated in the reign of James II., recut after the Revolution, but finally erased by an Act of Common Council, January 26, 1831.

Pope was unusually accurate when he wrote the lines :

'Where London's column, pointing at the skies,
Like a tall bully lifts the head and lies'

---

[1] *British Museum Catalogue*, vol. iii. pp 693-694.
[2] *Hogarth Illustrated*, vol. i. pp 198-199.

In Plate 8 we find Goodchild grown rich and become
Sheriff of London, dining at one of the City Companies' halls. John Ireland describes the Banquet-
ing Hall as the Guildhall, but this is clearly a
mistake, and the whole-length figure of Sir William
Walworth in a niche between the windows proves
that this is intended for the old hall of the Fish-
monger's Company which was built by Edward
Jerman, the City Surveyor, after the Great Fire. The
present hall, built 1831-33, is not on the site of the
old hall, but in an improved position formed in connection with the opening for the new London Bridge.

The imposing beadle in his state gown stands at
the entrance door with a letter in his hand directed
'To the Worship "Fra" Goodchild Es. Sher——
Londo—,' which has been delivered by a messenger
who, bareheaded and holding a hat in his hand,
awaits an answer. The principal seats are occupied
by the Sheriff and his wife, and a number of ladies
are seen sitting at the feast.

This picture is of great interest as showing the
manners at table in the eighteenth century. All
the dishes were put on at once and no wine was
placed upon the table. A black waiter is seen
handing it round. Sir Walter Besant says that a
writer in 1790 notes the fact that it had only lately
become the fashion to put wines upon the table,
and that the new custom was then very far from
being general. The dinner at the time of this print
was in the daytime, and the company retired to the

gardens, which were generally attached to the various halls, for dessert and wine.

The trees in the garden are seen through the windows in this plate.

It was not until well on into the nineteenth century when an improved system of service and better manners among the guests became general.

In Plate 10 the two former fellow-apprentices are brought together again under most painful circumstances. Goodchild having become an Alderman sits as a magistrate in the Guildhall, when Idle is brought before him as a criminal. The clerk is busily writing on a paper addressed 'To the Turnkey of Newgate,' a warrant for the committal of Thomas Idle to Newgate on the charge of having murdered the man whose plunder was shown in Plate 9 referred to in the Chapter on Crime. The appearance of the prisoner is abject. Mr. Stephens says of the man next him who is swearing on the book: 'The man in the knitted cap and having the patch over one of his eyes, appears as a witness against his accomplice and stands next to him in the character of a " King's evidence," swearing to the truth of his deposition by placing his *left* hand on the book held by an attendant of the court, who stands within the bar. This attendant has one of his hands behind his back, into that hand a slatternly woman is secretly placing a piece of money. This act of bribery is performed in order that the official may be induced not to notice that the witness uses his left instead of his right hand in attesting his oath on the book.   An assertion that an oath taken in this fashion was not binding on the swearer was frequently made by the vulgar before, at, and since the period in question.' [1]

The concluding Plate (12), in which Francis Goodchild is seen to have reached the summit of his ambition as Lord Mayor of London, contains a view of the greatest interest from a topographical point of view.

It is a brilliant representation of the west end of Cheapside.   Looking southwards across St. Paul's Churchyard, we see the eastern extremity of the cathedral.   In front a balcony projects from the first floor of a house at the corner of Paternoster Row. In the balcony are several personages, including Frederick, Prince of Wales, and his wife Augusta under a canopy of state. As to the persons attendant on royalty we have no information, with the exception of 'the lady in profile with a French cap, lappet and cloak' to the extreme right of the balcony, and we have Horace Walpole's authority for saying that this figure is intended for the Countess of Middlesex, Mistress of the Robes.[2]   The front of the balcony is decorated with two pieces of tapestry, the subjects of which have not been recognised.

The right of using these balconies was often

[1] *British Museum Catalogue*, vol. iii. pp. 708-709.

[2] This information is given in a MS. note in a copy of the first edition of Nichols's *Biographical Anecdotes*, 1781 (p. 109), in the author's possession, which originally belonged to Horace Walpole who annotated it.

reserved, and John Ireland refers to Wood's *Body of Conveyancing*, in which book (vol. ii. p. 180) there is a London lease; one of the clauses gives a right to the landlord and his friends to stand in the balcony 'during the time of the shews or pastimes, upon the day commonly called Lord Mayor's day.'

The favourite place for royalty to see the show was at Bow Church, but it is recorded that Frederick, Prince of Wales, on a previous occasion, wished to see it privately and he entered the city in disguise. He was discovered by some members of the Saddlers' Company, and was requested to occupy the Company's stand. He accepted the invitation and soon afterwards became a saddler.

The old Seldam or shed which was made by order of Edward III. on the north side of Bow Church for the purpose of accommodating the royal party on the occasions of shows and processions, was afterwards superseded by the balcony. In September 1677 Charles II. had advice at Newmarket that the Fifth Monarchy men had a design to murder him and the Duke of York on Lord Mayor's day in this balcony.

The crowded scene of Hogarth's plate is full of interesting details which it is needless to particularise here, although there is one which requires special attention as it helps to complete the series and causes us to remember the connection between the two apprentices. At the right-hand corner of the engraving is an emaciated boy, a hawker of broadsides, who holds a paper on which is printed, 'A full and true account of yᵉ Ghost of Tho. Idle which—'

We have, however, Chaucer's authority for the fact that every apprentice who is idle and neglects his proper duties does not necessarily come to the violent end of Hogarth's Idle Apprentice.

'A prentis whilom dwelled in our citee,

.   .   .   .   .

At every bridale wolde he sing and hoppe;
He loved bet the taverne than the shoppe;
For whan ther eny Riding was in Chepe,
Out of the shoppe thider wold he lepe;
Til that he had al the sight yseyn,
And danced wel he would nat come ageyn.'[1]

The passages from the Bible which are attached to the several plates of 'Industry and Idleness' were selected by Hogarth's friend, the Rev. Dr. Arnold King. John Nichols obtained this information from Dr. Ducarel.

There are a series of drawings by Hogarth for the engravings of 'Industry and Idleness' in the Print Room of the British Museum. Some of these are first thoughts, freely sketched; others represent more developed studies; others, again, are the final designs made for transfer to the copper. The description of these is very interesting (see Binyon's *British Museum Catalogue of Drawings by British Artists*, vol. ii. p. 316). There are also drawings for two subjects which were not engraved, viz. 'The Industrious 'Prentice when a Merchant giving Money

[1] *The Coke's Tale.*

Hogarth pinx[t] Barlow sculp[t]

Scene at a Banking house in 1745.

Pub. for S. Ireland May 1.1799.

SARAH, DUCHESS OF MARLBOROUGH, AT CHILD'S BANK.

to his Parents,' and 'The Idle Apprentice stealing from his Mother.' [1]

There is a very interesting tradition connecting Hogarth with sketches of the run upon Child's Bank, which was stopped with the help of Sarah, Duchess of Marlborough, but the accounts of this are so confused that it is difficult to obtain a satisfactory solution. A plain statement may help to draw attention to the subject and end in an explanation being suggested.

Samuel Ireland published in the second volume of his *Graphic Illustrations* (1799) an engraving by Barlow from a small picture in oil by Hogarth in his possession, which he entitled 'Scene at a Banking House in 1745.' Mr. Dobson says that the picture was bought at Ireland's sale in 1801 by George Baker for £3, 10s. At Baker's sale in 1825 it fetched £60, 18s. It was sold again in June 1899 at Forman's sale for £53, 11s.

Ireland's account of the picture is shortly as follows: 'The figure in the chair was intended for Sarah, the celebrated Dutchess of Marlborough. This circumstance is corroborated by the Ducal coronet on the back of the chair, which is supported by two boys. The figures represented in a sitting posture, are the principals of the banking-house of Mess[rs] Child and Co., who seem amply prepared to discharge all the demands pressing upon them. . . .

[1] Hogarth's original intention was to call the Idle Apprentice 'Thomas Fowler.'

The wealth of the house is allegorically represented by the bags of gold, which are piled over each other in the background of the picture.'

Ireland then relates the circumstances of the run upon the bank and relief supplied by the Duchess of Marlborough, which he says he obtained from an authority not to be doubted.   In 1745, owing to the Jacobite Rebellion, Bank of England notes were at a considerable discount, while the notes issued by Child's Bank and that of Hoare and Co. maintained their credit and circulated at par.   The directors of the Bank of England attempted to injure the credit of Child's Bank by collecting their notes with the intention of pouring them in for payment on the same day.   The Duchess heard of this plot and informed Messrs. Child, at the same time supplying them ' with a sum of money more than sufficient to answer the amplest demand ' that could be made upon them. The scheme was carried out, and the Bank of England was paid in its own paper to its own very great loss. This story breaks down owing to Ireland having overlooked the fact that the redoubtable Duchess Sarah was not alive in 1745, she having died in October 1744.

The late Mr. Hilton Price, partner in Child's Bank, gave an altogether different account of this 'run' in his octavo volume entitled *Ye Marygold*, 1875. He wrote: ' Child's Bank was saved from a run in 1689 by Sarah, Duchess of Marlborough (then Lady Churchill), who collected among her friends as much gold as she was able, which she brought down to the bank in her coach.   Hogarth made a spirited sketch of the Duchess's coach stopping at Temple Bar, and another sketch of her Grace appearing in the bank following porters carrying bags of gold.   No entry in the books of the firm respecting this, but there is no reason to doubt the fact.'[1]

We are not told where these sketches of Hogarth's are to be found; and if they were made by him, they must have been drawn from a relation of the events and not from sight, as the painter was not then born.

In 1902 Mr. Hilton Price published a larger book on the same subject, entitled *The Marygold by Temple Bar* (4to).   He there repeats what is quoted above, and adds an account of the run or ' push,' as it was then called, made upon Child's from John Francis's *History of the Bank of England.*   Francis gives Samuel Ireland as his authority, but adds some figures, and to some extent gets over the difficulty of the Duchess Sarah's death by dating the affair *about* 1745.   He says that Child's ' got scent of the plot ' and ' applied to the celebrated Duchess of Marlborough who gave them a single cheque of £700,000 on their opponents.'   Francis, while giving all this information, expresses the opinion that it is difficult to believe that any body of men could act so disgraceful a part.

Mr. Price adds that ' no entry of the above can be met with in the books of the firm, but we think it

---

[1] F. G. H. Price, *Ye Marygold*, 1875, p. 17 (privately printed).

worth mentioning as we have no reason for doubting it, these and other stories being mostly founded to a certain degree on facts.' It is to be hoped that some further facts may come to light which will settle the particular points of a story which is of interest both in the life of the Duchess of Marlborough and in that of Hogarth.

There are two more publications of Hogarth which, to a certain extent, belong to business life, although they are both instances of gambling in its worst form, viz. the 'South Sea Bubble' and the 'Lottery.' Both are dated 1721, and they form Hogarth's earliest contributions to pictorial satire. In the preface to the second volume of the *British Museum Catalogue of Prints and Drawings* (satires) it is said: ' The most numerous, the richest, and most varied series of satires in this Catalogue is that on the catastrophe of the South Sea Company and its allies the Mississippi and West India Companies, which begins with " The Bubblers Medley," and concludes with but few intervals in the sequence of entries with Hogarth's early work, " An Emblematical Print on the South Sea Scheme," comprising about one hundred entries which describe not fewer than two hundred and fifty distinct designs.'

The ' South Sea Bubble ' print represents a fancy London street at the foot of the Monument, the pedestal of which is decorated with statues of two foxes, emblematical of the directors of the South Sea Company, and inscribed: ' THIS MONUMENT WAS

ERECTED IN MEMORY OF THE DESTRUCTION OF THIS CITY BY THE SOUTH SEA IN 1720.'

In the centre of the print is a roundabout worked by South Sea directors and carrying persons of various grades—a Scotch nobleman, with his ribbon, an old woman, a shoeblack, a divine and a wanton, who chucks the last under the chin as he laughs at her. On the top of the machine is a goat with the label 'Who 'll Ride.' A crowd of women rush into a building, the gable of which is surmounted with horns; over the door is written, '*Raffleing for Husbands with Lottery Fortunes in Here.*' [1]

In the extreme right corner of the print is a figure lying exhausted or dead, which is labelled TRADE. This is one of Hogarth's early prints in which he followed the prevalent custom of using labels and letters to inform the spectator as to what is intended. D is Honesty, stretched upon a wheel, whose limbs are being broken by G—Self-Interest. F, a man with a dagger and mask, is flogging E—Honour fastened to a pillory. In front of the roundabout are three men, one of whom is said to be intended for Pope. Respecting this group it is said in a note by a friend contributed to Nichols's *Biographical Anecdotes*: 'That Pope was silent on the merits of Hogarth (as one of your readers has observed) should excite little astonishment, as our artist's print on the South Sea exhibits the translator of Homer is no very flattering point of view. He is represented

---

[1] *British Museum Catalogue,* vol. ıı p 590.

with one of his hands in the pocket of a fat personage, who wears a horn-book at his girdle. For whom this figure was designed, is doubtful. Perhaps it was meant for Gay, who was a fat man, and a loser in the same scheme.'

If these two figures were intended for Pope and Gay, their relative sizes can be illustrated by some lines in Pope's poem of *The Challenge* (1717):

> 'At Leicester Fields a house full high,
>   With door all painted green,
> Where ribbons wave upon the tie
>   (A milliner I mean);
> There may you meet us three to three,
> For Gay can well make two of me.'

The widespread misery caused by the Bubble Companies, chief of which was the South Sea Company, is so well known that it is unnecessary to expatiate upon it here. In spite of all this knowledge, it comes as a shock to find so many men distinguished in the State, literature, science, and even trade, who were mixed up in the scandals caused by this madness for gambling. Gay's stock given to him by Young Craggs was once worth £20,000. He was urged to sell, but he waited for a higher price, and even when importuned to sell so much as would make him sure of 'a clean shirt and a shoulder of mutton every day,' he still delayed till he lost all. Pope was more fortunate, as his stock was worth at one time between twenty and thirty thousand pounds, and he was one of the lucky few who had ' the good fortune to remain with half they imagined they had ' (letter to Atterbury). The learned Nonconformist divine, Samuel Chandler, D.D., F.R.S. (a fine portrait of whom, by M. Chamberlain, is in the possession of the Royal Society), in early life was ruined by the loss of his wife's fortune, and was forced to open a bookshop. A grandfather of Edward Gibbon was a Commissioner of Customs and a director of the South Sea Company. He was deprived of his whole fortune by the House of Commons, but the historian tells us in his autobiography that his grandfather lived to make another fortune which he bequeathed to his son.

The South Sea Company was formed in 1711 with the object of trading with Spanish America, but it was a swindle pure and simple. It was worse than Law's Mississippi Scheme, because England had very limited rights of trading with South America, while France possessed Louisiana. The verses engraved below the design are sad doggrel, and respecting them Nichols writes in his *Biographical Anecdotes*: ' It may be observed, that London always affords a set of itinerant poets, whose office it is to furnish inscriptions for satirical engravings. I lately overheard one of these unfortunate sons of the Muse making a bargain with his employer. " Your print," says he, " is a taking one, and why don't you go to the price of a half-crown epigram ? " From such hireling bards, I suppose, our artist purchased not a

few of the wretched rhimes under his early performances ; unless he himself be considered as the author
of them.'

The last line of the inscription is ' Guess at the
rest, you find out more,' and it has been said
that seems ' to imply a consciousness of such
personal satire as it was not prudent to explain.'

' The Lottery' (1721) is quite one of the least
interesting of Hogarth's productions, and does not
need much description.

Mr. Stephens describes the print as representing
' the interior of a large room with figures, having
various meanings, placed upon a raised platform.
In the centre is a pedestal of three stages, on the
topmost of which is a female figure representing
National Credit holding a church in her right hand,
and resting her cheek on her left hand, the elbow
of which is placed upon the summit of a pillar ; on
the next or middle stage sit Apollo and Justice with
their appropriate emblems.   The former points out
to Britannia, who sits on the lowest stage of the
pedestal, a picture which hangs on the wall behind
them. . . . On our right of the platform is Fortune,
a naked woman, blinded and standing on a wheel, in
the act of putting her hand into a great lottery
wheel or circular rotatory box which is placed on the
side of the platform.'[1]

There is a description or explanation added to the
design by the artist himself ; and, as Nichols says

---

[1] *British Museum Catalogue*, vol. ii. p 597.

in his *Biographical Anecdotes*, ' Had not Hogarth, on this occasion, condescended to explain his own meaning, it must have remained in several places inexplicable.' The corrupting influence of lotteries on the public, more particularly as they were arranged by the State, was considerable, and so far was a good subject for the satirist, but the subject is too confined to allow of a broad and interesting treatment.

CHAPTER IX

TAVERN LIFE

THE eighteenth century was essentially a pleasure-seeking period. The men met nightly in taverns and coffee-houses for social converse, and often for gaming and other amusements. There was then a greater mixture of classes than in later times, and here all ranks met on equal terms. This doubtless became irksome to some, and in order that persons of similar tastes should be able to meet together without mixture with uncongenial spirits Clubs were formed.

These meetings had been general in the sixteenth and seventeenth centuries, but coffee-houses increased greatly in the reign of Queen Anne, and still more so in the times of the Georges. References to many of these are found in Hogarth's works, but doubtless he frequented many more than we have authority to mention. Nowhere could the great satirist find more ample material for his pencil than in the taverns and coffee-houses of London.

In the City mention may be made of the Bell Inn in Wood Street, Cheapside, Pontack's Head in

"A Harlot's Progress." Plate 1. The Inn Yard.

Abchurch Lane, the Devil, and the Mitre in Fleet Street, the Bible in Shire Lane, and the Elephant in Fenchurch Street.

In Covent Garden the Bedford Coffee-House in the Great Piazza, the Bedford Arms in the Little Piazza, Button's in Russell Street, the Rose Tavern in Brydges Street, and Tom King's in the Market.

In Clare Market the Spiller's Head, in Gerrard Street, Soho, the Turk's Head, intimately associated with Samuel Johnson, the Feathers in Leicester Square, and the Rummer at Charing Cross.

The first plate of the 'Harlot's Progress' shows us one of the old inn yards so common in the eighteenth century at which the lumbering York wagon has just arrived. The sign of the Bell is seen by the door, and John Ireland informs us that this was situated in Wood Street, Cheapside. It is scarcely possible that Hogarth intended the poor clergyman on his half-starved horse to be the girl's father. If he had been such, he could not have allowed his daughter to fall into the hands of the brazen procuress, who is named as the notorious Mother Needham of Park Place, St. James's. This woman in 1731 (three years before the publication of the 'Harlot's Progress) was committed to the Gatehouse for keeping a disorderly house, and was so ill-used by the populace during her exposure in the pillory that she died shortly afterwards. In the doorway of the inn is her employer, Colonel Charteris, attended by his confidant, John Gourlay.

s

The very name of Charteris is a synonym for unmitigated villainy, and no more withering condemnation of a human being has ever been written than
Arbuthnot's epitaph on 'Francis Chartres, who
with an inflexible constancy, and inimitable uni-
formity of life, persisted in spite of age and
infirmities, in the practice of every human vice,
excepting prodigality and hypocrisy.   His insatiable
avarice exempted him from the first ; his matchless
impudence from the second.'

This London inn-yard, taken in conjunction with
the more lively and exciting 'Stage Coach or
Country Inn Yard' (1747), gives us an excellent idea
of the humours and troubles of travelling in Hogarth's
day.

Pontack's eating-house in Abchurch Lane was
the most expensive and esteemed resort of the
fashionable world from the Restoration to about the
year 1780.   Misson, the French refugee, did not
greatly esteem our mode of living, but he made an
exception in the case of Pontack's.   He says in his
Travels, 'Those who would dine at one or two
guineas per head are handsomely accommodated
at our famous Pontack's.'   The place was noted
for its wine, and Swift (Journal to Stella) says :
'Pontack told us, although his wine was so good,
he sold it cheaper than others ; he took but seven
shillings a flask.   Are not these pretty rates ?'

A tract entitled 'The Metamorphoses of the Town
or a view of the Present Fashion' (1730), shows

the position of Pontack's as the chief resort of extravagant epicures. Among the items in the bill-of-fare of a guinea ordinary figure 'a ragout of fatted snails,' and ' chickens not two hours from the shell.'[1]

The site of this ordinary was occupied before the Great Fire by the White Bear, but on the rebuilding a Frenchman, described by Evelyn as M. Pontack, the son of the President of Bordeaux, owner of a district whence are imported to England some of the most esteemed claret, was encouraged to establish a tavern with all the novelties of French cookery. Pontack was somewhat of a character, well read in philosophy, but chiefly of the rabbins, exceedingly addicted to cabalistic fancies and 'an eternal babbler.' He set up as his sign the portrait of his distinguished father. Pontack's portrait is introduced in the third plate of the ' Rake's Progress' as having been put up in place of that of Julius Cæsar.

In the early years of the Royal Society the Fellows dined at Pontack's, and this shows that the philosophers at that day had a taste for good living. Mrs. Susannah Austin, who kept the Pontack's Head in Hogarth's day, married William Pepys, banker in Lombard Street, at St. Clement's Church on January 15, 1736.

[1] Perhaps Bramston was thinking of this when he wrote in his *Man of Taste*, 1733,—

'Dishes I chuse though little, yet genteel,
Snails the first course, and *Peepers* crown the meal!'

'Peepers' are young chickens (Dobson's *De Libris*, 1908, p. 35 and notes).

The famous Devil Tavern in Fleet Street, so intimately associated with Ben Jonson, is shown in Hogarth's illustration of *Hudibras* (Part iii. canto 2) entitled ' Burning the Rumps at Temple Bar ':

> ' That beastly rabble—that came down
> From all the garrats—in the Town,
> And Stalls and Shop-boards,—in vast swarms
> With new chalk'd Bills,—and rusty arms,
> To cry the Cause—up heretofore,
> And bawl the Bishops—out of door ;
> Are now drawn up—in greater Shoals,
> To roast—and broil us on the Coals.
> And all the grandees—of our Members
> Are Carbonading—on the Embers ;
> Knights, citizens and burgesses—
> Held forth by Rumps—of pigs and geese,
> That serve for characters—and badges
> To represent their personages,
> Each bon-fire is a funeral pile,
> In which they roast and scorch and broil,
> And ev'ry representative
> Have vow'd to roast—and broil alive.
> And 'tis a miracle we are not
> Already sacrific'd incarnate.
> For while we wrangle here and jar,
> W' are grilly'd all at Temple-bar.
> *Some on the sign-post of an alehouse*
> Hang in effigy, for the gallows,
> Made up of rags to personate
> Respective Officers of State.'

Although the third part of *Hudibras* was not published until 1678, six years after Wren's Temple Bar was built, Hogarth would have been more correct if he had drawn the old bar which existed until the Great Fire of 1666 ; as the depicted scene occurred when that bar still stood on its old site.

"Hudibras." Plate II. 1726. Burning of the Rumps at Temple Bar.

He could have seen a figure of the timber bar in Hollar's seven-sheet map of London, but it is perhaps too much to expect such rigid accuracy from the artist. He painted what he saw.[1]

The original sign of the Devil Tavern represented St. Dunstan pulling the Devil by the nose, and probably originated from the house being situated opposite to St. Dunstan's Church. At the time the tavern was in chief repute, the Devil may be said to have been the more popular of the two personages, and his name formed a sufficient designation. At the latter end of the eighteenth century the house fell on evil days, and its history and brilliant associations were not sufficient to save it from decay. Messrs. Child the bankers, who occupied the next-door house (which in James the First's reign was a public ordinary with the sign of a Marygold), purchased in 1787 the freehold of the Devil, and added the premises to their own.

Close by was the Mitre, to which tavern Hogarth invited to dinner his friend Dr. Arnold King, who selected the texts for the series of prints of the two apprentices. John Nichols reproduced this drawing on the engraved title to his *Biographical Anecdotes*, and describes it as follows: A specimen of Hogarth's propensity to merriment on the most trivial occasions is observable in one of his cards requesting the company of Dr. Arnold King to dine with him at the

---

[1] The history of Hogarth's different illustrations of *Hudibras* is very complicated, and some notes on the subject will be found in the second chapter.

Mitre. Within a circle, to which a knife and fork are the supporters, the written part is contained. In the centre is drawn a pye, with a mitre on the top of it; and the invitation of our artist concludes with the following sport on three of the Greek letters— to Eta Beta Pi. The rest of the inscription is not very accurately spelt. A quibble by Hogarth is surely as respectable as a conundrum by Swift.'

The complete inscription is: 'Mr. Hogarth's comp^ts to Mr. King and desires the Honnor of his company at dinner on thursday next to Eta Beta Py.'

In a note Nichols gives the information that the original is now (1782) in Park Place in the possession of Dr. Wright. Some persons had doubted the existence of the card. The Mitre was a favourite sign, and many celebrated houses with this name were to be found in different parts of London. The two most famous were situated in Cheapside and in Fleet Street. The latter after many vicissitudes ceased to exist, and the site (No. 39 Fleet Street) was added to the banking house of Messrs. Hoare in 1829. This tavern was frequented (among other celebrities) by Ben Jonson, Samuel Pepys, and Samuel Johnson. Hogarth also appears to have found in it a convenient resort.[1]

The Royal Society and the Society of Antiquaries

---

[1] In *London, Past and Present* it is asserted, largely on the authority of T C. Noble and R H. Burn (*London Trade Tokens*) that Johnson's *Mitre* was a later house situated in Mitre Court, Fleet Street; but my friend Dr. Philip Norman, Treasurer of the Society of Antiquaries, has kindly given particulars which force me to the conclusion that this opinion is untenable.

were in the habit of dining there. Of the latter
Cawthorn wrote :

> 'Some Antiquarians, grave and loyal,
> Incorporate by Charter Royal,
> Last winter on a Thursday night were
> Met in full senate at the Mitre '

' A Midnight Modern Conversation ' (1734) is one
of Hogarth's first-rate performances, in which eleven
persons are brought together in various stages of
intoxication. There have been many conjectures as
to the scene of these orgies—two places have been
suggested—the St. John's Coffee-House in Shire
Lane and the Bible in the same place. The landlord
of the latter was a bookbinder named Chandler who
worked for Hogarth. John Ireland tells us this, and
adds that the conjecture is founded on the strong
resemblance of the man with a nightcap to Chandler,
who was very deaf. At the same time he himself
was inclined to pronounce the man from his consequential manner to be a justice of the peace. The
clergyman who is seen ladling out the punch is said
by Sir John Hawkins to be intended for Orator
Henley, but this has been disputed, and Dr. Johnson's
dissolute kinsman—Parson Ford—has been named
by some for the ' honourable ' post. Doubtless all
the characters introduced are taken from the life,
but it was only occasionally that Hogarth was
personal in his satire, and he seldom named his
subjects, as alluded to in the verses under the print :

> ' Think not to find one meant resemblance there,
> We lash the vices but the persons spare.'

His annotators were not so reticent, and attempted
to name all the persons in his pictures, often without
much probability. In this picture, besides those
already mentioned, one of the characters is said to
represent Kettleby, a blatant advocate, and another
John Harrison the tobacconist, who sold papers of
tobacco at the taverns he frequented. In this
picture there is a paper inscribed 'Freeman's Best.'
James Figg has also been named as one of the
company, but this is very doubtful. John Ireland
says that he was told that the original picture was
found in an inn in Gloucestershire, and ' is now (1793)
in the possession of J. Calverley, Esq. of Leeds.'

The engraving was very popular in France and
Germany as well as in England, and was transferred
to pottery and to fans. Mr. Dobson mentions
several copies—one, which had previously belonged
to Lord Chesterfield, was exhibited at Richmond in
1881 by the late Mr. Henry George Bohn; another
was sent to the Guelph Exhibition in 1891 by Mrs.
Morrison, of Basildon. There is a version in Lord
Leconfield's gallery at Petworth, and another is
referred to by Mr. J. Wade in the *Athenœum*
(September 24, 1881).

' A Chorus of Singers ' (1733) was the subscription
ticket for ' A Midnight Modern Conversation.'
John Ireland reports that ' On the 22nd of March
1742 for the benefit of Mr. Hippisley, was acted at
Covent Garden theatre, a new scene, called a Modern
Midnight Conversation taken from Hogarth's print,

in which was introduced Hippisley's Drunken Man, with a comic tale of what really passed between himself and his old Aunt at her house on Mendip Hills, in Somersetshire.'

Samuel Ireland includes in his *Graphic Illustrations* (ii. 105) a portrait of John Hippisley as Sir Francis Gripe in the *Busy Body*, which shows the distortion on the actor's face caused by an accidental burn in his youth. This portrait is not generally accepted as Hogarth's work, and as it is signed as engraver by Sykes, who was well known as a forger, it must be considered as more than doubtful.

Hogarth's name is associated by tradition with the Elephant Tavern in Fenchurch Street. The original house, named the Elephant and Castle, existed long before the Fire of London and was situated on the north side of the street between the Mitre and the Angel. The house was rebuilt soon after the Fire, and had a long life until 1826, when it was pulled down. Tradition reported that Hogarth in his early days of poverty lived at the Elephant, and ran in debt to the landlady. In order to wipe out his heavy score he is supposed to have painted on the walls of the tap-room four pictures. These represented Fenchurch in the eighteenth century, a Parish Club scene, the Humour of Harlow Bush Fair, and the Hudson Bay Company's Porters going to dinner.

When the building was condemned many persons flocked to the Elephant to see the supposed Hogarth pictures. A picture dealer bought the pictures and had them carefully transferred from the walls to canvas. They were exhibited in Pall Mall, but it is understood that experts were by no means convinced that they were Hogarth's work.[1]

Covent Garden must have been a happy hunting-ground for Hogarth, and he doubtless knew every inch of the place where all classes met, and where the manners of the society rakes were as bad as those of the lowest classes. First must be mentioned the Bedford Arms Tavern where Hogarth and several friends held a club, a few members of which in 1732 agreed together to go for a short tour in the Isle of Sheppey, and on their return the journal of their travels was read to the members of the club collected at the tavern. The original MS. with its illustrations is preserved in the British Museum.

Its title is 'An Account of what seem'd most remarkable in the Five Days perigrination of the five following persons vizt Messieurs Tothall, Scott, Hogarth, Thornhill & Forrest. Begun on Saturday May the 27th 1732 and Finish'd on the 31st of the same month.' Of these men William Tothall was the son of an apothecary in Fleet Street, who after many vicissitudes became a woollen-draper and earned a competence ; Samuel Scott was the excellent painter known as the English Canaletto; John Thornhill was the brother-in-law of Hogarth; and

---

[1] In a highly fanciful article in the *Builder* of Sept. 9, 1875, the scene of the meeting of the Parish Club is supposed to be the original of the 'Midnight Modern Conversation.'

Ebenezer Forrest was an attorney who lived in George Street, Adelphi. On the ninth illustration by Hogarth—a comical figure of Nobody, a head and two legs—is written by Forrest the following illustration: 'I think I cannot better conclude than with taking notice that not one of the Company was unemployed, For Mr. Thornhill made the map, Mr. Hogarth and Mr. Scott all the other drawings, Mr. Tothall was our Treasurer which (tho' a place of the greatest Trust) he faithfully Discharg'd, & the foregoing Memoirs was the work of E. Forrest.'

This was a most amusing freak, and the account contains much curious matter. When the party stopped at Rochester 'Hogarth and Scott . . . played at hop-scotch in the Colonnade under the Town Hall.' This is almost exactly opposite the Bull Hotel.

The headpiece representing a sort of human torso by Hogarth, is said to be representative of the journey which 'was a short tour by land and water, backwards and forwards without head or tail.'

The travellers sent the manuscript of their tour to the Rev. W. Gostling, a minor canon of Canterbury and author of *A Walk in and about Canterbury*. He wrote an imitation in Hudibrastic verse with additions of his own, twenty copies of which were printed in 1781 by John Nichols, who afterwards added it to his *Biographical Anecdotes* (second edition, 1782). The original was published in 1782 by Richard Livesay, who lived in Mrs. Hogarth's house

in Leicester Square. Two other members of the
Club had their portraits drawn by Hogarth, viz.
Gabriel Hunt about 1733, and Benjamin Read about
1757. These were engraved by Livesay in 1781.

The original drawings hung for many years on the
walls of the club-room, and afterwards came into the
possession of Theodosius Forrest, son of the author
of the *Five Days' Peregrination*. He gave them
to Mrs. Hogarth, who afterwards presented them to
the Marquis of Exeter. It is said that Read came
one night to the Bedford Arms after a long journey
and fell asleep there. Hogarth was about to leave
the club, but, struck by his friend's appearance, he
exclaimed ' Heavens ! what a character ! ' and took
the portrait immediately, without sitting down.
The Bedford Arms was situated in the Little Piazza
on the east side of the square, which was cleared
away and only partially rebuilt.

The Bedford Coffee-House, in the Great Piazza
near the entrance to the theatre, was another haunt
of Hogarth's ; and John Nichols was told by a friend
that, being once there with the painter, he observed
him to draw something with a pencil on his nail.
Inquiring what had been his employment, he was
shown the countenance (a whimsical one) of a person
who was then at a short distance off.

In Tavistock Street Richard Leveridge the singer
kept a famous house of entertainment. Hogarth
engraved a frontispiece to ' A Collection of Songs,
with the Musick, by Mr. Leveridge ' (1727). Captain

Coram was very poor in his later days, and a pension
of a little over one hundred pounds a year was raised
for him at the instigation of Sir Sampson Gideon and
Dr. Brocklesby by voluntary subscription. On
Coram's death in 1751 that pension was transferred
to Leveridge, who at the age of ninety had scarcely
any other prospect than that of parish relief.[1]

The Rose Tavern in Russell Street and Brydges
Street, Covent Garden, was next door to Drury Lane
Theatre, and afterwards, when that was enlarged
by Garrick in 1776, was cleared away and the site
added to that of the theatre. The Rose had a bad
name as the resort of the worst characters of the
town both male and female, who made it the headquarters of midnight orgies and drunken broils where
murderous assaults were frequently occurring among
the bullies of the time. It stood pre-eminent among
the dangerous houses in the neighbourhood. We
learn this from Dryden and Shadwell and other
dramatists of the seventeenth century, and it had not
improved in the eighteenth century. In the ' Rake
Reformed,' 1718, we read :

> 'Not far from thence appears a pendant sign,
> Whose bush declares the product of the vine,
> Where to the traveller's sight the full-blown Rose
> Its dazzling beauties doth in gold disclose,
> And painted faces flock in tallied cloaths.'

It is supposed that the night scene in the tavern
where Thomas Rakewell is surrounded by women of
the town (' Rake's Progress,' Plate 3) is laid at the

[1] John Ireland's *Hogarth Illustrated*, vol. iii. p. 54.

Rose.   On the rim of the large pewter dish on which
the female posturist was about to perform is inscribed ' John Bonvine at the Rose Tavern Drury
Lane.'   The porter of the Rose, known as Leathercoat, was a notorious man, and is supposed to be the
bearer of the dish.   Fielding makes this man a
principal character in his highly-objectionable *Covent
Garden Tragedy*, although he names him Leather-
sides.   It is amazing that such a play could have
been acted even in the eighteenth century, and that
so distinguished an actress as Miss Raftor (afterwards Mrs. Clive and the ' Clivey Pivey ' of Garrick)
should have demeaned herself by taking a part in it.

Leathercoat was a remarkably strong man, and
for a pot of beer he would lie down in the street and
allow a carriage to pass over him.   ' After his death
he was dissected by Dr. Hunter, and the appearance
of muscular strength was extraordinary, both in
form of the muscles and in the remarkable processes
of bones into which they were inserted.' [1]

In spite of its evil repute, some of us are apt to feel
a special interest in the tavern from the mistaken idea
that ' sweet Molly Mog ' of the Rose was a waitress
here.   Her charms happily bloomed in a purer air.
The delightful ballad we owe to John Gay—

> ' The schoolboy's desire is a play-day,
>   The schoolmaster's joy is to flog,
>   The milkmaid's delight is May-day,
>   But mine is sweet Molly Mog '—

---

[1] *London Chronicle*, Aug 26-29, 1806.

was written at the Rose Inn at Wokingham, in Berkshire, the landlord of which was John Mog, the father of Molly. Mr. Stander of Arborfield, who died in 1730, is said to have been the enamoured swain to whom the ballad alludes.

It is a curious fact that such taverns as the Rose in Covent Garden were fairly respectable resorts in the daytime, and we learn from the historian Gibbon that on January 19, 1763, the night of the production of Mallet's tragedy of *Elvira*, he and his father went to the Rose on their way to the play-house. They met Mallet and about thirty friends, dined together and then went to the pit, 'where we took our places in a body, ready to silence all opposition. However, we had no occasion to exert ourselves.'

Tom King's Coffee-House (after his death known as Moll King's), described by Arthur Murphy as 'well-known to all gentlemen to whom beds are unknown,' was one of the institutions of Covent Garden. It occupies an important position in Hogarth's 'Morning,' but it is needless to say more about it here as it is fully described in Chapter III. (Low Life).

Night houses were common enough in Covent Garden, and probably the death scene of the Earl of Squanderfield in the fifth plate of the 'Marriage à la Mode' took place in one of them. On the floor of the room is a bill inscribed 'The Bagnio,' with a cut of the Turk's Head.

The 'Marriage' series was engraved by Ravenet, and John Nichols says that the background of Plate 5 was the work of Ravenet's wife. This is, however, a mistake, and Charles Grignion, who knew Ravenet intimately, told John Ireland that Mrs. Ravenet could not engrave. 'Concerning the background of this print, Ravenet had a violent quarrel with Hogarth ; who thinking the figures in the tapestry, etc., too obtrusive, obliged him to bring them to a lower tone (without any additional remuneration), a process that must have taken him up a length of time, which no man but an engraver can form an idea of.'[1]

Samuel Ireland published in the first volume of his *Graphic Illustrations* (1794) four engravings of characters at Button's Coffee-House, taken from drawings in Indian ink in his possession, which he attributes to Hogarth. Ireland says that he purchased the originals ' (with three of the original drawings of *Hudibras*) from the executors of a Mr. Brent, an old gentleman, who was for many years in habits of intimacy with Hogarth.' He dates the drawings as having been made in 1720, which is possible, although Addison, who is figured in one of the drawings, died in 1719. Horace Walpole appears to have seen the drawings and to have named one of the figures in Plate 3 as that of Count Viviani, and George Steevens does not seem to have doubted the genuineness of the draw-

[1] *Hogarth Illustrated*, vol. iii. p. 345.

ings.[1] The originals are now in the Print Room of the British Museum. Button's Coffee-House was on the south side of Russell Street. Dryden made Will's the great resort of the wits, and Addison lorded it at Button's, which house was founded by Daniel Button in 1713, the year in which Addison's great reputation was confirmed by the success of *Cato*. James Moore Smythe, writing to Teresa Blount on August 13, 1713, says, 'The wits are removed from Will's over the way.'

Pope said that Button had been a servant of Addison's, but Johnson affirmed that he was a servant in the Countess of Warwick's family. We must remember that he did not marry the Countess until three years after he had become a constant habitué of Button's. Johnson's further statement that when Addison suffered any vexation from the Countess, 'he withdrew the company from Button's house' is incredible, and no one who loves Addison can for a moment believe in such an instance of littleness.

Plate 1 contains a portrait of Daniel Button repulsing a mendicant.

Plate 2.—Martin Folkes, afterwards President of the Royal Society, whose portrait Hogarth painted; and Addison.

Plate 3, four figures: the one in the centre is Dr. Arbuthnot, and the one to the right Count Viviani.

Walpole says that this Florentine nobleman

[1] *British Museum Catalogue*, vol II p 567.

T

showing the triumphal arch at Florence to Prince San Severino, assured him and insisted upon it, that it was begun and finished in twenty-four hours. Walpole writing to Mann on April 27, 1753, says, 'If you could send me Viviani with his invisible architects out of the Arabian tales I might get my house ready at a day's warning.' Viviani was a constant attendant at coffee-houses.

Plate 4, four figures: the left-hand one, Dr. Garth (died 1719), and the middle one Pope, who was a frequent visitor at Button's. He said that he met Addison there almost every day.

These sketches of coffee-house frequenters are fully described in Binyon's British Museum Catalogue of Drawings of British Artists (vol. ii. p. 321). The cataloguer says: 'These drawings are undoubtedly by Hogarth, but that is all that can be said with certainty about them. The assertions of a man of such unscrupulous credulity as Samuel Ireland must be well sifted. In the first state of his engravings from these sketches he made the date 1730, and this is perhaps about the actual date to which they belong, although it is probably nearer 1740. But while publishing them as drawings of 1730, he boldly claimed to recognise in them portraits of Addison and of Garth, who both died in 1719. The famous circle at Button's broke up on Addison's death, and Pope quarrelled with Addison and his coterie in 1713.'

These drawings are here critically discussed for

the first time, with the result that we may accept them as Hogarth's, but must reject most of the ascriptions. It is to be hoped that further evidence respecting them may be found, so that we may know who it was that Hogarth sketched.

Old Slaughter's Coffee-House was one of Hogarth's most favourite haunts; it was conveniently near his home, and it was largely the resort of his most intimate friends. A club of artists and literary men met regularly twice a week, and here authors, painters and sculptors were in the habit of showing any work they had produced before it was exhibited to the public. On these occasions the merits of the special work were discussed among the members, and possibly its demerits also.

Highmore, Roubiliac and Jonathan Richardson were among Hogarth's fellow-members; so also was that curious character, Dr. Mounsey, the physician to Chelsea Hospital, who, when he met Fanny Burney there, asked if she was the Queen's Miss Burney. I once possessed a letter from Mounsey to Garrick which was endorsed by the latter 'One of Mounsey's long lying epistles.'

Samuel Ireland says that Dr. Johnson and Isaac Hawkins Browne were members also, and relates an anecdote on the authority of Highmore of Johnson's remarkably retentive memory, which is not recorded in Boswell.

On one occasion at the club Browne 'entertained the company with a recital of his excellent Latin poem, *De Animi Immortalitate* ; this recital met with great applause from the parties present, and was accompanied by a strong wish on the part of some of them, to be favoured with the whole or extracts from it ; to which Mr. Browne replied that he could not comply with their request, as he had no copy of it. Dr. Johnson, who had listened with great attention during the recital, sent the next morning a manuscript of it to the author, which he had collected from his memory.' [1]

This coffee-house was established by Thomas Slaughter in the year 1692 on the west side of St. Martin's Lane three doors from Newport Street. Slaughter continued to be landlord for nearly fifty years, and was an attendant at the club.   In 1741 he was dead, and his business was carried on by Humphrey Bailey. About 1760 another coffee-house called ' New Slaughter's ' was established in St. Martin's Lane, and the original house came to be called ' Old Slaughter's,' a name which it retained until it was demolished in 1843 to make way for the new opening into Leicester Square.

' The Complicated Richardson,' in ridicule of Jonathan Richardson and his son, is so exceedingly coarse, and unkind as well that one can only hope that the engraving in the first volume of *Graphic Illustrations* (p. 118) is a forgery. Highmore says that Hogarth made a sketch, but finding that it hurt the

---

[1] The poem in two books was published in 1754   See *Graphic Illustrations*, vol 1 p. 121.

feelings of Richardson, ' he threw the paper in the fire and there ended the dissatisfaction.'[1]

The Rummer Tavern at Charing Cross is introduced into the picture of ' Night ' (' Four Times of the Day '), which is said to represent the annual rejoicing on the night of the 29th of May.

This was a famous place of entertainment kept in the reign of Charles II. by Samuel Prior, uncle of Matthew Prior, who was apprenticed to him and did not like the business, as is seen from his poems. The Prior family ceased to be connected with it in 1702, and the tavern was burnt down in 1750. A full account of the incidents in the picture of ' Night ' will be found in Chapter IV. (Low Life).

At a tavern in Oxford Street, The Man loaded with Mischief, there was a painted sign attributed to Hogarth, and an engraving of this was exhibited in the window. It represented a man carrying a woman, a magpie and a monkey, the woman with a glass of gin in her hand. This house was numbered 414, but some years ago the painted sign was removed and the name of the public-house was cut down to The Mischief. The house is now numbered 53, and the sign is the Shamrock. The sign had been so often renewed that if it was originally painted by Hogarth little of his work can have remained to our day.

The last place of entertainment to be mentioned is the most important of all, viz. White's Chocolate-

---

[1] *Graphic Illustrations*, vol. i. p. 120.

House in St. James's Street.   Clubs were established
at most of the coffee-houses and taverns, but these
were only given accommodation, and the houses
where they were held continued to be free to the
public who paid their fees.   The clubs often moved
from house to house, but the club at White's became
so important that in course of time it drove out the
public altogether and retained the house for itself,
becoming a proprietary club.   This occurred in
1755, twenty years after the publication of the
'Rake's Progress,' two of the plates of which
relate to White's.   The history of White's has been
found a very complicated and difficult one to recount
by the different writers on London topography, but
the Hon. Algernon Bourke has now made it clear, by
a thorough investigation of the books of the Club, and
the memoirs of the men of the time, in his most
interesting volumes entitled *The History of White's*
(1892).   He writes: 'When at the end of the seventeenth century a company of gentlemen founded the
club at White's by drawing up a few simple rules
to regulate their private meetings at the Chocolate-
House, there were few clubs in existence, and none
that have survived to the present day.   Clubs then,
were either assemblies of men bound together by
strong political feeling like the October; small groups
of philosophers and rhetoricians who met to discuss
abstract theories of ethics like the Rota ; or bands of
choice spirits, such as those whose very questionable
doings found a historian in Ned Ward of the London

"A Rake's Progress." No. 6. (White's.) 1735.

From the original painting in the Soane Museum.

Spy. Club life as we know it, began with the establishment of White's nearly two centuries ago, and
during those two centuries White's has seen the
origin of every other institution of its own kind
existing to-day, and the development of club life
into its huge modern proportions.'

White's Chocolate-House was opened in 1693 by
Francis White at a house on the site of Boodle's
Club (No. 38 St. James's Street). Francis White
removed the Chocolate-House in 1697 to the site of
the present Arthur's Club (69 and 70) on the opposite
side of the street. About this time the Old Club
was founded. White died in 1711, and his widow
succeeded him as proprietress. John Arthur succeeded Madam White as proprietor in 1725.

On April 28, 1733, White's at four o'clock in the
morning was entirely destroyed by fire, with two
houses adjoining. ' Young Mr. Arthur's wife leaped
out of a window two pair of stairs upon a feather bed
without much hurt.'

The King and Prince of Wales came from St.
James's Palace, and stayed above an hour encourag-
ing the firemen and people to work at the engines.
The King ordered twenty guineas among the firemen
and others, and five guineas to the guard. The
Prince ordered the firemen to receive ten guineas.

This was the fire, the commencement of which is
seen in Plate 6 of the ' Rake's Progress.' Here, as
John Ireland writes, every one present is so engrossed
by his own situation that the flames, which are

sufficiently visible, are disregarded, and it needs the
entrance of the watchman crying 'Fire' to draw
attention to the serious danger in which all the
company are placed.   The Rake is seen kneeling in
the front of the picture imprecating vengeance on
his own head.   He has pulled off his wig and dashed
it on the floor in a frenzy of rage and despair at the
loss of his fortune.   The loss of his all drives him to
the Fleet Prison in the next plate, to be followed in the
last one by his incarceration in Bedlam as a hopeless
maniac.   J. B. Nichols points out that in the original
sketch in oil belonging to Mrs. Hogarth the Rake is
sitting, and not, as in the finished picture, on his
knees.

The scene in the sixth plate shows how miscellaneous was the company gathered together at White's.
By the fire is a highwayman, with a horse pistol and
black mask in a skirt pocket of his coat.   He wears
long horseman's boots with spurs and a large riding-
coat, and carries a hat under his arm.   He is so
engrossed in his thoughts that he observes nothing
that is going on around him, and he does not observe
the boy by his side, who endeavours to attract attention to the glass of liquor which he carries on a tray.[1]

In connection with this we may quote Farquhar's
Beaux Stratagem (act iii. sc. 2), where Aimwell says
to Gibbet, who is a highwayman, 'Pray, sir, ha'nt
I seen your face at Will's Coffee-House ?'   'Yes, sir,
and at White's too,' answers the highwayman.

---

[1] *British Museum Catalogue*, vol. iii p. 155.

It would appear that some of the frequenters of the Club, not satisfied with the possibilities of gambling in the club-room, searched for further opportunities in the public room. The figure in the background who is giving his note of hand to a usurer is said to represent ' Old Manners,' brother to the Duke of Rutland, who is reported to have been the only person of rank of his time who amassed a considerable fortune by the profession of a gamester.

White's was always the headquarters of gaming, and Robert Harley, Earl of Oxford, in the time of his ministry never passed the house ' without bestowing a curse upon that famous academy, as the bane of half the English nobility.' [1] On the left of the picture is a richly-dressed nobleman borrowing from a moneylender, who is writing in a memorandum book ' Lent to Ld Cogg 500l.' On the wall above the highwayman is a card bearing the royal arms and an inscription, ' R Justian, Card-maker to his Maj[esty] —royal family.'

As an instance of the serious losses of members of the aristocracy by gaming, John Ireland relates that a Lord C—— lost in one night thirty-three thousand pounds to General Scott. He was warned of his probable complete ruin by three ladies dressed as witches at a masquerade. He was much struck by the warning, and vowed never to lose more than one hundred pounds at a sitting, and by keeping his vow he retrieved his fortune !

[1] Swift's *Essay on Modern Education*. *Works* (Bell's edition), vol. xi. p. 53.

After the fire the Club and Chocolate-House were removed to Gaunt's Coffee-House on the west side of the street and two doors from the end of the street and Cleveland Row. This removal is announced in the *Daily Post* of May 3: 'This is to acquaint all noblemen and gentlemen that Mr. Arthur having had the misfortune to be burnt out of White's Chocolate-House is removed to Gaunt's Coffee-House, next the St. James's Coffee-House in St. James's Street, where he humbly begs they will favour him with their company as usual.'

The fourth plate represents St. James's Street with the palace in the background closing the vista; the clock on the gateway indicates the hour as 1.40 P.M. The time of the year is shown by the Welshman on the right of the picture wearing a large leek, which fixes the day as the 1st of March (St. David's Day). He also carries a muff. The fact that it was the anniversary of St. David is only an incident; the really important event connected with March 1 then was that it was Queen Caroline's birthday and therefore a Court day. The Rake overwhelmed with debt is apparently proceeding to Court, and with the blinds of his sedan-chair drawn hopes to escape the bailiffs who are in search of him. He is, however, stopped, and the faithful woman (Sarah Young) whom he deserted sets him at liberty by paying the present demand. The lamp-cleaner behind the Rake is so much interested in the arrest that he pours the oil from his can over

St. James's Street "A Rake's Progress" Nº 4.

the lamp to the inconvenience of any one beneath him.

Hogarth appears to have made alterations in the plate after the fire, as in the second state he indicated the site of Gaunt's Coffee-House with a label marked Black's, and specially points to it by means of a flash of lightning. In this second state a group of gambling boys take the place of the shoeblack who steals the Rake's cane.

The posts which marked the edge of the pavement in most of the London streets are seen in this picture. John Ireland (i. 43) alludes to this in a note on this plate. 'On new paving the streets soon after his present Majesty's accession [George III.] they were removed. During the short time of Lord Bute's administration an English gentleman reprobated the idea of making a Scotch pavement in the vicinity of St. James's. Being asked by a North Briton, who was present, how he or any other Englishman could reasonably object to even Scotchmen mending their ways in the neighbourhood of a palace ? "We do not object to your mending our ways," replied the other, "but you have taken away *all our posts.*"'

In 1736 the Club was removed to the premises rebuilt on the site of the present Arthur's Club. Robert Arthur succeeded John Arthur as proprietor.

In 1753 a little book was published entitled '*The Polite Gamester ; or the Humours of Whist :* a dramatick satyre as acted every day at White's and other coffee houses and assemblies.' Mr. Bourke quotes from this : 'In the Club at White's being a select company above stairs, where no person of what rank soever is admitted without first being proposed by one of the Club.'   Mr. Bourke says that this is the last mention of the Chocolate-House which he has found, and he adds ' there is little doubt that the Chocolate-House was extinguished on the removal of the Clubs [Old and New] to the present building in 1755.'

It is interesting to notice in *The History of White's* that, although so great stress is laid upon the importance and greatness of the Club, the historian is proud to illustrate his book with two plates from the ' Rake's Progress,' in order to show its interest is enhanced by the fact that Hogarth saw fit to make it the subject of his satire.

This chapter contains some miscellaneous notes on tavern life in London in the eighteenth century, but it may be well to show succinctly how the life of the man of the world was daily spent.   Pope has told us how Addison apportioned his day :

' Addison's chief companions, before he married Lady Warwick (in 1716) were Steele, Budgell, Philips, Carey, Davenant and Colonel Brett. He used to breakfast with one or other of them at his lodgings in St. James's Place, dine at taverns with them, then to Button's, and then to some tavern again, for supper, in the evening, and this was the usual round of his life.' [1]

---

[1] Spence's *Anecdotes*, ed. Singer, 1829, p. 196.

This does not seem to leave much time for work or study, but such a life was general.

A distinction continued to be made between taverns and coffee-houses, but the latter seem to have encroached very largely upon the privileges of the former. Taverns did not sell coffee, but coffee-houses occasionally did provide dinners.

CHAPTER X

HOGARTH was quite at home at the theatre, and he was well acquainted with many actors, so that we find sufficient materials from his pencil to help us to form a very accurate idea of the theatre in the eighteenth century. In fact a very large number of his engravings bear upon the various phases of theatrical life, so that the present chapter has grown to be one of the longest in the book.

The pleasures of all classes were catered for with eagerness by a large number of persons who made their living by the frivolity of the people. Probably at no period of our history were the various forms of dissipation more generally sought after by large numbers of the population of great cities than in the first half of the eighteenth century. The satirical representation of some of the many features of this life was specially agreeable to Hogarth, who found on all sides an endless exhibition of character suited for his particular purpose. Two of his pictures give us a vivid representation of the interior of a play-house of his time, viz. the ' Beggar's Opera ' (1728) and the ' Laughing Audience ' (1733).

Rec.ᵈ   of

Half a Guinea being the first Payment for Nine Prints, 8 of Which
Represent a Rakes Progress & the 9ᵗʰ a Fair, Which I Promise to
Deliver when finish'd   on Receiving one Guinea more, the
Print of the Fair being Deliver'd at the time of Subscribing.
NB the Rakes alone will be two Guineas after the time of Subscribing.

"THE LAUGHING AUDIENCE."   1733.

The 'Laughing Audience' was at one time styled 'A Pleased Audience at a Play.' It was used as the subscription ticket for 'Southwark Fair' and a 'Rake's Progress.' Below the design the following form of receipt was engraved: 'Rec^d of Half a guinea being the first Payment for Nine Prints, 8 of which represent a Rake's Progress and the 9th a Fair, which I Promise to Deliver at Michaelmas next on receiving One Guinea more, the Print of the Fair being Deliver'd at the time of Subscribing.'

There are three varieties of this inscription: the above is in the first state; in the second 'when finish'd' is substituted for 'at Michaelmas next,' and the price was raised after the subscription was closed. Hogarth filled in the receipt himself.

After this etching had served its purpose as a subscription ticket it was issued separately as a distinct print.

The original picture belonged to Richard Brinsley Sheridan in 1814, when it was exhibited at the British Institution. In 1832 it realised twenty guineas at G. Watson Taylor's sale, and in 1848 forty-nine guineas, when were sold the effects of Richard Sanderson of Belgrave Square. In the engraving a part of the orchestra, pit, and boxes are represented. The heads of three musicians are shown in the orchestra, and eleven men and women sit in the pit. The latter are the only persons in the audience who seem to be enjoying the performance,

and the expressions of their faces are varied and full
of humour.   The figures in the boxes are too much
interested in their own concerns to pay attention to
what is going on upon the stage.   Two points are
worthy of special attention, one being the iron spikes
on the wooden barrier between the orchestra and the
pit.   This awkward protection was also common
to French theatres until a serious mishap caused its
abolition.   A young English nobleman visiting Paris
near the end of William the Third's reign, had a
quarrel at the opera with a French gentleman and
pitched him bodily from the box tier into the
orchestra.   In his fall the Frenchman was impaled
upon the spikes.   After this the management cleared
them away from the barrier.   In Churchill's earlier
days in London, when he was gathering materials for
his *Rosciad,* he sat in the front row of the pit, and
it was noticed that he grasped the spikes on the
partition between the orchestra and pit.   Arthur
Murphy, in his ' Ode to the Naiads of the Fleet
Ditch,' described how Churchill used to sit

> ' In foremost row before th' astonish'd pit,
> And grin dislike,
> And kiss the spike,
> And twist his mouth and roll his head awry.'

In those days Churchill was a somewhat unclerical
fop with ruffles, leathern breeches, and gold-laced hat.
The other point for notice is the mode of lighting,
which must have been very inefficient.   Candles in
sconces will be seen in front of the boxes.

Scene from the "Beggar's Opera." Act III.

This picture shows the front of the house, that of the ' Beggar's Opera ' gives us a representation of the stage of the period.

The picture which represents the scene of Lucy and Polly wrangling over Macheath, and appealing to their respective fathers, as represented in the third act, is said to have been painted for Rich, the manager, in 1729. Another picture of the same scene was painted in the same year for Sir Archibald Grant; this afterwards came into the possession of Mr. William Huggins, at the sale of whose effects it was bought by Dr. Monkhouse of Queen's College, Oxford.[1] John Ireland says that the frame had a carved bust of Gay on the top, which proves that this is the picture now in possession of Mr. John Murray who lent it to the exhibition in the Whitechapel Art Gallery, 1906, and to the Royal Academy Winter Exhibition, 1908.

At the sale of Rich's pictures in 1762 the first-mentioned picture was purchased by the Duke of Leeds for £35, 14s., and it is now in the possession of the present Duke. It was not engraved until 1790, when it was undertaken by William Blake and published by Messrs. Boydell.[2] Another picture was in the possession of Mr. Louis Huth.

The *Beggar's Opera* was written by Gay in 1727 on the suggestion by Swift that a Newgate Pastoral would be effective. Although Gay took the hint so

[1] John Ireland's *Hogarth Illustrated*, 1793, vol. ii p. 330.

[2] J. Ireland says that it was 'engraven by Mr. Tew.' *Hogarth Illus. trated*, vol. ii p. 328

far as to choose his characters from the dangerous
classes, he really threw his work into the form of a
parody of Italian opera, which, for a time, he caused
to be less popular than it was before he figured as the
Orpheus of highwaymen.   John Ireland relates that
an Italian he knew 'concluded an harangue calculated to throw Gay's taste and talents into contempt
with "Saire, this simple signor did tri to pelt mi
countrymen out of England with *lumps of pudding* "'[1]
(one of the tunes used by Gay).

The *Beggar's Opera* was first offered to Colley
Cibber for Drury Lane Theatre, but was refused by
him.   It was then accepted by John Rich (son of
Christopher Rich), and brought out at Lincoln's Inn
Fields Theatre on January 29, 1728.   It was not
only Cibber who was doubtful of success, for, according to Boswell, the Duke of Queensberry said, 'This
is a very odd thing, Gay; it is either a very good
thing or a bad thing.'   At its first appearance success
was not certain for some time after the opening of
the play.   Pope and a party of Gay's friends attended the first night 'in very great uncertainty of
the event,' until they overheard the Duke of Argyll
in the next box say, 'It will do, it must do.   I see it
in the eyes of them.'   Pope told Spence that this
gave them all ease of mind, 'for that duke (besides
his own good taste) has a particular knack, as any one
living, in discovering the taste of the public.   He
was quite right in this as usual.'

[1] *Hogarth Illustrated*, vol. ii. p. 328

Macklin was present at the first representation, and from him we learn that success was doubtful until the opening of the second act, when, after the chorus song of ' Let us take the road,' the applause was as universal as unbounded. Others affirm with more probability that success was assured rather when Polly sang her pathetic appeal to her parents :

> ' Oh ponder well I be not severe ;
> To save a wretched wife ;
> For, on the rope that hangs my dear,
> Depends poor Polly's life '

There were several circumstances that went to make the play a success. (1) It was a thoroughly English production, so that those who resented the popularity of Italian opera were whole-hearted in their support of the *Beggar's Opera*. (2) All the wits of the day supported and assisted the author. (3) The bitter satire levelled at Sir Robert Walpole and his ministry was eagerly taken up by his many enemies.

The minister was not a coward, however, and he attended the performance. The following anecdote of what happened is related in Baker's *Biographia Dramatica* : ' Being in the stage boxes at its first representation, a most universal encore attended the following air of Lockit, and all eyes were directed on the minister at the instant of its being repeated :

> " When you censure the age,
> Be cautious and sage,
> Lest the courtiers offended should be ;
> If you mention vice or bribe
> 'Tis so pat to all the tribe,
> Each cries—That was levelled at me "

'Sir Robert, observing the pointed manner in which the audience applied the last line to him, parried the thrust by encoring it with his single voice, and thus not only blunted the poetical shaft, but gained a general huzza from the audience.'

In addition to these causes of success we must remember that the play had great merits, was quite fresh, and the songs and music were sufficiently pretty not only to carry it triumphantly through the longest run that the English stage had ever known up to that date, but also to continue it as a stock piece for considerably more than a century.

Not being an experienced playwright Gay did not introduce his songs until about the middle of the play. This had to be remedied, so the wits set to work to help their colleague and produced a series of additional songs. 'Virgins are like the fair flower in its lustre,' was written by Sir Charles Hanbury Williams; 'The gamesters and lawyers are jugglers alike,' by William Fortescue, Master of the Rolls; 'When you censure the age,' by Swift, and 'The modes of the court so common are grown,' by Lord Chesterfield.[1]

It was originally intended that no music should accompany the songs, as the junto of wits objected to it. Music was, however, tried at a rehearsal, and the Duchess of Queensberry (Gay's kind patroness) was so strongly in favour of introducing an orchestra that she settled its adoption. This was not large, as

Lady Townshend (*European Magazine*, 1800, vol. xxxvii. p. 25).

it consisted only of three or four fiddles, a hautboy, and an occasional drum. Dr. Pepusch arranged and scored the notes.

Henry Angelo in his *Reminiscences* claims for Pope the success of the *Beggar's Opera*, on account of his having contributed the most satirical hits at the Court.

He wrote :

> ' And the statesman, because he's so great
> Thinks his trade is as honest as mine.'

These lines stood in Gay's MS. :

> ' And there's many arrive to be great
> By a trade not more honest than mine '

Also Pope contributed these lines in the song of Macheath :

> ' Since Laws were made for every degree,
> To curb vice in others as well as in me,
> I wonder we hadn't better company
> Upon Tyburn tree.'

The question must often have been asked, What was the meaning of the title of the *Beggar's Opera* ? This was answered in the original edition, when in the Introduction a beggar offers his opera to the players. He says :

' The piece I own was originally writ for the celebrating the marriage of James Chanter and Moll Lay, two most excellent ballad singers. I have introduced the similes that are in all your celebrated operas : the Swallow, the Moth, the Bee, the Ship, the Flower, etc. Besides I have a prison scene, which the ladies always reckon charmingly pathetic. As to the parts, I have observed such a nice impartiality to our two ladies, that it is impossible for either of them to take offence.'

This was not considered a good beginning, and was perhaps wisely struck out.

The parts of the Beggar and the Player are left in at the end, and therefore they appear to come from nowhere. The Player complains that the play has an unhappy ending, which is against all precedent, so the Beggar says that can be easily changed. 'So you rabble there—run and cry, A Reprieve! Let the prisoner be brought back to his wives in triumph.' Macheath returns, and the opera ends happily with a dance. We all know the saying that the success of the *Beggar's Opera* made Gay rich and Rich gay; but it did more than this, for it made the fortunes of the two principal actors who had not previously been possessed of much fame.

Lavinia Fenton (1708-1760) made her first appearance on the stage in 1726 as Monimia in Otway's *Orphans* at the New Theatre in the Haymarket. John Rich was so much struck with her appearance as Cherry in the *Beaux' Stratagem* that he tempted her away from the Haymarket with the 'magnificent' offer of 15s. per week.

When shortly afterwards he was arranging for the presentation of the *Beggar's Opera*, in order to secure the services of Miss Fenton for the principal female character, he doubled her salary. She appeared as

LAVINIA FENTON (POLLY PEACHUM), AFTERWARDS DUCHESS OF BOLTON.
From the original painting in the National Gallery.

Polly Peachum on the opening night, January 29, 1728, and at once became the idol of the town. On June 19 the opera was played for the sixty-second and last time that season, when she made her last appearance on the boards of a theatre, so that her career as an actress was a short one. She was succeeded in the character of Polly by Miss Warren.

Charles Paulet, third Duke of Bolton, said that he was first captivated by Polly's song, ' Oh, ponder well,' which has already been alluded to as the turning-point in the success of the performance. The Duke was a constant attendant at the theatre, and after the first season he took Miss Fenton from the stage and she remained his mistress for twenty-three years. Soon after the death of the Duchess, from whom he had been separated for many years, the Duke married Lavinia at Aix in Provence (on the 20th of September 1751). She was highly thought of in her new sphere, and the famous Dr. Joseph Warton gave her a high character.

' She was a very accomplished and most agreeable companion, had much wit, good strong sense, and a just taste in polite literature. Her person was agreeable and well made, though I think she could never be called a beauty. I have had the pleasure of being at table with her, when her conversation was much admired by the first characters of the age, particularly old Lord Bathurst and Lord Granville.'

Hogarth's portrait of her, now in the National

Gallery, is a fine work, and gives a pleasing idea of the charming actress.[1]

Gay wished his friend Quin to take the part of Macheath, but that great actor had no taste for the part, for which he felt he was unfitted, although he had a good ear for music and was famous for singing ballads with ease.   He did, however, drudge through two rehearsals, but at the close of the second Tom Walker was observed behind the scenes humming some of the songs in a tone and manner that attracted notice.   Quin laid hold of this circumstance to get rid of the part, and exclaimed: 'Ay, there is a man who is more qualified to do you justice than I am.' Walker was called on to make the experiment, and Gay, who instantly saw the difference, accepted him as the hero of his piece.

Walker was an indifferent musician and knew little of music scientifically, but he could sing a song in good ballad time.   He had a speaking eye and admirable action; the ease and gaiety of his style was very marked.   He showed great judgment in his treatment of the character which he created and made as great a success as Lavinia Fenton did in Polly.   He did not make Macheath a town beau or a gentleman, but his manner, deportment, and voice

[1] This picture was in the possession of Samuel Ireland who published an engraving of it by C. Aposteel in 1797.   It faces p. 49 of *Graphic Illustrations*, vol. ii.   The picture was bought by Mr. William Seguier at Ireland's sale in 1801 for £5, 7s. 6d , and was afterwards in the collection of Mr. George Watson Taylor.   He exhibited it in 1814, and at his sale it fetched £52, 10s   It was purchased for the National Gallery in 1884 from Sir Philip Miles's collection for 800 guineas.

all partook of the roughness and simplicity of the character. Walker was not famous before the opportunity of his life occurred, but he had made his mark in his profession. His Macheath, however, obliterated all remembrance of his former successes.

Barton Booth saw Walker playing Paris in a droll named *The Siege of Troy*, and at once recommended him to the management of Drury Lane. Davies tells us that his Bajazet and Hotspur had hardly been rivalled, and that his Falconbridge was better than that of Garrick, Sheridan, Delane, and Barry, which indeed is high praise.

In the same year that he gained his great fame as Macheath he brought out at Lee and Harper's booth in Bartholomew Fair a sort of imitation of the *Beggar's Opera* entitled the *Quaker's Opera*.

During the run of the *Beggar's Opera* and for many years afterwards Walker was more in requisition with the public than the highest performers on the stage. To have spent an evening with him at the tavern was a feather in the town buck's cap, and not to know him personally off the stage was reckoned a piece of gross incuriosity. His portrait was set in every print-shop, and all the fashionable fans and screens of the day represented some scene between him and Lavinia Fenton as Macheath and Polly.

This popularity was his ruin, as he gave way to intemperance and lost his memory, with the consequence that he was discharged from the London stage. He attempted to recover his character and went to Ireland to change the scene, but bad habits were too deeply fixed, and he died in Dublin in great wretchedness in 1744.

Mrs. Egleton was the original Lucy Lockit, and she shared with Polly much of the appreciation of the public.   She had been much admired as a good comic actress before she undertook this part.

John Hippisley was the original Peachum, a character drawn after Jonathan Wild.   He was well known for his acting of many of Shakespeare's low comedy characters, and his representation of Fluellen was considered an artistic performance.   Davies describes him as a comedian of lively humour and droll pleasantry.

There is a portrait of him at the Garrick Club attributed to Hogarth.

John Hall was the original Lockit.   He was a dancing-master before he took to the stage, and he was not much known until he acted this character, but by it he acquired a great reputation.

Mrs. Martin was the original Mrs. Peachum, and she also took the character of Diana Trapes.

To return to Hogarth's picture after this digression respecting the chief actors and actresses.   It represents Macheath in the centre of the stage with Lucy on the left pleading for him to her father Lockit, and Polly on the right pleading to Peachum.

Hogarth has given us a good representation of the stage of the theatre in Lincoln's Inn Fields, and no other picture of the interior of this old playhouse is known. It shows how inconvenient it must have been to have a crowd of fashionable loungers seated on the stage and leaving little room for the actors. This was a bad old custom which continued for many years in spite of protests. A royal proclamation of Queen Anne, dated November 15, 1711, forbade the practice, but no notice was taken of the prohibition.

'Whereas we are informed that the orders we have already given for the reformation of the stage by not permitting anything to be acted contrary to religion or good manners, have in great measure had their good effect we proposed and being further desirous of reforming all other indecencies and disorders of the stage, our will and pleasure therefore is, and we do hereby command that no person of what quality soever shall presume to stand behind the scenes, or go upon the stage either before or during the acting of any opera or play, and that no person go into either of our houses for opera or comedy without first paying the established prices for their respective places.'

Originally the portion of the audience who were allowed on the stage sat about in chairs, but here, in 1728, we find that the visitors were confined in boxes or pews.

It was Garrick who cleared away from the stage every one but the actors.

On the right hand of the stage we see the Duke of Bolton (who sits in front) giving all his attention to Polly; next to him is Major Paunceford, and then in the following order Sir Robert Fagg, M.P., Rich the manager, Cock the auctioneer, and Gay the author.

On the left-hand side is Lady Jane Cook, Anthony Henley, Lord Gage, Sir Conyers d'Arcy, and Sir Thomas Robinson.

The lights on the stage consisted of candles set round in a hoop of tin sockets.   This mode of lighting continued till Garrick's return to the stage in 1765, when he introduced side lights, invisible to the audience.

In the same year (1728) Hogarth produced a plate entitled ' The Beggar's Opera Burlesqued,' of which there are five states.   Under the design are engraved the following four lines :

> ' Brittons attend—view this harmonious stage,
> And listen to those notes which charm the age :
> Thus shall your taste in sounds and sense be shown,
> And Beggar's Op'ras ever be your own.'

The design is rather confused and difficult of comprehension.   It shows a representation of the *Beggar's Opera* and a rehearsal of an Italian opera. The characters of the former are drawn with the heads of different animals, as Polly with a cat's ; Lucy with a sow's ; Macheath with an ass's ; Lockit, Peachum and Mrs. Peachum with an ox, a dog, and an owl respectively.

It is not clear why Hogarth burlesqued the characters in this way, as he evidently wished to point out the inferiority of the Italian opera.

Mr. F. G. Stephens explains this as follows :

' At our left are the boxes of a theatre, and on the right is a scene at the Italian Opera, where a female singer is surrounded by noblemen offering homage and presents ; this, by the motto at the top of the plate " et cantare pares et respondere paratæ," seems to be held out as worthy of equal estimation with the satirical representation of *The Beggar's Opera*, which occupies the left of the design.' [1]

A copy from Hogarth's print was published in 1735 with the title ' The Opera House or the Italian Eunuch's Glory, Humbly Inscribed to those Generous Encouragers of Foreigners and Ruiners of England.'[2]

The dangerous tendency of the *Beggar's Opera* has been the subject of a considerable amount of dispute.

Dr. Herring, preacher at Lincoln's Inn and afterwards Archbishop of Canterbury, ' censured it as giving encouragement not only to vice but to crimes, by making a highwayman the hero, and dismissing him at last unpunished.' On the other side Swift defended the opera against the attacks of his fellow Churchmen.

Sir John Fielding, the Bow Street magistrate, tried to stop the performance on more than one occasion, but unsuccessfully. He once told Hugh Kelly that ever since the first representation of this piece there had been on every successful run a proportionate number of highwaymen brought to the office, as he

[1] *British Museum Catalogue of Political and Personal Satires*, vol. ii. p. 670
[2] *British Museum Catalogue*, vol. iii. p. 95.

would show him by the books any morning he took the trouble to look over them. Kelly had the curiosity to do so, and found the observation to be strictly true.[1]

About the year 1772 Fielding sent letters to the managers of Drury Lane and Covent Garden urging them not to perform the *Beggar's Opera*, as it tended to increase the number of beggars. Garrick, not having any good singers, expressed his approval of the magistrate's suggestion ; but Colman was not so complacent, and sent this answer : ' Mr. Colman's compliments to Sir John Fielding, he does not think his the only house in Bow Street where thieves are hardened and encouraged—and will persist in offering the representation of that admirable satire the *Beggar's Opera*.' (Lee Lewes's *Memoirs*.)

John Ireland corroborated Sir John Fielding's judgment by cases which came under his own observation. ' With three instances that I had an accidental opportunity of seeing, I was very forcibly impressed. Two boys, under nineteen years of age— children of worthy and respectable parents—fled from their friends, and pursued courses that threatened an ignominious termination to their lives. After much search they were found engaged in midnight dissipations, and in each of their pockets was the *Beggar's Opera*.'

The third case was more conclusive. ' A lad of seventeen, some years since tried at the Old Bailey,

[1] *European Magazine*, Jan. 1800, vol xxxvii. p. 26.

for what there was every reason to think his first offence, acknowledged himself so delighted with the spirited and heroic character of Macheath, that on quitting the theatre, he laid out his last guinea in the purchase of a pair of pistols, and stopped a gentleman on the highway.'[1]

It will be remembered that Dr. Johnson took a different view both in conversation and in writing. In his Life of Gay (*Lives of the Poets*), after referring to Dr. Herring's condemnation and the observation 'that after the exhibition of the *Beggar's Opera*, the gangs of robbers were evidently multiplied,' Johnson writes: 'Both these decisions are surely exaggerated. The play, like many others, was plainly written only to divert, without any moral purpose, and is therefore not likely to do good; nor can it be conceived, without more speculation than life requires or admits, to be productive of much evil. Highwaymen and house-breakers seldom frequent the playhouse, or mingle in any elegant diversion; nor is it possible for any one to imagine he may rob with safety, because he sees Macheath reprieved upon the stage.'

Boswell tells us that Johnson expressed the opinion that more influence had been ascribed to the play than it in reality ever had, and he added, 'At the same time I do not deny that it may have some influence by making the character of a rogue familiar and in some degree pleasing! Then collecting himself as it were, to give a heavy stroke: There is

[1] *Hogarth Illustrated*, vol. ii. p. 324.

in it such a *labefactation* of all principles as may
be injurious to morality.'

This discussion on the influence of the *Beggar's
Opera* was a favourite one with Boswell, and he had
made collections for the purpose of publishing a
quarto volume. Mr. Percy Fitzgerald says that it is
supposed that his many visits to Newgate, attending
on convicts, etc., were made with a view to this
publication.

One can hardly expect any instance of a bad
influence to follow a performance of the opera in the
present day, but in a time when highwaymen were
admired as heroes by persons of weak and ill-
regulated minds it was likely to have an evil effect.

Samuel Ireland mentions benefit theatre tickets
for three of the actors in the *Beggar's Opera*, which he
attributes to Hogarth, viz. for Walker, Milward, and
Spiller. The one 'For the benefit of Mr. Walker,'
represents the same scene in the play as Hogarth
painted which has already been described. It is
not, however, a copy, but an entirely different treatment of the five chief characters. Below is the
inscription : ' Theatre Royal Covent Garden. Pitt.'
The etching is signed 'W. Hogarth int, J. Sympson
Jun. sculp.' The original is in the Royal Collection.
S. Ireland published a copy ' A. M. Ireland sculpt ' in
his *Graphic Illustrations* (vol. i. p. 58).

J. B. Nichols (*Anecdotes of W. Hogarth*, 1833, p. 300)
quotes the following MS. note by W. Richardson
(printseller, Strand), in the *Graphic Illustrations*: ' A

palpable fiction; Sympson etched much better. See the frontispiece to Ned Ward's Works. Powell's daughter brought me this, with a few common prints, for sale. She asked for them 15s. I said " Why do you ask me so much for such trumpery?" She said there was one of Hogarth's worth a good deal more. She then sold them to N. Smith, May's Buildings, who sold this print to S. Ireland for eight guineas—a proof that neither of them was possessed of much real judgement in Hogarth's works.'

This is a very interesting piece of information, but Nichols is not inclined entirely to agree with Richardson's decision.

The benefit ticket for Milward represents a scene from the *Beggar's Opera*, in which that actor represented the Player who disputes with the Beggar, the supposed author of the play. The inscription is : ' Theatre Royal, Lincolns Inn Fields, Tuesday April 23. A Bold Stroke for a Wife wth Entertainments for y[e] Benefit of M[r] Milward.'

John Nichols (*Anecdotes*, 1785, p. 423) refers to this benefit ticket, and writes : ' This careless but spirited engraving has more of Hogarth's manner than several other more laboured pieces which of late have been imputed to him. Let the connoisseur judge.'

The date of Milward's benefit is not positively recorded, but it must have been after 1728 and before 1733. Mrs. Centlivre's play, *A Bold Stroke for a Wife*, was first performed in 1718. Ireland etched a copy of the original print which was published by

Motton and Co. in 1788, and another impression was issued in the *Graphic Illustrations* (vol. i. p. 98).

James Spiller, who sustained the character of Mat o' the Mint, was reduced to a state of great distress soon after the first success of the *Beggar's Opera*. The ticket for his benefit is mentioned by John Nichols and J. B. Nichols. The former describes it as a 'beautiful little print,' and the latter expressed the opinion that ' this is immeasurably superior to all the other tickets both in design and execution. It makes one suspect all the rest to be not by Hogarth.' (*Anecdotes of Hogarth*, 1833, p. 299.) Samuel Ireland etched a copy from the original print in 1788 ; subsequently it was included in the *Graphic Illustrations*. The ' print represents a large balance, suspended in the open space before a prison on the one hand, and on the other a tavern, in front of which is the sign of the " Sun." A leg of mutton hangs before the adjoining house, which is thus probably indicated to be that of Spiller himself. Entwined with the beam of the balance is a label with " For the benefit of Spiller." Under the beam stands Spiller, eagerly selling tickets for his benefit at the theatre in Lincoln's Inn Fields to several gentlemen.'[1]

Spiller was a publican in Clare Market, where a club was held of which Hogarth was a member. The original sign was the Bull and Butcher, but on Laguerre painting Spiller's portrait, which he presented to the Club, it was changed to the Spiller's

---

[1] *British Museum Catalogue of Satires*, vol. ii. p. 677.

Head. This was the scene of a picture by Hogarth called ' Oysters ; or St. James's Day.' [1]

Spiller's last appearance on the stage was on January 31, 1729. He died on February 7 following, aged thirty-seven years, and was buried at the expense of Rich the manager in the churchyard of St. Clement Danes. He was a favourite of the public, but intemperance was the bane of his career.

Hogarth produced several portraits of actors, and he must have had a varied acquaintance with the players at the different theatres, but his associations were more intimate with the actors of the chief theatre—Drury Lane.

Joe Miller took his benefit as Sir Joseph Wittol in Congreve's *Old Bachelor* at Drury Lane on April 25, 1717. There is a theatre ticket for this occasion representing a scene in the third act of this play. Samuel Ireland attributes this to Hogarth, and suggests that it was designed about the time of the publication of the ' Rake's Progress ' (1735). [2]

It is generally believed to be a forgery, and W. Richardson supposes the forger to have been Powell.

S. Ireland also gives a copy of a ticket for the benefit of Fielding, author of the *Mock Doctor*, which occurred on April 20, 1732. [3] Theophilus Cibber filled the part of the Mock Doctor, and the scene represented in the picture contains a portrait of him. This is not accepted as a true work of Hogarth.

---

[1] Dobson's *Hogarth*, 1907, p 218
[2] *Graphic Illustrations*, vol. ɪ. p. 128.   [3] *Ibid.*, p. 104.

'A just View of the British Stage, or three Heads are better than one. Scene Newgate, by M. D[e]v[o]to' (1725), has been attributed to Hogarth, but it is of very doubtful authenticity. Devoto was scene-painter at Drury Lane, Lincoln's Inn Fields, and Goodman's Fields. This print is called in Walpole's Catalogue, 'Booth, Wilks and Cibber contriving a Pantomime.'

In 1733 Theophilus Cibber produced at Drury Lane a short grotesque pantomime entitled *The Harlot's Progress, or the Ridotto al Fresco,* founded on Hogarth's pictures. It was printed with a dedication to the painter. The tract is very rare, and some copies contain portraits of Hogarth and Cibber, the latter in his favourite character of Pistol.

In this same year Theophilus Cibber promoted a quarrel between the manager of Drury Lane and some of the actors, which caused a secession of the latter to the Haymarket. John Laguerre, the scene-painter, produced an interesting etching on the subject entitled 'The Stage Mutiny,'[1] which is worthy of special mention here because Hogarth used the design on a show-cloth in his representation of Southwark Fair. Laguerre was a friend of Hogarth, who obtained his services as a witness in his action against Joshua Morris. He is said also to have designed a benefit ticket for him.

The manager of Covent Garden Theatre was glad to have a laugh at his rivals, and in 1734 a tragi-

[1] See *British Museum Catalogue of Satires,* vol. ii. p. 794

comi-farcical opera called *The Stage Mutineers, or a Playhouse to be Let,* was produced with some success.

The pit ticket for Fielding's benefit, already alluded to, brings the names of Fielding and Theophilus Cibber in conjunction in 1732, but in the following year they are found on different sides. Fielding considered that Highmore, the manager, was ill-used, and he stuck to the fortunes of Drury Lane Theatre. He has been said, on little authority, to be the author of the '*Apology for the Life of Mr. The. Cibber,* being a Proper Sequel to the Apology for the Life of Mr. Colley Cibber, Comedian,' in which the actor is unmercifully satirised in a vein of sustained irony. We must now pass on to notice the friendship of Hogarth and Garrick, which is in every way pleasing to the admirers of both men, for it is said that they never had a misunderstanding. Mr. Joseph Knight, in his valuable *Life of Garrick* (1894), gives us several glimpses of their mutual relations.

On one occasion it had been hinted to Garrick that he had been remiss in his visits to Hogarth. In consequence of these hints he wrote a very agreeable letter of which this is the concluding part:

' If Mrs. Hogarth has observed my neglect I am flattered by it, but if it is your observation woe betide you !

' Could I follow my own wishes I would see you every day in the week, and not care whether it was in Leicester Fields or Southampton Street, but what

with an indifferent state of health and the care of a
large family [Drury Lane Theatre], in which there
are many froward children, I have scarce half an
hour to myself. However, since you are grown a
polite devil, and have a mind to play at lords and
ladies, have at you. I will certainly call upon you
soon; and if you should not be at home I will leave
my card.—Dear Hogarth, yours most sincerely,

'D. GARRICK.' [1]

Hogarth painted Garrick as Richard III. in 1746
for Mr. Duncombe of Duncombe Park, and he was
proud of receiving two hundred pounds for the picture,
which he observed in his *Autobiography*, ' was more
than any English artist ever received for a simple
portrait.' It still remains in the possession of Mr.
Duncombe's descendant, the Earl of Feversham.

The picture was engraved by Hogarth and Charles
Grignion. The latter informed John Ireland 'that
Hogarth etched the head and hand, but finding the
head too large he erased it, and etched it in a second
time, when seeing it wrong (*sic*) placed upon the
shoulders, he again rubbed it out, and replaced it as
it now stands, remarking, "I never was right until I
had been wrong." '

On October 21, 1746, Hogarth sent a sketch of
Garrick and Quin to a member of a literary society
at Norwich, styled the Argonauts. He wrote,
' S^r, If the exact figure of Mr Quin were to be
reduc'd to the size of the print of Mr Garrick it

[1] Knight's *David Garrick*, p. 157.

ל

DAVID GARRICK AND MRS. GARRICK. 1757.

would seem to be the shortest man of the two, because Mr Garrick is of a taller proportion.'

A facsimile of this letter was published in 1797 by Laurie and Whittle, and a print of the two figures is included in Hogarth's works.[1]

The portrait of Garrick writing the prologue to Foote's comedy of *Taste*, with Mrs. Garrick behind him taking the pen from his hand, is interesting on account of the anecdote connected with it. The actor found fault with the picture. Hogarth, in a fit of irritation, drew his brush across the face of Garrick, and the picture remained in his possession till his death. Mrs. Hogarth sent the portrait to Garrick after the painter's death. At Mrs. Garrick's sale in 1823 the picture was bought by Mr. Edward Hawke Locker of Greenwich Hospital for £75, 11s. Mr. Locker sold it to George IV., and it is now at Windsor. Mr. Austin Dobson, who gives this account, quotes from Mr. F. G. Stephens (*Grosvenor Gallery Catalogue*, 1888) the corroboration of Hogarth's supposed action: 'The eyes of Garrick being coarsely painted, ill-drawn, and evidently by another hand than Hogarth's, attest the truth of this story.' It is related by Murphy that Hogarth saw Garrick in *Richard III.* on one night, and on the following night in *Abel Drugger*. He was so much struck that he said to the actor, 'You are in your element when you are begrimed with dirt or up to your elbows in blood.'

[1] *British Museum Catalogue of Satires*, vol. iii. p. 618.

Garrick is said to have allowed himself to be drawn as a rustic whose height is being taken by a recruiting sergeant in Plate 2 of the ' Invasion.'

He wrote the descriptive verses to the two prints, twelve lines each.   The verses are :

Plate 1, ' France.'

' With lantern jaws, and croaking gut,
See how the half-starv'd Frenchmen strut,
   And call us English dogs !
But soon we'll teach these bragging foes,
That beef and beer give heavier blows,
   Than soup and toasted frogs.

The priests inflam'd with righteous hopes,
Prepare their axes, wheels and ropes,
   To bend the stiff-neck'd sinner !
But should they sink in coming over,
Old Nick may fish 'twixt France and Dover
   And catch a glorious dinner.'

Plate 2, ' England.'

' See John the soldier, Jack the Tar,
With sword and pistol arm'd for war,
   Should Mounseer dare come here !
The hungry slaves have smelt our food,
They long to taste our flesh and blood,
   Old England's beef and beer !

Britons to arms ! and let 'em come,
Be you but Britons still, strike home,
   And lion-like attack 'em ;
No power can stand the deadly stroke,
That's given from hands and hearts of oak,
   With Liberty to back 'em.'

In 1762 Hogarth drew an excellent frontispiece for Garrick's successful interlude of *The Farmer's*

GARRICK IN "THE FARMER'S RETURN." 1762.

Return from London, which was dedicated to the artist 'as a faint testimony of the sincere esteem which the writer bears him.'

Forster, in his *Life of Goldsmith,* among some disparaging remarks on Boswell, relates the following improbable story: 'The youthful Scot . . . had seen Garrick in the new farce of the *Farmer's Return,* and gone and peeped over Hogarth's shoulder as he sketched little David in the Farmer, hitting off in half a dozen minutes with magical facility of pencil, a likeness that was held to be marvellous' (vol. i. p. 295).[1]

Garrick and his wife went to Italy in 1763. From Savoy he wrote to his man George, bidding him 'take care of Hogarth's pictures and keep them out of the sun by which they might be spoilt.'[2]

A little later, when Churchill was writing his *Epistle to William Hogarth,* Garrick wrote to 'The Bruiser' with admirable loyalty though without success:

'I must entreat of you by the regard you profess to me that you don't tilt at my friend Hogarth before you see me. . . . He is a great and original genius. I love him as a man and reverence him as an artist.'

In connection with the history of Drury Lane

[1] To the recent *Fasciculus J. W. Clark dicatus,* Cambridge, 1909 (pp. 406-422), Mr. Sidney Colvin contributed a learned and very interesting study of Hogarth's original sketch for *The Farmer's Return,* now in the possession of the Hon Mrs. A. E. Gathorne-Hardy. It originally belonged to Mr. H. P. Standly, afterwards to Mr. William Mitchell. Mr. Colvin's paper includes a facsimile of Hogarth's pen-drawing.

[2] Knight's *David Garrick,* 1894, p. 203.

there are two pictures of the green-room attributed to Hogarth which claim our special attention. Both were exhibited at the Whitechapel Art Gallery in 1906.

No. 50, ' Garrick in the Green Room,' lent by Mr. J. E. Reiss,[1] and No. 70, ' Green Room, Drury Lane,' lent by the late Sir Charles Tennant. ' Garrick in the Green Room ' is the title of a picture which was discovered early in the nineteenth century and purchased for a few shillings. It was ' engraved in mezzotinto by William Ward Jan. 1, 1829,' for the possessor, James Webb Southgate, who published it at 22 Fleet Street. George Daniel wrote a description of the picture, also published in 1829, and entitled ' *Garrick in the Green Room!* a Biographical and Critical Analysis of a Picture.'

The key given of the persons represented is as follows : 1, Mr. Beard ; 2, Mr. Baddeley ; 3, Mrs. Garrick ; 4, Mr. Woodward ; 5, Unknown ; 6, Gentleman Aickin ; 7, Mr. Macklin ; 8, Gentleman Smith ; 9, Mrs. Yates ; 10, Mrs. Abingdon ; 11, Mr. Hogarth ; 12, Mr. O'Brien ; 13, David Garrick ; 14, P. Garrick. This is a distinguished party, and the figures are arranged in a well-grouped picture, but one would like to know more of its history before accepting it as an undoubted original. One would have expected that such collectors of Hogarthiana as Walpole, Nichols, the two Irelands, and Trusler would have heard of the picture from Mrs. Hogarth

---

[1] This picture was exhibited in 1880 by Mr. Samuel Addington

if they had not seen it themselves. J. B. Nichols expressed his doubt as to its authenticity, although he considered it a carefully-painted picture. He writes: ' I cannot believe it to have been painted by Hogarth. It is not unlikely to be a French painting, with alterations adapted to the English market.'[1]

There does not appear to be any good reason for the latter suggestion.

Of the picture styled ' The Green Room, Drury Lane,' we know even less than we do of ' Garrick in the Green Room.' We have neither information as to the date of the picture, nor of how or where it was discovered.

The catalogue of the Whitechapel Gallery contains a very strongly-worded eulogy of the picture, and the writer places it in the very front rank of Hogarth's work. He writes: ' A magnificent work, unequalled for brilliance among the painter's achievements. The grave lighting is magical in its arresting power ; the way this light seems to come and go, now discovering and now obscuring the objects, means illumination profoundly understood, and the result is a picture inevitable and mysterious as life itself.' I do not question this statement respecting the technique, although it appears somewhat exaggerated, and I should not have quoted this criticism if I had found any earlier description of the picture in the literature of Hogarth's work.

[1] *Anecdotes of W. Hogarth*, 1833, p 314

As a picture it is certainly much inferior in interest to the ' Garrick in the Green Room.' The figures are fewer and not so representative of ' Old Drury.'

The picture is reproduced in Mr. Austin Dobson's folio *Hogarth* (Heinemann), and the names of the persons represented are there given, as they appear on the frame. They are : Miss Pritchard, Mrs. Pritchard, Barry, Fielding, Quin, and Lavinia Fenton. The figures between Barry and Quin are in the background and are very indistinct ; one is said to be intended for Fielding, and the other is unnamed.

Two points in the picture which are worthy of special attention are the portraits of Quin and Lavinia Fenton. The former is a mere caricature and quite unworthy of Hogarth, who knew the actor well and painted his portrait more than once. Lavinia Fenton seems out of place in this green-room, as she never had any connection with Drury Lane, and she was not likely to be a frequenter of a green-room after 1728 when she finally left the stage.

In dealing with the authenticity of the picture the first thing to find out is the supposed date of the scene represented. A clue to this seems to present itself in the presence of Mrs. Pritchard and her daughter.

Miss Pritchard made her *début* at Drury Lane as Juliet to Garrick's Romeo in 1756. Her appearance caused a great sensation, but she was not able to keep up her high reputation. We may therefore take the year 1756 as the date of the picture, and if we do so we cannot but be astonished at the absence from the green-room of Drury Lane of Garrick himself and of such stars as Mrs. Cibber and Kitty Clive, not to mention the names of Woodward, Palmer, and Mossop.

Of those persons who are represented, Fielding had been dead two years in 1756; Quin was sixty-three years of age, and had retired from the stage five years before; Lavinia Fenton was forty-eight, and, moreover, was the widowed Duchess of Bolton.[1]

Having referred to that great actress, Mrs. Pritchard, one of the mainstays of Drury Lane Theatre, we cannot resist the temptation of inserting here an anecdote from an old magazine, which places her in a pleasing light.

' Mrs. Pritchard, in one of her summer rambles went with a large party to see the *Beggar's Opera* at a remote country town, where it was so mangled as to render it almost impossible to resist laughing at some of the passages. Mrs. Pritchard perhaps might have indulged this too much, considering one of her profession; however she escaped unnoticed till after the end of the performance, it was necessary for her and company to cross the stage to go to their carriages —the only musician who filled the orchestra happened likewise to be the manager, and having no

---

[1] I have no wish to dispute the authenticity of this picture, but until we know more of its history and pedigree it seems necessary to set down the apparent difficulties in the way of accepting it as an undoubted work of Hogarth.

other way of showing his revenge, he immediately
struck up the opening tune—

> "Through all the employments of life,
> Each neighbour abuses his brother."

'This had such an effect on Mrs. Pritchard that she
felt the rebuke, and threw Crowdero a crown for his
wit, as well as a tribute of her own humiliation.' [1]

Passing from Drury Lane to the Haymarket we
have to take note of some of Fielding's successes in
which his friend Hogarth was interested.

Fielding's version of Molière's *Médecin Malgré lui*,
which he called *The Mock Doctor, or The Dumb Lady
Cured*, has already been alluded to because it was
acted at Drury Lane.

Fielding's first play, *Love in Several Masques*, was
performed at Drury Lane in February 1728, and on
publication the author acknowledged in his preface
the kindness of Wilkes and Cibber the managers.

His *Tom Thumb, a Tragedy* (in two acts), was
brought out at the Haymarket in 1730. In the following year Fielding enlarged it into three acts. It was
published in 1731 with the following title : *Tragedy
of Tragedies*, or the Life and Death of Tom Thumb
the Great . . . with the annotations of H. Scriblerus
Secundus. London, J. Roberts, 1731.' Hogarth designed a frontispiece (1731) for this book, which was
engraved by G. Vandergucht.

This is an excellent burlesque written on the same
principle as *The Rehearsal*. The scene between

---

[1] *European Magazine*, 1800, vol. xxxvii. p. 26.

Glumdalca and Huncamunca is a parody of the meeting between Octavia and Cleopatra in Dryden's *All for Love*. Swift told Mrs. Pilkington that he had only laughed twice in his life, and one of the occasions was when he saw Tom Thumb killing the ghost.[1] This, however, was omitted after the first edition of the piece.

On the 3rd of May 1732 the play was transferred to Drury Lane, and was acted on that day for the benefit of William Rufus Chetwood, the well-known prompter and bookseller in Covent Garden.

The authenticity of the 'Pasquin' ticket for the benefit of the author, Henry Fielding, has been doubted, but many will agree with Mr. Dobson when he writes: 'There is a doubt whether this is really the work of Hogarth, but the strokes at political morality in that " dramatic satire on the times " would have been so much to the taste of the artist who later designed the inimitable Election Prints, that one is inclined to give him the benefit of any uncertainty.'

Moreover, Hogarth was so great a friend of Fielding that to assist him at his benefit was just what he would be glad to do.

Mr. Stephens gives a description of this ticket, and a facsimile of it by A. M. Ireland will be found in the first volume of his *Graphic Illustrations*. 'The design represents a stage scene, the background

---

[1] 'Mrs. Pilkington's memory served her imperfectly, since it is not Tom Thumb who kills the ghost, but the ghost of Tom Thumb which is killed by his jealous rival, Lord Grizzle' (Dobson's *Fielding*, 1907, p. 22).

comprising a colonnade from the respective wings of which a tight-rope is stretched. On this rope dancers are performing and holding their balancing poles; an ape sits astride of the rope on our right.' [1]

The inscription on the ticket is 'The Author's Benefit Pasquin. At ye Theatre in the Haymarket.' On S. Ireland's copy is written in Fielding's handwriting, 'Tuesday, April 25th. Boxes.'

The success of the *Beggar's Opera* is the first instance of a long run on the English stage, and Fielding's *Pasquin*, eight years afterwards (1736), had almost as long a one. It contained severe satirical reflections on the Ministry, which were greatly appreciated by the audience. The Government, naturally, did not appreciate the satire, and in consequence they passed the Licensing Act by which the number of playhouses was limited and the liberty of the stage was restrained. As Mr. Cyril Maude says in his *Records of the Haymarket Theatre*, it is indirectly to the little theatre in the Haymarket that Mr. George Redford enjoys ' his enviable position of Examiner of Plays.'

The scene of action shown in the ticket is at the conclusion of the fifth act, where the Queen of Common Sense is stabbed by Firebrand, and the Queen of Ignorance declares to Harlequin, his allies, and to Squeekaronelli that she will be to them all a most propitious queen.

Samuel Ireland says in his *Graphic Illustrations*

---

[1] *British Museum Catalogue of Satires*, vol. III. p. 186.

that he had a larger print on this subject from a design by Hogarth that includes all the characters in the piece ; in a corner of which Pope appears to be quitting the theatre, and by the label issuing out of his mouth is exclaiming, ' There is no whitewashing this stuff.' [1]

This is very suspicious, and the larger print mentioned is certainly a forgery, for Hogarth did not use labels containing speeches at this date. It may be remarked, however, that Pope was said to have been present at one of the performances. Some verses were written on seeing ' Mr. Pope at the Dramatic Satire call'd Pasquin.' The satirists of the time were busy with making fun over the ' illegitimate ' drama of the period, and Hogarth was to the fore with his ' Masquerades and Operas,' etc., which will be referred to later in this chapter.

In this year, 1736, was issued an engraving entitled ' The Judgment of the Queen o' Common Sense. Address'd to Henry Fielding, Esqr. A Satire on Pantomimes, and the professors of Divinity, Law and Physic.' This is described by Mr. Stephens as ' representing the stage of a theatre, with an alcove in the background on which, raised a step above the floor, stands a crowned female, the Queen of Common Sense, who holds in her right hand a well-filled purse, and in her left hand an halter. On her right kneels a gentleman, Henry Fielding, offering to the Queen a piece of paper inscribed PASQUIN ; to him she is

---

[1] *Graphic Illustrations,* vol. i. p. 131.

giving the contents of the purse; the halter she extends to her left, and its extremity is in the hand of a harlequin, who is capering on the stage in front of the design.' The description is too long to copy here. Below the design are engraved some verses commencing :

'With bounteous hands yᵉ Queen of Common Sense,
Appears her honest favours to dispence,
On Pasquin's Author show'rs of Gold bestows,
And Hamlet's Ghost the impartial Poet shows
Tho' Shakespear's merit in his bosom glows.' [1]

The last production of George Colman, the elder, was acted at the Haymarket in 1789. It was a slight musical interlude of little merit entitled, *Ut Pictura Poesis, or The Enraged Musician*. As its title indicates, it was founded upon Hogarth's celebrated picture.

Hogarth painted several portraits of actors which are of interest, such as those of Lavinia Fenton, already alluded to as in the National Gallery, Quin and William Bullock. There are two portraits of Peg Woffington in a reclining position at the Garrick Club, one by Hogarth and the other by Mercier. Hogarth's picture was sold by Henry Angelo to Charles Matthews. The one by Mercier is the more pleasing picture.

Among the books illustrated by Hogarth are several plays for which he designed frontispieces. Two of these have already been referred to, viz.

[1] *British Museum Catalogue of Satires,* vol. iu. p. 200

Fielding's *Tom Thumb* (1731), and Garrick's *Farmer's Return* (1762).

Others are ' *The Humours of Oxford*, a Comedy. By a Gentleman of Wadham College ' [Rev. James Miller], 1729, which was acted at Drury Lane.

' *The Highland Fair, or The Union of the Clans*, an Opera. Written by Mr. [Joseph] Mitchell,' 1731, also acted at Drury Lane. Fielding tells us in *The Covent Garden Journal* (No. 19) an amusing anecdote of the dulness of the author:

' A certain comic author produced a piece on Drury Lane stage called *The Highland Fair*, in which he intended to display the comical humours of the Highlanders; the audience, who had for three nights together sat staring at each other, scarce knowing what to make of their entertainment, on the fourth joined in an unanimous exploding laugh. This they had continued through an act; when the author, who unhappily mistook the peals of laughter which he heard for applause, went up to Mr. Wilks, and with an air of triumph, said, "Deel o' my sal, Sare, they begin to tauk the humour at last." '

' *The Lawyer's Fortune, or Love in a Hollow Tree*, a Comedy,' 1705, is somewhat of a curiosity. It was written when its author, William Grimston, was only thirteen years of age, and was never acted except by a strolling company of actors at Windsor. The author was in 1719 created Baron of Dunboyne and Viscount Grimston in the Peerage of Ireland. He was unfortunate in the strong opposition of the old Duchess of Marlborough, when he contested successfully the borough of St. Albans. He had attempted to suppress his play, but the Duchess reprinted it in order to make him ridiculous.

Lord Grimston was apparently an estimable man, but the wits were against him. Alluding to his residence at Gorhambury Pope wrote :

> 'Shades that to Bacon could retreat afford,
>   Become the portion of a booby Lord.'

And Swift, attacking him for his unfortunate play, said :

> 'The leaden crown devolved to thee,
>   Great poet of the *Hollow Tree.*'

Hogarth's frontispieces to these three plays were all engraved by Gerard Vandergucht.

The frontispiece to Henry Carey's *Chrononhoton-thologos* (1734) is attributed to Hogarth, but this attribution is very doubtful, and it has not received a favourable reception.

' *The Tragedy of Chrononhotonthologos.* Written by Benjamin Bounce. London. Printed by J. Suckburgh.'

The engraving represents a scene in a prison-cell.

There is a picture in existence representing a scene from Dr. Benjamin Hoadly's *Suspicious Husband.* This belonged to Mrs. Hoadly in 1782.

Dr. John Hoadly, the younger son of Bishop Hoadly, had a private theatre in his house. Few visitors were allowed to leave until they had exhibited their powers here as amateur actors. Hogarth

" THE CONQUEST OF MEXICO."

From an engraving by Robert Dodd.

was one of Hoadly's failures, for when he performed with Garrick and Hoadly in a parody of the scene in *Julius Cæsar*, where the ghost appears to Brutus, he entirely forgot the few words he had to recite. The host was not to be disappointed, so to help his friend he had the verses written in large letters on the paper lantern which the ghost carried in his hand when on the stage. Hogarth designed a playbill with characteristic ornaments which was preserved but not engraved.

Hogarth was interested in two instances of private theatricals. He painted a picture of the performance of Dryden's *Indian Emperor, or the Conquest of Mexico* at Mr. Conduit's house, and designed a ticket for an entertainment at Cliefden, given on August 1, 1740, before the Prince and Princess of Wales, that being the birthday of their daughter the Princess Augusta. The picture of the fourth scene of the fourth act of the *Indian Emperor* is preserved at Holland House.

John Conduit was the Master of the Mint in succession to Sir Isaac Newton, whose niece (Mrs. Catherine Barton) he married. Their only child (also Catherine), who acted in this piece, married on the 8th of July 1740 Viscount Lymington, the eldest son of the first Earl of Portsmouth, who died before his father, and his son succeeded the first Earl in the title. The eldest sons of this noble family have usually borne the name of Newton. The four characters on the stage are: 1, Cortez, acted by Lord Lempster ; 2, Cydaria, by Lady Caroline Lennox ; 3, Almeria, by Lady Sophia Fermor ; 4, Alibeck, by Miss Conduit.

Hogarth appears to have continued his acquaintanceship with Lady Lymington from her childhood. There is a tradition that he was proud to be allowed to draw figures from her, and that she was so obliging as to sit to him for the Viscountess in the 'Marriage à la Mode.'

The audience included in the picture are : 5, the Duke of Cumberland ; 6, Princess Mary ; 7, Princess Louisa ; 8, Lady Deloraine ; 9 and 10, her daughters ; 11, Duchess of Richmond ; 12, Duke of Richmond ; 13, Earl of Pomfret ; 14, Duke of Montague ; 15, Tom Hill or Captain Poyntz ; 16 (on the stage), Dr. Desaguliers.

The picture was engraved by Robert Dodd, and published by J. and J. Boydell in 1792. There is a key-plate in John Ireland's *Hogarth Illustrated* (ii. 331).

Leslie in his *Handbook for Young Painters* (1855, p. 151) praises this picture very highly. He writes : ' Three girls and a boy are on the stage, and seem to be very seriously doing their best ; but the attitude and expression of one little girl in a front seat among the audience, is matchless. She is so entirely absorbed in the performance, that she sits bolt upright, and will sit, we are sure, immovably, to the end of the play, enjoying it as a child only can, and much the more because the actors are children.'

The ticket for the performance of Thomson and Mallet's *Masque of Alfred*, written by command of the Prince of Wales, and performed in the gardens of Cliefden House in 1740, has had more than one date given to it. It consists of an oval with the two figures of Hymen and Cupid in the foreground, and a view of a handsome mansion (Cliefden) in the background.

When originally acted, the chief character of the *Masque* was the Hermit, taken by Quin, Alfred by Milward, the Earl of Devon by Mills, Corin by Salway, Eltruda by Mrs. Horton, and Emma by Mrs. Clive. Mallet remodelled the *Masque*, making Alfred the chief character, when it was acted at Drury Lane in February 1751. Garrick took Alfred, Berry the Hermit, Lee the Earl of Devon, Miss Bellamy Eltruda, and Mrs. Bennet Emma. The play was revived at Drury Lane in October 1773, when Reddish played Alfred.

John Nichols (in his *Biographical Anecdotes*, 1785, p. 436), says that the ' print was intended as a ticket for Sigismunda, which Hogarth proposed to be raffled for. It is often marked with ink 2l. 2s. The number of each ticket was to have been inserted on the scroll hanging down from the knee of the principal figure. Perhaps none of them were ever disposed of. This plate however must have been engraved about 1762 or 3. Had I not seen many copies of it marked by the hand of Hogarth, I should have supposed it to have been only a ticket for a concert or music-meeting.'

The suggested date is much too late, but the guess as to a ticket is a shrewd one.

J. B. Nichols says that the ticket was used as a receipt for the Election Prints as well as for ' Sigismunda.'   The subscription for the latter was 10s. 6d. and that for the former two guineas.   Mr. Standly had a copy on which is written ' Nº 12 ' in the scroll, and under the print ' Election Entertainment 2l 2s Wm. Hogarth.' [1]

No copy of the original ticket (1740) is registered, but 1748 is given as the date of the reprint by John Ireland.[2]

Hogarth was greatly interested in everything that tended towards the amusement of the people, and he had many opportunities of understanding the history of the theatre.   He was well acquainted with actors, and he was the honoured friend of three of the great managers of the chief theatres of London.

Of Garrick at Drury Lane little further need be added.   The Haymarket, at which Fielding presided for a time, was the small theatre which was superseded by the present building in 1821.

Fielding's fame will ever live in English literature on account of his immortal novels.   His plays occupy five octavo volumes of the most modern edition of his works,[3] but his fame cannot be aug-

[1] *Anecdotes of W. Hogarth*, 1833, p. 334.
[2] *Hogarth Illustrated*, Supplement, p. 349
[3] *Complete Works of Henry Fielding*.   New York . Printed for Subscribers only by Croscop and Sterling Company, and published in England by W Heinemann. 16 vols 8vo.

mented by them. Although his *Tom Thumb* and *Pasquin* are productions of great power and were highly successful on the stage, they do not affect the truth of the general verdict that his genius naturally tended to narrative rather than to the dramatic.

John Rich, the manager of Lincoln's Inn Fields and introducer of pantomimes, was successful, and will ever be remembered for his production of the *Beggar's Opera.* His theatre was the third and last house to bear the name of Lincoln's Inn Fields.

In December 1732 Rich removed to Covent Garden Theatre, which was built for him. There is a print entitled 'Rich's Glory, or his Triumphant Entry into Covent Garden,' which is attributed to Hogarth, but is of very doubtful authenticity. It is, however, an interesting illustration of Hogarth's London.

Although the works of Hogarth, already alluded to in this chapter, are satirical, the actors at the ordinary theatres were acceptable to him because they were English and their performances racy of the soil. The most intense prejudice in Hogarth's nature was a hatred of the introduction of foreign customs into this country, and Italian opera excited his keenest displeasure as he considered it an unwelcome exotic. He satirised the great Italian singers who were the fashion, and thus displayed his national prejudice. We are, however, grateful, because his sketches help us to understand the intense feeling exhibited in favour of and against the Italian opera which forced itself upon the country, and in the end became an established institution. Before treating of Hogarth's attitude towards this branch of the stage, reference must be made to his altogether admirable ' A Chorus of Singers ; or, the Oratorio.' This was reproduced in small by George Cruikshank for Major's edition of Trusler (1831), but the later artist cannot be said to have done justice to his original, although his ' Four Groups of Heads,' given in that book, are excellent in themselves.

The original print was used as the subscription ticket for ' A Midnight Modern Conversation.'

Below the design is engraved a form of receipt :

' Rec^d　　　　　　　　　　　of

Five shillings being the whole Payment for a Print call'd the Midnight Moddern Conversation which I Promise to Deliver on ye 1st of March next at farthest. But Provoided the number already Printed shall be sooner Subscribed for, then ye Prints shall be sooner Delivered & time of Delivery will be advertiz'd.'

In the British Museum copy the blank spaces are filled in, probably by Hogarth, thus: 'December 22th, 1732,' and ' Mr Tho. Wright.' In the second state of this plate the word ' Provoided ' is corrected to ' Provided.'

The print represents a rehearsal of ' Judith : an Oratorio or Sacred Drama.' The author of this was Hogarth's friend, William Huggins, and the composer of the music was William Defesch. Some of

the editors of Hogarth supposed the composer to be
Handel, and stated absurdly enough that the con-
ductor was intended for the great composer himself,
whose portrait he did at one time paint.[1]

Huggins was painted by Hogarth and his portrait
was engraved. An original of the ticket has been
spoken of, and Bishop Luscombe bought such a
picture in Paris. Sir William Knighton told the
Bishop that Hogarth's picture had belonged to the
Dukes of Richmond, and had been in their house in
Paris until the first Revolution, since which time it
had not been heard of.[2]

Besides this design, Hogarth prepared a frontispiece
for the Oratorio when Huggins published it in
1733.

In his *Autobiography* Hogarth writes: ' But here
again I had to encounter a monopoly of printsellers,
equally mean, and destructive to the ingenious ; for
the first plate I published, called *The Taste of the
Town*, in which the reigning follies were lashed, had
no sooner begun to take a run, than I found copies of
it in the printshops, vending at half price, while the
original prints were returned to me again ; and I was
thus obliged to sell the plate for whatever these
pirates pleased to give me, as there was no place of
sale but at their shops.'[3]

[1] A portrait of Handel was engraved by C Turner and published in
1821 (see Chapter VII., Professional Life).
[2] *Notes and Queries*, First Series, vol VII. p 484.
[3] For further particulars respecting Hogarth's fight with the pirates see
Chapter II.

John Ireland writes respecting this : ' The print here alluded to, I apprehend to be that now entitled the small *Masquerade Ticket* or *Burlington Gate*, published in 1724, in which the follies of the town are very severely satirised, by the representation of multitudes, properly habited, crowding to the Masquerade, Opera, pantomime of *Doctor Faustus*, etc., while the works of our greatest dramatic writers are trundled through the streets in a wheel-barrow, and cried as waste paper for shops.' [1]

This plate, also named ' Masquerades and Operas,' is very interesting from its richness of detail.   In the background is the entrance gate of Burlington House, surmounted by a statue of Kent standing between two reclining figures of Michael Angelo and Raphael. It is quite possible to understand Hogarth's hatred of Kent, who was a contemptible painter set up as a rival to Sir James Thornhill, although he had some merit as an architect and a landscape gardener. In the front are three figures looking up at the gate : these are the Earl of Burlington, accompanied by his architect, Colin Campbell, and another person who, as Mr. Stephens says, has been ' erroneously called his lordship's postilion.' We can understand Hogarth's feeling towards Burlington, although we may judge that it was unjust. The inscription on the gate ' Academy of Arts ' is prophetic, for the enlarged Burlington House is now the home of the Royal Academy of Arts, which did not then exist.

[1] *Hogarth Illustrated*, 1798, vol. iii. p. 16.

MASQUERADES AND OPERAS. BURLINGTON GATE. 1724.

In the foreground on the left is the home of Masquerades. John Ireland notes that the leader of the figures hurrying to a masquerade crowned with a cap and bells and a garter round his right leg, has been supposed to be intended for George the Second, who was very partial to these nocturnal amusements, and is said to have bestowed a thousand pounds towards their support. The purse with the label £1000, which the satyr holds immediately before him, gives some probability to the supposition.

Heidegger, the great promoter of masquerades, is seen looking out of a window. Of him there will be more to be said later on. A show-cloth hanging from the front of the building is inscribed 'Opera.' It represents the famous singers Berenstadt, Senesino, and Cuzzoni. To the right are three figures kneeling; the foremost, the Earl of Peterborough, a prominent supporter of the opera, exclaims, 'Pray accept £8000.' Cuzzoni is seen raking in the gold which the Earl pours out of a purse. A signboard next to the show-cloth is inscribed 'The Long Room. FAUX. Dexterity of Hand.' Fawkes was a famous mounteback of the time, who gave entertainments at Bartholomew Fair and elsewhere. His portrait will be found in Caulfield's Portraits, etc., of Remarkable Characters.

To the right of the plate opposite to the masquerade building is the theatre where Rich performed his pantomimes. A crowd is seen rushing into a colonnade over which is a harlequin pointing to a show-cloth representing the head of a devil, which is inscribed ' Dr. Faustus is Here.'

The pantomime entitled *The Necromancer, or Harlequin Doctor Faustus* was brought out at Lincoln's Inn Fields in 1723, and was so great a success that Rich's rival managers were forced to imitate his example.

It will be seen from this description that there was but little of topographical accuracy in the introduction of these different buildings in one picture. The print entitled ' Berenstat, Cuzzoni and Senesino ' has been the cause of a considerable amount of dispute. It represents the stage of a theatre at the performance of the opera of *Julius Cæsar*, the three singers taking the characters in the following order: Julius Cæsar, Cleopatra, and Mark Antony, and a child representing the train-bearer of Cleopatra. This is nothing but a caricature, and it has been supposed not to be Hogarth's work. Mr. Stephens points out that under the Duchess of Portland's copy is written ' This print of Senesino, Berenstadt and Cuzzoni was given me by Vanderbank the younger's mother. He drew it from seeing it at the opera.' The chief reason for believing it to be the work of Hogarth is the fact that he repeated the three figures in his picture of ' Masquerades and Operas,' already described, but this is not a very strong argument, as Hogarth imitated other artists' work in some of his pictures ; as, for instance, we have seen that he copied Laguerre in ' Southwark Fair.'

John Ireland replaces the name of Farinelli for that of Berenstadt, but this necessitates our dating this print after 1734, when Farinelli came to England, and this is not very probable, as the 'Masquerades and Operas' was produced in 1724. Ireland also says that the characters are Ptolemy, Cleopatra, and Julius Cæsar, from Handel's opera *Ptolomeo*, which was first performed in 1728.[1]

A picture of Farinelli seated on a pedestal lies on the floor in the second plate of the 'Rake's Progress.'

A print entitled 'A Satire on Cuzzoni, Farinelli and Heidegger' has been attributed to Hogarth, but it is believed to be the design of Dorothy, Countess of Burlington, who is said to have had it etched by Goupy. In Mr. Stephens's *Catalogue of Satirical Prints in the British Museum* there are notices of several satirical prints connected with the celebrated Italian singers by others than Hogarth.

The opera dancers were not overlooked, and Hogarth produced in 1742 a print in ridicule of Desnoyers, the dancing-master, and Signora Barberini, under the title of 'The Charmers of the Age.' An original print was in the Strawberry Hill Collection. It was re-engraved by R. Livesay, and published by him in 1782 at Mrs. Hogarth's.

At the Whitechapel Exhibition, 1906, a picture entitled 'A Pantomime Ballet on the English Stage (about 1750),' attributed to Hogarth, was lent by Mr. Charles E. Newton Robinson. It

---

[1] The print is reproduced in *Hogarth Illustrated*, vol iii p. 255.

is an interesting picture, but the ascription is doubtful.

As has already been noticed, the fashion for masquerades in connection with the foreign introduction of opera became very general, and the fosterers of these entertainments were in many instances the same persons.

There is no doubt that very great evils were caused by the public welcome of masquerades, and therefore Hogarth's attacks upon them did him credit. Reference has already been made to the print of ' Masquerades and Operas,' or the small Masquerade Ticket (1724). The large Masquerade Ticket was published in 1727 at the price of one shilling. This is engraved as a frontispiece to the third volume of *Hogarth Illustrated* from the original print given to John Ireland by Sir James Lake. There is a full description by Ireland, and also one in Mr. Stephens's *British Museum Catalogue*.[1] The print shows the interior of a large room which serves as a vestibule to the chamber where the masquerade is held. A multitude of grotesque characters press towards the door. It is not necessary to describe fully the surroundings of the place which are all indicative of the orgies performed there. The head of the high priest of the mysteries, the renowned Heidegger, is placed on the front of a large dial, fixed lozenge fashion at the top of the print. The ball of the pendulum is labelled *nonsense*. On the minute

[1] Vol. ii. p 661

hand is written *impertinence*, and on the hour hand *wit*.

Recumbent on the upper line of this print and resting against the sides of the dial the lion and the unicorn are seen lying on their backs, and this parody of the royal supporters is supposed to allude to George II.'s patronage of masquerades.

John James Heidegger was a remarkable man. He was the son of the Swiss pastor of Zurich, and came to England at the age of about fifty, after having lived a Bohemian life for some years in almost every capital in Europe. In 1713 he was manager of the Opera House in the Haymarket. Again in 1728 he was connected with Handel in the same venture. He was appointed by George II. Master of the Revels, and in his attempts to introduce masquerades he was supported by the King.

For some years great opposition to this form of amusement was set in motion by the more sober portion of the population. On January 6, 1726, a sermon was preached at Bow Church by the Bishop of London before the Society for the Reformation of Manners, which created a great effect. Futile attempts were made to obtain an Act of Parliament for the suppression of masquerades, but a royal proclamation against the evils produced by them was published.

In 1729 a Middlesex Grand Jury presented Heidegger 'as the principal promoter of vice and immorality.' In spite of all this opposition there was no abatement of the evil, and the only concession to the popular outcry was to change the name of a masquerade to a Ridotto.

Bramston in his *Man of Taste* alludes to this :

'Thou Heidegger, the English taste has found,
And rul'st the mob of quality with sound,
In Lent if Masquerades displease the town,
Call 'em Ridottos, and they still go down.
Go on, Prince Phiz, to please the British nation,
Call thy next Masquerade a Convocation.'

The name 'Prince Phiz' refers to Heidegger's ugliness, which was so patent to all that he himself made a jest of it. Mrs. Delany describes him as 'the most ugly man that ever was formed.' Fielding introduces him as Count Ugly in the puppet show called *The Pleasures of the Town* at the end of *The Author's Farce.*

The Count speaks :

'I disdain
O'er the poor ragged tribe of bards to reign.
Me did my stars to happier fates prefer,
Sur-intendant des plaisirs d'Angleterre,
If Masquerades you have, let those be mine,
But on the Signior let the laurel shine.'

When asked, 'Hast written ? ' he answers :

'No, nor read.
But if from dulness any may succeed,
To that and nonsense I good title plead.
Nought else was ever in my masquerade.'

He was, however, a highly successful man, and starting with nothing he soon made about five thousand pounds a year. He was a member of

White's exclusive club, and entertained George II. at his house at Barn Elms.

John Nichols gives an anecdote which shows the careless humour which caused him to succeed in this country.

' Being once at supper with a large company, when a question was debated, which nationalist of Europe had the greatest ingenuity ; to the surprise of all present, he claimed that character for the Swiss, and appealed to himself for the truth of it. " I was born a Swiss," said he, " and came to England without a farthing, where I have found means to gain £5000 a year, and to spend it. Now I defy the most able Englishman to go to Switzerland, and either to gain that income or to spend it there in eating and drinking." '

A slight pencil sketch entitled ' Heidegger in a Rage ' (*circa* 1740) belonged to John Ireland, who engraved it in the third volume of his *Hogarth Illustrated*. The ascription is untenable, but the well-known anecdote of Heidegger's confusion which is here represented is just such an incident as would appeal to the humour of Hogarth. The sketch is now in the Print Room of the British Museum, and is described by Mr. Stephens in his *Catalogue* (vol. iii. p. 360). Mr. Binyon catalogues it under Philip Mercier's name.[1]

---

[1] This little sketch (a black-chalk drawing) belonged to John Ireland who inserted a facsimile of it by J. Mills in his *Hogarth Illustrated*, 1798, vol. iii. p. 323. He attributed it to Hogarth on little or no evidence, but having been given this authority it has been treated as one of his works.

Heidegger would never allow any portrait of himself to be taken, and he managed to evade George II.'s expressed wish that he should be painted. What could not be obtained by fair means was undertaken by a ruse. The Duke of Montagu, who was a prince of practical jokers, succeeded where others had failed. He invited Heidegger to make one of a choice party at the Devil Tavern. The rest of the company, all chosen for their powers of hard drinking, were in the plot, and a few hours after dinner the Swiss Count was carried out of the room dead drunk. A daughter of Mr. Salmon, the wax-work maker, was in attendance, and took a model from the unconscious man's face, from which she was ordered to make a cast in wax, and colour it to nature.

The Duke bribed Heidegger's valet to give him information as to the clothes his master would wear at the next masquerade. A man of a similar figure was found, and with the help of the mask was made up into a striking reproduction of the Master of the Revels.

George II. was apprised of the plot and he promised to be present with the Countess of Yarmouth. On the King's arrival Heidegger at once bade the band play 'God save the King,' but no sooner was his

The drawing was purchased for the British Museum in 1858. Mr. Laurence Binyon says that it was originally attributed to Philip Mercier (1689-1760), and as that ascription is doubtless correct it is described under his name in his *Catalogue of Drawings by British Artists* in the Department of Prints in the British Museum (vol. ii p. 326 ; vol. iii. p. 102).

back turned than the impostor with a fine assumption of the voice and manner of the true master ordered the Jacobite song 'Charlie over the Water' to be struck up. Heidegger then raged, stamped and swore, commanding the continuation of 'God save the King.' Immediately he retired the impostor returned and ordered the band to resume 'Charlie.' The musicians thought their master was drunk, but dared not disobey the order. All this confusion caused an uproar, and the courtiers who were not in the plot were in dismay. Some of the officers of the guard who attended the King wished to turn the musicians out of the gallery, but the Duke of Cumberland interposed. The Duke then told Heidegger that the King was in a violent passion and advised him to go instantly and make an apology. At the same time he told the impostor to do the same. When the two met Heidegger stared, staggered, grew pale and could not utter a word. Montagu then explained the situation, but Heidegger swore that he would never attend any public entertainment if the waxwork-maker did not break the mould, and melt down the mask before his face.

Samuel Ireland contributed to the second volume of his *Graphic Illustrations* an etching by Le Cœur (1797), from a slight sketch by Hogarth, entitled 'Ill Effects of Masquerades.' The picture speaks for itself, but Ireland gives a rather florid description of it which may be condensed.

A husband called away to the country for a short time left his young wife with her sister. During his absence the two ladies resolved to go to a masquerade, the wife adopting the dress of a gallant and the sister acting as his betrothed. All went well, and they returned home. The husband unexpectedly followed them, and rushing with impatience to his wife's apartment saw on the floor the clothes of a man. Imagining that he had full proof of his wife's inconstancy he stabbed both sisters in a frenzy of revenge. The picture shows the fatal ending and the man's remorse. A not very probable story, unless he was completely blinded by passion.

Mr. Dobson notes that the picture belonged to Mr. Peacock of Marylebone Street. There is still another picture of a masquerade attributed to Hogarth, which was engraved in 1804 by T. Cook, 'from an original picture painted by Hogarth in the collection of Roger Palmer, Esq.' It is described as 'Royal Masquerade, Somerset House.' There are several masquerades recorded as having been held at Somerset House; thus one, in 1716, which is amusingly described in the *Freeholder*, and the more famous one in 1749, when the scandalous Elizabeth Chudleigh (afterwards Duchess of Kingston) appeared so thinly clothed that the Princess of Wales thought it expedient to throw a thick veil over her maid of honour. Horace Walpole told Mann in one of his letters that ' Miss Chudleigh was Iphigenia, but so naked you would have taken her for Andromeda.'

It is difficult to fix the date of the masquerade shown in this picture, as the figures are not very accurately described in J. B. Nichols's *Anecdotes*, 1833, p. 287; but perhaps this does not matter, as it is very doubtful if Hogarth had anything to do with the painting of it.

In concluding this long notice of masquerades and Hogarth's strong feeling as to the evils connected with them, it will be appropriate to quote from Fielding, who was capable of giving an unbiassed opinion. He writes: 'I cannot dismiss this head, without mentioning a notorious nuisance which hath lately arisen in this town; I mean, those balls where men and women of loose reputation meet in disguised habits. As to the masquerade in the Haymarket, I have nothing to say; I think really it is a silly, rather than a vicious, entertainment; but the case is very different with those inferior masquerades; for these are indeed no other than the temples of drunkenness, lewdness, and all kinds of debauchery.'[1]

[1] *An Enquiry into the Causes of the late Increase of Robbers, etc.*, 1751 (Section I.).

CHAPTER XI

HOSPITALS

THE subject of the present chapter is one that shows Hogarth on his best side, and exhibits instances of his great charity and kindness of heart.   After many struggles and much hard work he succeeded in obtaining a competence, but he does not appear to have been at any time what we may call a rich man. In spite of this he was munificent in his presentations to the Foundling and St. Bartholomew's Hospitals, and of both these institutions he was made a governor.

The Foundling is not what one now understands by a hospital, but as in the case of Christ's Hospital, the term is unalterably attached to it.

The Foundling Hospital is one of the most interesting institutions in London, and at the same time the very form and body of the eighteenth century at its very best pervades the buildings and the gardens.   A continued sense of responsibility in respecting the tradition of its originators united with a proper determination to keep it abreast of the times has been the great aim of the management.   The rooms are filled with works of art, and as the delighted visitor passes through them he feels that a shrine has been reserved for the good men who founded and fostered the Hospital—Coram, Hogarth, Handel, and many others. It is the earliest home of representative English pictorial art, and it possesses a proud claim to distinction as one of three places in London where Hogarth may be seen at his best. The National Gallery contains the 'Marriage à la Mode' and many other fine pictures, the Soane Museum the 'Rake's Progress' and the 'Election,' and the Foundling Hospital the grand portrait of Captain Coram, the 'March to Finchley,' and 'Moses brought to Pharaoh's Daughter.' The contents of the rooms and the beauty of the gardens glorify the plain old building, and as we look around our eyes are satisfied and our minds are full of thankfulness that no imp of mischief has been allowed to put into the minds of the governors a wish to replace the delightful old buildings by some important-looking new structure without charm or association.

May the rural beauties of the Foundling Hospital in the midst of London long remain an oasis in a barren land! The house where Hogarth lived for so many years in Leicester Square has been rebuilt, and few of the places associated with him still exist, so that the Foundling Hospital, which he so often visited, is of special interest in connection with his fame, and the more so that his memory is specially cherished there, and the rulers are proud of what he did for the institution. The Foundling Hospital

was founded by Captain Thomas Coram in 1739, the
date of the charter in which Hogarth figures as ' a
Governor and Guardian.' Its first home was in
Hatton Garden, and the arms in an heraldic shield
which Hogarth designed were placed over the door
of this house.[1] The engraving of the arms was
published in 1781, and is described as being engraved
from the original in the possession of the Earl of
Exeter. The artist also designed the pleasing
heading to a Power of Attorney for collecting
subscriptions, the plate of which is still in the
possession of the Hospital. It represents Coram
with the charter under his arm and a mother kneeling
to him, while a beadle, bearing a mace and carrying
a child in his arms, is leading the way to the door of
the Hospital, around which are congregated many
children. A village church is seen to the left in the
distance, and the sea with ships on it in the middle
of the design.

Hogarth was busy with work for the Foundling in
1739-40, for in May of the latter year he presented the
noble full-length portrait of the founder, which is so
well known from the numerous engravings, but the
painting itself requires to be seen by any one who
wishes to obtain an adequate idea of Hogarth's great
merits as a portrait painter. Although there are
several good portraits in the gallery, one of them by

[1] Hogarth's original draft for these arms will be found in the *Genuine
Works* (vol. iii. p. 139). The arms are a naked child, the crest a lamb, and
the motto 'Help' The supporters are 'Nature' and 'Britannia'

To all to whom these Presents shall come.

Whereas our sovereign Lord the King hath been graciously pleased to take into His Princely and tender Consideration the deplorable Case of great Numbers of Newborn Children daily exposed to Destruction, by the cruelty or poverty of their Parents, and having by His **Royal Charter** bearing date the 17th day of October 1739, constituted a Body Politick and Corporate, by the Name of The Governors and Guardians of the Hospital for the Maintenance and Education of exposed and deserted young Children; which Corporation is fully impowered to raise & apply the Charities of all compassionate Persons who shall contribute towards erecting & establishing the same. And Whereas His Majesty for the better & more successful carrying on the said good Purposes, hath by His said **Charter** granted to the said Corporation and their Successors full & ample Power to authorize such Persons as they shall think fit to take subscriptions, and to ask and receive of all or any of His Majesty's good subjects, such Monies as shall by any Person or Persons, Bodies Politick and Corporate, Companies and other societies be contributed and given for the Purposes aforesaid. Now know Ye that We the said Governors & Guardians being well assured of the great Charity & Integrity of and that

greatly desire the Success & Accomplishment of so excellent a Work, Have by Virtue of the said Power granted to Us, authorized & appointed, and by these Presents Do authorize & appoint the said to take Subscriptions and to receive gather & collect such Monies as shall by any Person or Persons, Bodies Politick & Corporate, Companies & other Societies, be contributed & given for the Purposes aforesaid, and to transmit with all convenient speed, the Monies so Collected and Received, into the Bank of England for the use of this Corporation. And the Receipt for the same to our Treasurer for the time being, together with the Names of the Contributors, except such as shall desire to be concealed, and in that Case to insert the Sums only, in order that We the said Governors & Guardians may be enabled from time to time to Publish perfect Accounts of such Benefactions. Given under our Common Seal the Day of 17

By Order of the said Governors & Guardians.

"THE FOUNDLINGS." 1739.

CAPTAIN THOMAS CORAM.   1739.

From Nutter's engraving, 1796.

Reynolds, this picture dominates its surroundings, and proves itself pre-eminent as a work of art of which all Englishmen may be proud.

The Hospital was opened on March 25, 1741, for the reception of nineteen boys and eleven girls. The first boy was named Thomas Coram and the first girl Eunice Coram, after the Captain and his wife. In an account of the opening in the *Gentleman's Magazine* (vol. xi. p. 163) it is said that 'the orphans received into the Hospital were baptised there—some nobility of the first rank standing godfathers and godmothers. . . . The most robust boys being designed for the sea service, were named Drake, Norris, Blake, etc., after our most famous admirals.'

The house in Hatton Garden was only a temporary residence, and a very advantageous purchase of fifty-six acres of land in Lamb's Conduit Fields was made from the Earl of Salisbury for £6500. It is believed that there was a good-humoured controversy as to price. The hospital would only give £5000, and the Earl asked £7000. He offered to take off £500, but he would not budge a jot from his price of £6500. However, he allowed it to be understood that as he was an admirer of the charity he would be pleased to subscribe £500. As there was more land than was required for the buildings and ground, the unused portion was let on building leases, which has produced a valuable source of income to the institution.

The new ground was laid out and the building was designed by Theodore Jacobsen, architect. The west wing was completed in December 1746, and the chapel in 1747, in the vaults under which the founder was buried, pursuant to his own desire. Coram died at his lodging near Leicester Square on March 29, 1751.

When the new building was ready for occupation an annual dinner was instituted. Many artists had followed the lead of Hogarth in painting and presenting works to the Hospital, so that the rooms became a fashionable lounge as being a sort of headquarters of British art.

Mr. Dobson says regarding the annual dinners: ' The assembled painters were accustomed to commemorate the landing of William the Third, using for their loyal libations a fine old white and blue dragon china punch bowl, generally described as Hogarth's, which is still carefully preserved in one of the cases of the Court room, and is beautifully copied in Pye's *Patronage of British Art*.' In illustration of this there is an interesting entry in Stukeley's Diary: ' November 4, 1752. Dined at the annual feast at the Foundling Hospital : Present : Judge Taylor White, treasurer ; Hayman, Wills, *Hogarth*, Hudson, Scot, Brown, Dalton, painters ; Roubiliac, statuary ; Pine, engraver ; Houbraken, Jacobsen, the architect of the house, etc., a cozen of my late friend, Chancellor Stukeley.'

The fine picture of ' The March to Finchley,' one

of the painter's masterpieces, was disposed of by public lottery, and owing to Hogarth's generosity in giving the unsold tickets to the Foundling Hospital it came into the possession of that institution.

The result is announced in the *General Advertiser* of May 1, 1750, as follows: 'Yesterday Mr. Hogarth's subscription was closed. Eighteen hundred and forty-three chances being subscrib'd for, Mr. Hogarth gave the remaining hundred and sixty-seven chances to the Foundling Hospital; at two o'clock the Box was open'd, and the fortunate chance was Number 1941 which belongs to the said Hospital; and the same night Mr. Hogarth delivered the Picture to the Governors.'

J. B. Nichols in his *Anecdotes of W. Hogarth* (1833, p. 360) quotes a very improbable story from the *Gentleman's Magazine* for November 1832 (p. 390), which is too late in date to be of any value, but must be noted as he refers to it in his book: 'A lady was in possession of the fortunate number, and intended to present it to the infant institution; but some persons having suggested that a door would be open for scandal were any of her sex to make such a present, it was given to Hogarth, on the express understanding that it should be presented in his own name.'

John Ireland says that Hogarth acquainted the Treasurer 'that if the Trustees thought proper they were at liberty to dispose of the picture by auction,' but afterwards he changed his mind and requested that they would not dispose of it.[1]

This Hospital holds a remarkable position in the history of British art through the liberality of our painters.

John Nichols quotes from Sir Robert Strange's *Inquiry into the Rise and Establishment of the Royal Academy of Arts in London*, 1775, the author's opinion as to the origin of the Academy: 'The donations in painting which several artists presented to the Foundling Hospital, first led to the idea of those Exhibitions which are at present so lucrative to our Royal Academy, and so entertaining to the publick. Hogarth must certainly be considered as the chief of these benefactors.'[2]

Mr. Dobson writes (p. 62 n.): 'To complete the record of Hogarth's connection with the Foundling Hospital, it may here be added that his patronage of the institution took the practical form of watching over the welfare of some of the children, who in accordance with custom were put out to nurse. In a case in the court room is still to be seen his discharged account for the keep, etc., at Chiswick, of two little girls, Susan Wyndham and Mary Woolaston, who, when he died, were sent back to the Hospital by his widow.'

The Hospital was not only distinguished for its gallery of pictures, but through the liberality of

[1] *Hogarth Illustrated*, vol ii p 134.
[2] Nichols's *Biographical Anecdotes* (1782), p. 247.

Handel it was a gathering-place for musicians and lovers of music. The great composer frequently performed his *Messiah* in the chapel, and as he engaged most of the performers to contribute their assistance gratis, the profits to the charity were very considerable. These performances were generally crowded, and in the notices the audience were desired to leave at home—the ladies their hoops and the men their swords. Handel bequeathed the score of the *Messiah* to the Hospital.

Hogarth's presentation of two large pictures to St. Bartholomew's Hospital took place before his gifts to the Foundling Hospital; they are dated 1736. He was so well acquainted with Smithfield and its neighbourhood that he must early have been interested in the Hospital.

'The Good Samaritan' (16 ft. 9 in. by 13 ft. 8 in.) and 'The Pool of Bethesda' (20 ft. 3 in. by 13 ft. 8 in.) on the grand staircase were painted gratuitously by Hogarth, and for this generosity he was made a Governor of the Hospital. The subjects are surrounded with scrollwork painted at Hogarth's expense by his pupils. These pictures are very uninspiring, particularly 'The Good Samaritan,' but the painter does not appear to have been dissatisfied with the result, although he acknowledged that they did not suit the taste of the public at large. The pictures were not engraved until after his death, but were published by John Boydell in 1772.

They have, however, an interest for us which has

not been specially alluded to by writers on Hogarth. Dr. Norman Moore has made a particular study of the pictures from a medical and surgical point of view, with the remarkable result that that accomplished student is able to praise the correct delineations of disease by the great painter. He says: 'The Good Samaritan employs the method of treating a wound by pouring oil into it which was in use till the time of Ambroise Paré; while the Physicians will admire in the painting of the Pool of Bethesda the accurate representation of the distribution of psoriasis on the well-rounded limbs of one patient, the contrast of hypertrophy and atrophy on the left of the picture, the wasted figure with malignant disease of the liver and the rickety infant.'

Dr. Leonard Mark, in an interesting address on 'Art and Medicine' (1906), has given more fully the views of Dr. Moore on the subject with the addition of his own observations. He says the tradition at the Hospital is that the woman with patches of psoriasis on both knees and on her right elbow, who turns her face away from the Saviour, is a portrait of a courtesan named Wood who lived at the time in the City. Gout, acute melancholia, cancer of the liver, and abscess of the breast are all represented in the picture. He adds: 'The last two female figures represent the two different forms of consumption that used to be talked of. The extremely emaciated woman is clearly a case of very advanced phthisis. The other one with the red cheeks, the thick lips, the short, thick nose, represents the strumous or scrofulous type. In the front there is a woman with bandaged feet.' Dr. Mark says further: ' Hogarth has been very successful in representing sufferers, and no doubt had excellent opportunities for choosing his subjects from patients in the hospital.'

This is a singularly interesting illustration of the care with which Hogarth worked on his paintings. Doubtless he was not contented with observing the cases in the wards, but consulted the physicians and surgeons of the Hospital. If he had not done so he would scarcely have escaped some rebuke from the authorities of to-day. John Freke (1688-1756), a surgeon of St. Bartholomew's, we know to have been a friend of the painter from the well-known anecdote told to Nichols by John Belchier, F.R.S., the surgeon.[1]

Hogarth designed a ticket for the ' London Infirmary for relieving sick and diseased manufacturers, seamen, etc.,' with the arms of the Duke of Richmond as President, which was engraved by T. Ramsay. It was used as a certificate for pupils in surgery and anatomy. The background was afterwards altered to a view of the Infirmary. It was engraved on a large scale in an oval by C. Grignion, 1745. It is not known whether this was done in the way of business or was a gift to the institution.

The London Hospital was originally instituted in

_____
[1] See _ante_, p. 44.

1740 in Prescot Street, Goodman's Fields, but it soon outgrew the accommodation there provided, and a new site was purchased 'in an airy situation near the Mount in Whitechapel Road,' and the first stone of the new hospital was laid on June 10, 1752.

The last scene (Plate 8) of 'A Rake's Progress' contains a remarkable picture of the horrors of the great madhouse known as Bedlam, which was situated in Moorfields, on the south side of what is now Finsbury Square. The original hospital stood in Bishopsgate Without on the site of the North London and Great Eastern Railway Stations in Liverpool Street. It was originally founded as 'a Priory of Canons with brethren and sisters' in 1246 by Simon Fitzmary, one of the sheriffs of London. On the petition of Sir John Gresham, Lord Mayor, Henry VIII. gave in 1547 the building of the dissolved priory to the City of London in order that it might be converted into a hospital for lunatics. In 1557 the management was given to the governors of Bridewell Hospital.

The old building escaped the Great Fire, but being found to have become very dilapidated and quite inadequate for its purpose, a new one was built in Moorfields from the designs of Robert Hooke, which was finished in July 1676. Like its predecessor it was open as an exhibition, payment being made for admission. There were 'spacious and agreeable walks' in front of the building, which became a favourite promenade. At one time the Hospital

"A RAKE'S PROGRESS." No. 8. (BEDLAM.)

From the original painting in the Soane Museum.

'derived a revenue of at least £400 a year from the indiscriminate admission of visitants.' An illustration of the practice is seen in Hogarth's picture, where two fashionable and well-dressed women (apparently a lady and her maid) are seen in the background, their frivolity being singularly out of place in such a scene of terror. In 1770 it appeared at last to have dawned upon the intelligence of the authorities that the introduction of visitors 'tended to disturb the tranquillity of the patients.' In May 1775 Johnson and Boswell visited the Hospital, but in July 1784 Cowper writing to Newton speaks of the custom having been abolished. He writes: 'In those days when Bedlam was open to the cruel curiosity of holiday ramblers I have been a visitor there. Though a boy, I was not altogether insensible of the misery of the poor captives nor destitute of feeling for them. But the madness of some of them had such a humorous air, and displayed itself in so many whimsical freaks, that it was impossible not to be entertained, at the same time that I was angry with myself for being so.'

Hogarth's picture of the interior of a room in Bedlam is one of the most valuable of his illustrations of London Life, which gives a terrible picture of the sufferings of the poor afflicted patients.

The wealth and variety of physiognomical display in this picture is extraordinary, and it might be made the subject of a volume of illustrations and comment. The main incident of the Rake in the foreground is appalling in its reality, while the faithful Sarah Young, who, after all her ill-usage, is present at the last to soothe her dying lover by her tears and self-devotion, helps to humanise the whole scene.

John Ireland makes some just remarks on the preposterous comment of the Rev. William Gilpin on the presence of this ill-fated woman. 'The Reverend Mr. Gilpin, in his elucidation of these eight prints, asserts that this thought is rather unnatural, and the moral certainly culpable ! With the utmost deference for his critical abilities, I must entertain a different opinion. We have many examples of female attachment being carried still farther. If it be culpable to forgive those who have despitefully used us, to free those which are in bonds, to visit those which are in prison, and to comfort those which are in affliction, what meaning have the divine precepts of our holy religion ? ' [1]

Respecting the Rake himself Gilpin appears to have affirmed that ' the expression of the principal figure is rather unmeaning.' In answer to this Ireland refers to the opinion of John Hamilton Mortimer, A.R.A. We are told that Mortimer was once requested to delineate several of the Passions as personified by Gray. One of the subjects proposed was ' Moody madness, laughing wild, amid severest woe.' The instant this line was read to him, he opened a portfolio, took out the eighth plate of the ' Rake's Progress,' and pointing to the principal

[1] *Hogarth Illustrated*, 1793, i. 61.

figure, exclaimed, ' Sir, if I had never seen this print, I should say it was not possible to paint these contending passions in the same countenance. Having seen this, which displays Mr. Gray's idea with the faithfulness of a mirror, I dare not attempt it. I could only make a correct copy; for a deviation from this portrait in a single line would be a departure from the character.'

In the cell out of the principal room is seen a reclining figure with a cross leaning against the wall. Ireland says that it is designed from one of the stone figures of Madness by Caius Gabriel Cibber, which formerly stood on the outer gates of the Hospital, and are now preserved in the Victoria and Albert Museum at South Kensington. J. B. Nichols refers to a painting by Hogarth, ' A View of Bethlehem Hospital,' exhibited in 1814 by Mr. Jones (*Anecdotes of William Hogarth*, 1833, p. 364). The Hospital was removed to St. George's Fields in 1815, and it still remains there.

In *Low Life* (1764), already referred to, we read under Hour xiii., from twelve till one o'clock on Sunday noon: ' The nurses of Bethlehem Hospital, carrying the appointed messes in wooden bowls, to the poor people under their care, and putting by the best part of it for their ancient relations and most intimate friends, who are to come and visit them in the afternoon.'

In Hour i., from twelve o'clock on Saturday night to one o'clock on Sunday morning, we are told of 'the unhappy Lunaticks in Bethlehem Hospital in Moorfields, rattling their chains and making terrible out-cry, occasioned by the Heat of the weather having too great an effect over their rambling brains.' We also read of some disagreeable things done by nurses and 'women called Watchers in Hospitals,' which need not be quoted here.

The Governors of St. George's Hospital possess a picture of the building at Hyde Park Corner with a portrait on horseback of Michael, the son of the last Count Soleirol, a Huguenot, who fled to England on account of his religion. It was exhibited at Whitechapel (Georgian England) in 1906, No. 26, the horseman being described as 'Count Solacio,' the name given to him by a writer in *Notes and Queries*, sixth series, i. 125.

In 1713 Michael Soleirol, the son of John and Jeanne, was born at Monteile [?], and was subsequently naturalised in England.

The picture was presented to the Hospital in 1870 by Mr. Charles Hawkins, F.R.C.S., perhaps the 'C. H.' of *Notes and Queries*, who was Treasurer of St. George's Hospital, 1865-70. The following particulars are obtained from a letter of Mr. Robert F. D. Campbell, engineer and surveyor, a descendant of the Count, who sold it to Mr. Hawkins, which is preserved in the Minute Book of the Hospital.[1]

[1] I am greatly indebted to Mr. George Peachey, who has kindly communicated this information to me. The engraving here given is taken from the original picture, which does not appear to have been previously reproduced.

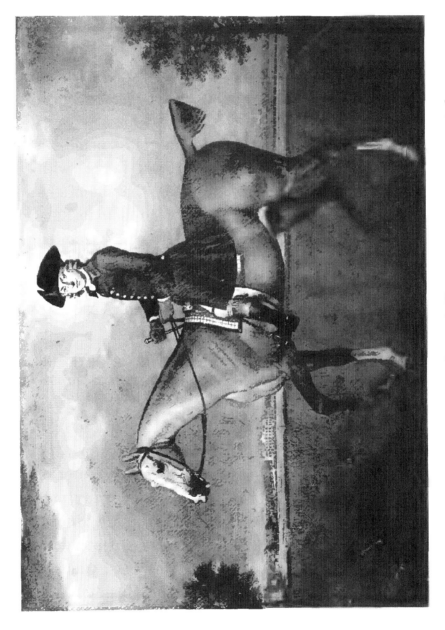

COUNT SOLIRAUL, WITH ST. GEORGE'S HOSPITAL IN THE DISTANCE. 1746.

From the original painting in the Hospital.

The view of the Hospital and Hyde Park is merely a background for the portrait of the horseman painted by Hogarth. Michael Soleirol was the proprietor of the Cocoa Tree Club, originally in Pall Mall and afterwards in St. James's Street, and was friendly with Steele, Addison, and others connected with the *Spectator*. It has even been hinted that he wrote himself an occasional contribution. The picture is said to have been painted at the expense of the club, and a sum of sixty guineas was voted and paid to Hogarth. Apparently he only painted the figure, as the horse was the work of John Sartorius (father of Francis Sartorius and, according to the *Dictionary of National Biography*, the first of four generations of animal painters); and the view was by a third artist whose name is not recorded. The horse is a portrait, as also is the dog named Rose. Mr. Peachey says that the only signature he can discover on the picture is 'J. S. 1748.' The proprietor of the Cocoa Tree had four daughters, and one of them married Mr. Burke. Mrs. Burke had two sons and one daughter, Maria, who married James O'Brien. The eldest daughter of the latter, Elizabeth Helen, married a Mr. Campbell. The picture came into the possession of Mr. O'Brien in the early part of the nineteenth century, and he gave it to Mrs. Campbell. She bequeathed it to her son, who sold it to Mr. Hawkins, so that the history of the picture is fully traced. Mr. R. F. D. Campbell says that two of the daughters of Soleirol, proprietor of the Cocoa Tree Club, were either brought up by Hogarth or lived at his house. They survived to a considerable age, as they did not die until a period between the years 1812 and 1820. These ladies affirmed that the picture was very much approved of on account of its accuracy, in respect to the representations of the man, the horse, the dog and the view. The pose of the rider was said to be a faithful representation of his resolute air and mien.

CHAPTER XII

PRISONS AND CRIME

CRIMES of violence were common in the eighteenth century, and at few times in our history was Society coarser and more depraved than during a portion of the period when there was little or no fear of public odium on account of ill-conduct.   The Court, during the reigns of George I. and II., did not set a good example to those who are apt to follow persons in high places.

Criminals figure largely in Hogarth's works, and those in authority whose duty it was to bring criminals to justice were sometimes little behind those whom they condemned.   The system by which magistrates were appointed and governed was not satisfactory, but the magistrates seem to have been vigilant, and gradually a better system grew up.

It is evident that in the eighteenth century people did not depend upon the protection of the police. The watchmen were quite incompetent and unable to keep the roughs in order.   The men of the day therefore took the matter in their own hands and made themselves capable of carrying out their own means of protection by instruction in the use of the

sword or of their fists.   Watchmen were either feeble
old men, or if they were of any use they often received
pay from the housebreakers to keep out of the way.
The author of *Low Life* makes this special charge:
'Watchmen taking fees from House-breakers for
liberty to commit burglaries within their beats, and
at the same time promise to give them notice, if
there is any danger of their being taken—or even
disturbed in their villainies.'

Gay's *Trivia* contains a description of the watchmen's less criminal venality.   To understand the
picture it is needful to remember that the watch
consisted of watchmen with staves and lanterns led
by a constable, who carried a staff but not a lantern.
The scene scarcely differed in any respect from the
immortal one in which Dogberry and Verges figured.

> 'Yet there are Watchmen who with friendly light
> Will teach thy reeling steps to tread aright;
> For sixpence will support thy helpless arm,
> And home conduct thee, safe from nightly harm,
> But if they shake their lanthorns, from afar
> To call their brethren to confed'rate war
> When rakes resist their power; if hapless you
> Should chance to wander with the scowring crew;
> Though fortune yield thee captive, ne'er despair,
> But seek the constable's consid'rate ear;
> He will reverse the watchman's harsh decree,
> Moved by the rhet'ric of a silver fee.
> Thus would you gain some fav'rite courtier's word,
> Fee not the petty clerks, but bribe my Lord.'

Ned Ward gives a vivid sketch of the constable's
authority when a 'strayed reveller' is said to be
drunk.   'My friend puts his hand in his pocket,

plucks out a shilling. Indeed, Mr. Constable, says he, we tell you nothing but the Naked Truth. There is something for your Watch to drink. We know it is a late hour, but hope you will detain us no longer. With that Mr. Surly Cuff directs himself to his right Janizary: Hem hah, Aminadab, I believe they are civil gentlemen; Ay, ay, said he, Master you need not question it; they don't look as if they had fire balls about 'em. Well gentlemen you may pass; but pray go civilly home. Here Colly, light the gentlemen down the hill, they may chance to stumble in the dark and break their shins against the Monument.'

Of the more capable officers of the law the vocation of a bailiff or catchpole or a sheriff's officer was considered infamous by Englishmen, and in consequence of this a large number of them were Dutchmen or Flemings.

Three active magistrates were associated with Hogarth, viz. Saunders Welch, Sir Thomas de Veil, and Sir John Gonson. The first was a personal friend of the painter, the other two were introduced incidentally into his pictures; but the greatest magistrate was Henry Fielding, who, with his brother and successor Sir John Fielding, did more than any one else at this period to improve the police and the administration of justice. The novelist worked for this improvement both as a magistrate and a writer.

Fielding was appointed a justice of the peace for Westminster, in December 1748, and moved to

Bow Street to a house belonging to the Duke of Bedford.

In the dedication of *Tom Jones* to George Lyttelton (afterwards Lord Lyttelton) Fielding seems to refer to this appointment. He writes: 'Lastly, it is owing to you that the history appears what it now is. If there be in this work, as some have been pleased to say, a stronger picture of a truly benevolent mind than is to be found in any other, who that knows you, and a particular acquaintance of yours, will doubt whence that benevolence hath been copied? The world will not, I believe, make me the compliment of thinking I took it from myself. I care not: this they shall own, that the two persons from whom I have taken it, that is to say, two of the best and worthiest men in the world, are strongly and zealously my friends. I might be contented with this, and yet my vanity will add a third to the number; and him one of the greatest and noblest, not only in his rank, but in every public and private virtue. But here, whilst my gratitude for the princely benefactions of the Duke of Bedford bursts from my heart, you must forgive me reminding you that it was you who first recommended me to the notice of my benefactor.'

Fielding was shortly afterwards qualified to act for Middlesex, and on May 12, 1749, he was unanimously chosen Chairman of Quarter Sessions at Hicks's Hall. His charge to the Westminster Grand Jury on June 29, 1749, was published, and is well worth reading now. In it he said, ' The fury after licentious and luxurious pleasures is grown to so enormous a height, that it may be called the characteristic of the present age.'

Fielding's *Enquiry into the Causes of the late Increase of Robbers, etc., with some Proposals for remedying this growing Evil,* is a practical and most interesting book which had a great effect. Sir John Fielding, who was blind from birth, was associated with his brother as assisting magistrate for three or four years, and succeeded him in office on his death in 1754. He carried on Henry Fielding's plan for breaking up bands of robbers and died in 1780. Sir Walter Besant (*Eighteenth Century*) refers to a scandalous book published in 1755 and entitled, ' *Memoirs of the Shakespear's Head in Covent Garden,* by the Ghost of Shakespear,' one chapter of which ' is devoted to the most venomous delineation of Henry Fielding in his official capacity. That there should be no possible mistake as to the person intended, he is mentioned by name without any disguise at all.' One of the most discreditable circumstances connected with the eighteenth century was the very existence of such an unmitigated scoundrel as Jonathan Wild, and the scathing satire *The Life of Mr. Jonathan Wild the Great* will keep the recollection of this miscreant alive. Fielding did honour to an office which sadly wanted it. He was partly paid in fees, and he said himself that his appointment did not bring him in, ' of the dirtiest money upon earth,' £300 a year.

Saunders Welch, a magistrate of Westminster, was a great friend of Fielding, and saw the last of him when he set forth on his voyage to Lisbon. The novelist wrote in his *Journal*, ' By the assistance of my friend Mr. Welch, whom I never think or speak of but with love and esteem, I conquered this difficulty.' This was when he was getting into the vessel at Rotherhithe. When they were at Gravesend, Monday, July 1, 1754, he says, ' This day Mr. Welch took his leave of me, after dinner.'

Welch was also a friend of Johnson, and in a letter from the latter to him when at Rome, dated February 3, 1778, we learn the doctor's feelings towards him :

' DEAR SIR,—To have suffered one of my best and dearest friends to pass almost two years in foreign countries without a letter has a very shameful appearance of inattention. But the truth is that there was no particular time in which I had anything particular to say ; and general expressions of good will, I hope our long friendship is grown too solid to want.'

Welch's second daughter Mary was married to Joseph Nollekens, R.A., and it is said that Johnson had serious thoughts of marrying her, and jokingly observed on one occasion, ' Yes, I think Mary would have been mine if little Joe had not stepped in.' If this were so, and J. T. Smith is correct in his character of Mrs. Nollekens, we may consider Johnson as happy in his escape. It was partly through

Johnson's influence that Welch obtained two years' leave of absence to visit Italy for his health.

Boswell tells a very amusing and instructive anecdote of Johnson's power of simple speech, when he found it necessary. In his ' eager and unceasing curiosity to know human life in all its variety ' he attended Welch's office for a whole winter ' to hear the examinations of the culprits, but he found an almost uniform terror of misfortune, wretchedness and profligacy.' Sir Joshua Reynolds happened to be present at an examination of a little blackguard boy. ' Welch, who imagined he was exalting himself in Dr. Johnson's eyes by using big words, spoke in a manner that was utterly unintelligible to the boy ; Dr. Johnson perceiving it, addressed himself to him, and changed the pompous phraseology into colloquial language. Sir Joshua Reynolds, who was much amused by this procedure, which seemed a kind of reversing of what might have been expected from the two men, took notice of it to Dr. Johnson as they walked away by themselves. Johnson said that it was continually the case ; and that he was always obliged to translate the justice's swelling diction (smiling) so that his meaning might be understood by the vulgar, from whom information was to be obtained.'

It speaks well for the character of Welch that he possessed three such distinguished friends as Hogarth, Fielding, and Johnson. He wrote an excellent description of the ' March to Finchley ' in Christopher

Smart's publication *The Student*. Hogarth and Welch differed on some points in the article, but very amicably, and the former is said to have observed, 'I generally thought with the author of this paper, and whenever I differed from him I have found reason to take shame to myself.'

Miss (Anne) Welch said that 'when Mr. Hogarth advertised the sale of his pictures without reserve, her father, apprehensive of the event, mentioned his intention of bidding for them on his own account, as he knew Mr. Hogarth would not permit a fictitious bidding.   To this Mr. H. strenuously objected, and with great earnestness intreated him not to attempt it; "for," said Mr. Hogarth, "you are known to be my friend; I have promised to sell my pictures without reserve, and your bidding will ruin my reputation with the public, as it will be supposed I have broke my word and the pictures were bought in."' [1]

J. T. Smith, in *Nollekens and his Times*, tells us that Welch was born at Aylesbury, educated in the workhouse of that town, and apprenticed to Mr. Clements, the trunkmaker at the corner of St. Paul's Churchyard.   For some years he was a grocer in Queen Street, Bloomsbury (now Museum Street).

Smith does not tell us how Welch's improved fortunes came about, but he states that William Packer of Great Baddow, Essex, and many other venerable persons, recollected 'seeing him as High

[1] S. Ireland, *Graphic Illustrations*, vol. i. p. 157.

Constable of Westminster dressed in black, with a large nine-story George II.'s wig, highly powdered, with long flowing curls over his shoulders, a high three-cornered hat, and his black baton tipped with silver at either end, riding on a white horse to Tyburn with the malefactors.' Hogarth painted (it is said in a quarter of an hour) a portrait of Welch in a short wig, which is engraved and published in S. Ireland's *Graphic Illustrations* (1794). Welch was popular on account of the justness of his actions and his kindness to the poor.

The questionable honour was done him of taking his portrait as the sign of a low public-house in Dyot Street, Bloomsbury. A story is told that in 1766 he went unattended into Cranbourne Alley to quell the riotous meetings of the journeymen shoemakers there who had struck for an advance of wages. One of the crowd recognised him and he was at once mounted on a beer barrel, when the men patiently listened to his expostulations. He quieted the rioters, and prevailed on the master shoemakers to grant an additional amount to the workmen's wages.

Sir Thomas de Veil (1684-1746) was a most unpopular magistrate. John Ireland said that he 'raised himself from the rank of a common soldier to a station in which he made a considerable figure,' and he was 'both intelligent and active.'[1] Mr. Dobson writes of him: 'Sir Thomas De Veil was an

---

[1] *Hogarth Illustrated*, vol. III. p 260 note.

able but not very worshipful Justice of the Peace for London and Westminster, and a predecessor of Henry Fielding at Bow Street.'   His figure in the picture of 'Night' as a drunken Freemason is fully described in Chapter IV. (Low Life).

Fielding's comedy, *The Coffee-House Politician, or the Justice caught in his own Trap*, 1730, contains an exposure of Justice Squeezum's unmitigated villainies, and Squeezum is believed to represent de Veil.

So well was this man known among the dangerous classes that it is said an elegy published on his death went through nine editions, and that there was hardly a thief or a harlot who did not buy a copy.

John Ireland has a note in the first volume of his *Hogarth Illustrated* to the effect that ' on the resignation of Mr. [Charles] Horatio Walpole in February 1738 de Veil was appointed Inspector-General of the imports and exports, and was so severe against retailers of spirituous liquors, that one Allen headed a gang of rioters for the purpose of pulling down his house, and bringing to a summary punishment two informers who were there concealed.   Allen was tried for this offence, and acquitted, upon the jury's verdict declaring him *lunatic*.'   There is a life of de Veil in the *Gentleman's Magazine*, 1747, p. 562, and *Memoirs of the Life and Times of Sir Thomas de Veil* were published in the same year.   Mr. Stephens says that the justice in the picture of ' A Woman swearing a Child to a grave Citizen ' is intended to represent Sir Thomas de Veil.

The magistrate in Plate 3 of the 'Harlot's Progress,' who apprehends the heroine, is intended to represent Sir John Gonson, who gained the name of the 'harlot-hunting justice.' The introduction of this figure conduced to the success of the prints.

Nichols relates, in the *Biographical Anecdotes*, an interesting anecdote respecting this plate. 'At a board of Treasury which was held a day or two after the appearance of that print, a copy of it was shewn by one of the lords as containing among other excellencies a striking likeness of Sir John Gonson. It gave universal satisfaction; from the Treasury each lord repaired to the print shop for a copy of it, and Hogarth rose completely into fame. This anecdote was related to Mr. Huggins by Christopher Tilson, Esq., one of the four chief clerks in the Treasury, and at that period under secretary of state. He died August 25, 1742, after having enjoyed the former of these offices fifty-eight years. I should add however that Sir John Gonson is not here introduced to be made ridiculous, but is only to be considered as the image of an active magistrate identified.' In *The Lure of Venus, or a Harlot's Progress*, by Captain Breval, under the name of Joseph Gay, Gonson is specially mentioned in the third canto:

> 'Sir John and all his myrmidons appear'd,
> With clubs and staves equipt, a numerous Herd,
> The surly Knight intrepid, led the van.'

Gonson's charges to juries were very energetic, and

frequently referred to in the newspapers of the time. Pope alludes to 'the storm of Gonson's lungs.'

PRISONS.—Newgate is supposed to be represented in the scenes from the 'Beggar's Opera,' but the only two prisons actually pictured by Hogarth are the Fleet and Bridewell. The painting of the Committee of the House of Commons examining Bambridge is one of the greatest importance as a record of the attempted reformation of the long-continued enormities permitted in ancient prisons. There is every reason to believe that in giving way to his abominably cruel nature Bambridge was following the precedent set by former Wardens of the Fleet. In the *Calendar of State Papers* (Domestic, 1619-23) there is note of a letter from Rookwood to Sir Clement Edmondes (August 2, 1619), in which it is stated that 'the Warden has put into the dungeon called Boulton's Ward, a place newly made to exercise his cruelty, three poor men, Pecke, Seager and Myners, notwithstanding the express command of the Council that they should be favourably dealt with till further orders, they are starving from want of food.' In the spring of 1727 a Committee of the House of Commons was appointed to inquire into the management of Debtors' Prisons, and they brought to light a series of extortions and cruelties which would have been considered incredible were not the evidence so incontrovertible. When the Committee paid their first and unexpected visit to

SCENE IN THE FLEET PRISON. (COMMITTEE OF THE HOUSE OF COMMONS EXAMINING BAMBRIDGE) 1729.

the Fleet Prison, they found Sir William Rich confined in a loathsome dungeon and loaded with irons because he had given some slight offence to Bambridge. It was reported that a poor Portuguese, who had been manacled in a filthy hole for months, on being examined, supposed from something that was said that Bambridge might return to his post, and was so overcome with fear that he fainted and blood started out of his mouth and nose.

The picture was painted in 1729 by Hogarth for Sir Archibald Grant of Monymusk, a member of the Committee, and it is suggested that Hogarth may have obtained facilities for painting the picture through the good offices of Sir James Thornhill, who was also a member of the Committee.

The Committee appointed February 25, 1728-9, ' to examine the state of the gaols within the Kingdom ' was a large one. John Nichols gives in *Genuine Works*, vol. iii. (1817), the following as the principal members: James Oglethorpe, Esq., Chairman; The Right Hon. the Lords Finch, Morpeth, Inchiquin, Percival, Limerick; Sir Robert Sutton, Sir Robert Clifton, Sir Abraham Elton, Sir Edward Knatchbull, Sir Humphrey Herries, Hon. James Bertie, Sir Gregory Page, Sir Archibald Grant, Sir James Thornhill, Gyles Earle, Esq., General Wade, Humphrey Parsons, Esq., Hon. Robert Byng, Edward Houghton, Esq., Judge Advocate, Captain Vernon, Charles Selwyn, Esq., Vetters Cornwall, Esq., Thomas Scawen, Esq., Francis Child, Esq.,

William Hucks, Esq., Stampe Brookshank, Esq., Charles Withers, Esq., John La Roche, Esq., Mr. Thomas Martin. Many attended daily, and some of them twice a day.

In the foreground of the picture a prisoner explains the mode by which his hands and neck were fastened together by metal clasps. Some of the Committee are examining other instruments of torture in which the heads and necks of prisoners were screwed, and which seem rather to belong to the dungeons of the Inquisition than to a London debtors' prison.

The chairman (General Oglethorpe) is seen in an arm-chair at the head of the table. Sir Andrew Fountaine is on the chairman's left, and Lord Percival behind him. The prominent figure seated to the right of the table, examining the instrument of torture worn by a prisoner, is Sir William Wyndham. The man to the left addressed by the chairman is Bambridge.[1]

Hogarth gave his oil sketch for the picture to Horace Walpole, who greatly appreciated it. At the

[1] This picture and the 'Beggar's Opera' both belonged to Sir Archibald Grant and afterwards passed into the possession of William Huggins, son of the (at one time) Warden of the Fleet. Nichols thinks it probable that Huggins bought the pictures in 1731 when Sir Archibald was expelled from the House of Commons owing to an irregularity connected with the financial affairs of a Corporation for Relieving the Poor. Both pictures possessed a similarity in the ornamentation of the frames The frame of the 'Committee' was surmounted by a bust of Sir Francis Page with a halter round his neck, that of the 'Beggar's Opera' has a bust of Gay above. The picture of the 'Committee' at the National Portrait Gallery has no bust on its frame, but Mr. John Murray's picture of the 'Beggar's Opera' is still ornamented with Gay's bust.

Strawberry Hill sale it fetched £8, 5s., and now it is in the possession of Mr. Fairfax Murray. Walpole described this in his *Anecdotes of Painting*:

'The scene is the Committee; on the table are the instruments of torture. A prisoner in rags, half starved, appears before them; the poor man has a good countenance, which adds to the interest. On the other hand is the inhuman gaoler [Bambridge]. It is the very figure that Salvator Rosa would have drawn for Iago in the moment of detection. Villainy, fear and conscience are mixed in yellow and livid on his countenance; his lips are contracted by tremor, his face advances as eager to lie; his legs step back as thinking to make his escape; one hand is thrust precipitately into his bosom, the fingers of the other are catching uncertainly at his button holes. If this was a portrait, it is the most striking that ever was drawn; if it was not it is still finer.'

John Huggins purchased the Wardenship of the Fleet (a patent office) from the Earl of Clarendon for £5000. The term of the patent was for his own and his son's life, but his son William Huggins having no wish to take upon himself the responsibility of such an office, John Huggins, in August 1728, sold it to Thomas Bambridge and Dougal Cuthbert for the same amount he paid for it.

Huggins, no doubt, had much to answer for; but Bambridge managed to better such instructions as he had received, and bring things to a crisis within a year. The late G. A. Sala, in his little book on

Hogarth, draws a sort of distinction between the two men. He says Huggins's chief delight was to starve his prisoners unless they were rich enough to bribe him, but Bambridge's genius lay more towards confining his victims, charged with fetters, in underground dungeons, with the occasional recreation of attempting to pistol and stab them. The moneyed debtors both rascals smiled upon. Both Bambridge and Huggins were declared 'notoriously guilty of great breaches of trust, extortions, cruelties, and other high crimes and misdemeanors.' They were sent to Newgate, and Bambridge was disqualified by Act of Parliament from enjoying the office of Warden of the Fleet.

John Nichols, in a note on p. 19 of his *Biographical Anecdotes*, says that Mr. Rayner in his Reading on Stat. 2 Geo. II., chap. xxxii., whereby Bambridge was incapacitated to enjoy the office of Warden of the Fleet, has given the reader a very circumstantial account, with remarks on the notorious breaches of trust, etc., committed by Bambridge and other keepers of the Fleet Prison. For this publication see Worral's *Bibliotheca Legum*, by Brooke (1777), p. 16.

The picture painted for Sir Archibald Grant afterwards passed into the possession of William Huggins of Headly Park, Hants, at whose death in 1761 it was purchased by the Earl of Carlisle. It was exhibited in 1814, and in 1892 it was presented to the National Portrait Gallery by the present Earl.

The seventh plate of ' A Rake's Progress ' (Prison

"A Harlot's Progress." Plate 4. (Bridewell.) 1732.

Scene) represents the interior of a stone cell in the Fleet where Rakewell is confined after his ruin in a gambling-house (White's), as seen in Plate 6. Sarah Young falls into convulsions and is attended by three persons. At Rakewell's side stands his one-eyed wife, with clenched fists, vehemently denouncing him. The man sits helpless, bewildered, and despairing amid the overwhelming troubles that have fallen upon him.[1] He is in the first stage of that madness that has fallen upon him in the eighth and last scene.

The Fleet Prison was burned down in the Great Fire of 1666, rebuilt four years later; destroyed in the Gordon Riots 1780, and rebuilt in 1781. It was finally taken down in 1844.

The fourth plate of the 'Harlot's Progress' exhibits a scene in Bridewell, in which the peculiar features of that miserable place are shown. Men and women are beating hemp under the eye of a savage taskmaster, and a lad, too idle to work, is seen standing on tiptoe to reach the stocks, in which his hands are fixed, while over his head is written, ' Better to work than stand thus.' The harlot is the principal figure standing at the left of the picture handsomely dressed in a flowered brocade petticoat. She is about to beat with a heavy mallet a thick hank of oakum which lies before her on a large wooden block; very little of her work has been performed, and the warder who stands beside her

---

[1] *British Museum Catalogue*, vol. iii. p. 162.

angrily points to the state of the oakum and, holding
a rattan, is about to beat his prisoner.

The flogging at Bridewell is described by Ned
Ward in his *London Spy*. Both men and women
were whipped on their naked backs before the
Court of Governors. The president sat with his
hammer in his hand, and the culprit was taken from
the whipping-post when the hammer fell. The calls
to knock, when women were flogged, were loud and
incessant: 'O good Sir Robert, knock! Pray, good
Sir Robert, knock!' This became a common cry of
reproach among the lower orders, to denote that a
woman had been whipped as a harlot in Bridewell.

As a specimen of the atrocious manners of the time
it may be noted that it was one of the sights to see the
women flogged.

John Ireland quotes a paragraph from the *Grub
Street Journal* (1730) to show that there is no
exaggeration in respect to the dress of the harlot.
Here one Mary Moffat is described ' as beating hemp
in a gown very richly laced with silver.'

As a corroboration of the fact that Sir John
Gonson was the magistrate who apprehended the
harlot and committed her to Bridewell is seen, in
the hanging figure drawn in chalk on the wall, with
the inscription over it, 'Sir J. G.' Mr Stephens
expresses the opinion that this print was used as a
plea for the amelioration of the treatment of these
unfortunates in the prisons.[1]

[1] *British Museum Catalogue*, vol. iii. p. lxi.

Bridewell continued for many years to be used as a
'house of correction,' but on the erection of the City
Prison at Holloway in 1863 the materials of the
Bridewell Prison were sold by auction and cleared
away in the following years.

Hogarth made portraits of such criminals as Mary
Malcolm (1733), Elizabeth Canning (1753), Lord
Ferrers (1760), and Theodore Gardelle (1761).

Those miscreants, Francis Charteris and Mother
Needham, who are represented in the first plate of the
'Harlot's Progress,' have been already mentioned in
Chapter IX. (Tavern Life).

A highwayman is among the company at White's
in the sixth plate of the 'Rake's Progress,' and in the
third plate of the 'Harlot's Progress' the wig-box of
James Dalton, another notorious highwayman, is
seen among the miscellaneous contents of the harlot's
room, when she is about to be apprehended by Sir
John Gonson.

Sarah Malcolm, a laundress in the Temple, was
executed in March 1733 at the Fetter Lane end of
Fleet Street, opposite Mitre Court, for three murders,
viz. Mrs. Lydia Duncomb and her two servants,
Elizabeth Harrison and Ann Price, living in Tanfield
Court, Temple. When she sat to Hogarth for her
portrait in the condemned cell she had, according to
Walpole, put on red to look the better. When he
was at work the painter said to Sir James Thornhill,
'I see by this woman's features that she is capable of
any wickedness.'

The portrait was painted for Horace Walpole, who gave Hogarth five guineas for it. It was sold at the Strawberry Hill sale in 1842 to Charles Kirkpatrick Sharpe for £24, 3s.

Hogarth painted another portrait,—a whole length (the original being three-quarters), which was in the possession of Joshua Boydell in 1793. An engraving of this is to be found in John Ireland's *Hogarth Illustrated* (vol. ii.). It was exhibited in 1814 by the Earl of Mulgrave.

She was twenty years of age when she was executed, and therefore a fine portrait of a comely middle-aged woman exhibited by Sir Frederick Cook, Bart., at the Winter Exhibition of the Royal Academy (1908) cannot well be a portrait of the murderess.

A portrait of Elizabeth Canning, painted in prison, belonged to the Earl of Mulgrave in 1833. The extraordinary case of this woman's false swearing produced a great public excitement. She fully described her alleged abduction and ill-treatment, and on her false statement Mary Squires, a gypsy, and Susannah Wells were indicted. Being found guilty Squires was condemned to death, and Wells to be branded and imprisoned for six months. The case is not likely to be forgotten, for one reason, that Fielding was deceived by the woman and wrote a pamphlet in her favour, entitled *A Clear State of the Case of Elizabeth Canning*, 1733. Sir Crisp Gascoyne, the Lord Mayor, was convinced of the fraud, and succeeded in obtaining the pardon of

Squires. Canning was brought to trial in 1754 and found guilty of perjury. She was transported to New England, but was afterwards released, and a subscription being raised for her she became a schoolmistress. She married a Quaker and lived till 1773. The public feeling was all along strongly in favour of Canning, and Gascoyne suffered much obloquy from his labours in bringing her to justice. The full-length portrait of Lawrence Shirley, Earl Ferrers, the murderer, who was executed in 1763, was exhibited at Whitechapel (Georgian England) 1906, by Mr. Frederick M. Cutbush of The Hobby, Maidstone.

A portrait of Theodore Gardelle, engraved by S. Ireland, will be found in his *Graphic Illustrations*, 1794. The sketch was by Mr. Richards, and only touched on by Hogarth. Gardelle was born in Geneva in 1721, and only arrived in London from Paris in 1760. He found employment as a miniature painter, and lived in Leicester Square at the house of a Mrs. Anne King. He murdered her in a brutal manner and concealed her body. He was arrested on the 27th of February 1761, and was executed at the corner of Panton Street, Haymarket, on the following 4th of April. His body was hung in chains on Hounslow Heath.

We have already dealt in Chapter VIII. (Business Life) with the incidents of the life of the Industrious Apprentice, who was Hogarth's favourite, which are all of the greatest interest. The incidents of the life of the Idle Apprentice, naturally, come under the heading of crime, but they need not detain us long. The artist was not careful to mark his fall with the same elaboration, and in consequence it seems to be too violent. Plate 3, where the Idle Apprentice is seen at play in the churchyard, is one of the best of the series. Plate 5 shows him sent to sea, and contains a view of a reach in the Thames known as Cuckold's Point in the distance, and three vessels off that promontory; the pathetic element of the picture centres in the poor widowed mother, who is weeping over the sad state of her son, and filled with horror at his recklessness. In Plate 7 Tom Idle returned from sea is in a garret with a prostitute. In Plate 9 he is betrayed by this woman. The cellar in which he is found is said to have been a notorious place called Blood Bowl House, Blood Bowl Alley, Fleet Street, afterwards known as Hanging Sword Alley, Whitefriars.[1] The latter appears always to have been the official name, and the former to have been only the popular name. Dickens refers to Hanging Sword Alley in *Bleak House*; Mr. Marks, in his *Tyburn Tree*, gives an account of the robbery of Mr. or Captain George Morgan by James Stansbury and Mary his wife. He writes : ' The case is very

[1] In Chapter VIII. (Business Life) there is a notice of a series of drawings by Hogarth for the engravings of 'Industry and Idleness' in the Print Room of the British Museum. Mr Dobson points out that in the sketch for Plate 7 a rat is added, and there is a sword in place of the petticoat over the bed, and he suggests that probably this is intended to indicate that the garret was in Hanging Sword Alley, the scene of the cellar in Plate 9 (See *W. Hogarth*, 1907, p. 250, note.)

"Industry and Idleness." Plate 11. 1747. (The Idle Apprentice executed at Tyburn.)

interesting as having furnished to Hogarth the motive of one of his prints in the series of " The Effects of Industry and Idleness." ' Captain Morgan going home in the early hours of the morning of July 17, 1743, seeing a lady in the street, feared for her safety and gallantly offered to escort her home. He was taken into a house where he was robbed and assaulted. The house in Hanging Sword Alley, Fleet Street, bore an execrable reputation, in virtue of which it was known as ' Blood Bowl House.' At the trial Mary Stansbury asked a witness, ' Have I not let you go all over the house, to see if there were any trap-doors as it was represented ? ' The witness Sharrock replied that he had looked all over the house and saw no trap-door. It will be recollected that in Hogarth's print the body of a murdered man is being thrust through a trap-door. The same witness spoke of the house as ' Blood Bowl House.' Stansbury asked him how he came to know of the Blood Bowl, to which Sharrock replied that he had seen it in the newspapers. Mr. Marks adds that he had been less fortunate; he had not found accounts in contemporary newspapers referring to the name or to the trap-door.

Plate 10, where Tom Idle is brought up before his former comrade, now an Alderman of London, in the Court-house at Guildhall, has already been referred to. We now come to Plate 11, the finest picture of all, in which Idle is executed at Tyburn. This is the best view of Tyburn in existence, and gives a vivid picture of the scenes which were constantly occurring. The Rev. Mr. Gilpin wrote: 'We seldom see a crowd more beautifully managed than in this print,' and he is quite right. The composition, in spite of innumerable details, is thoroughly harmonious. Mr. Marks gives this as the best illustration of the Triple Tree in 1747 in his interesting work on *Tyburn Tree*, which is a monument of well-planned research and by far the best authority on the subject.

Like the ' March to Finchley,' the picture of the execution of the Idle Apprentice is admirably arranged and the figures grouped with all Hogarth's remarkable facility. In the background are seen the hills of Hampstead and Highgate.

An execution was made the occasion of regular holiday-making and a round of diversions. It was one of the sorriest sights to be seen in the eighteenth century, and naturally the vivid delineator of the manners of the century painted the scene. Nevertheless the very thought of such orgies taking place on the occasion of the ignominious death of a human being fills one with horror, and sorrow for the brutality of our ancestors.

The ' Four Stages of Cruelty ' (1751) are the most painful and repulsive of Hogarth's works, and one's first impulse is to pass them by, but this cannot be done. The atrocities of Tom Nero seem to be too horrible for representation, but the artist had his reasons for his work. He remarks : ' The leading points in these, as well as the two preceding prints (*i.e.* 'Beer Street' and 'Gin Lane') were made as obvious as possible in the hope that their tendency might be seen by men of the lowest rank. Neither minute accuracy of design, nor fine engraving were deemed necessary, as the latter would render them too expensive for the persons to whom they were intended to be useful. And the fact is, that the passions may be more frankly expressed by a strong bold stroke, than by the most delicate engraving. To expressing them as I felt them I have paid the utmost attention, and as they were addressed to hard hearts, have rather preferred leaving them hard, and giving the effect, by a quick touch, to rendering them languid and feeble by fine strokes and soft engraving; which require more care and practice than can often be obtained, except by a man of a very quiet turn of mind. . . . The prints were engraved with the hope of in some degree correcting that barbarous treatment of animals the very sight of which renders the streets of our Metropolis so distressing to every feeling mind. If they have had that effect and checked the progress of cruelty, I am more proud of having been the author, than I should be of having painted Raffaelle's 'Cartoons.'[1]

We may pass by the First Stage in which Tom Nero is shown as one of the boys in St. Giles's Charity School. In the Second Stage he is a hackney coach-

[1] *Anecdotes of William Hogarth*, by J. B. Nichols, 1833, pp. 64-5.

man.   The scene is laid at the gate of Thavie's Inn,
Holborn.   The longest shilling fare in London was
from that Inn of Chancery to Westminster, and the
foreground of the picture is occupied by four lawyers
in wigs and gowns who have clubbed their three-
pence each for the hackney coach No. 24, T. Nero,
driver, to carry them to Westminster Hall.   The
coach comes to a stop from the horse having fallen
on its knees, broken its legs and overthrown the
vehicle.   The driver beats the horse on its head
with the butt of a whip.

John Ireland says with respect to this scene:
' A man taking the number of the coach is marked by
traits of benevolence, which separate him from the
savage ferocity of Nero, or the guilty terror of these
affrighted lawyers.'

' Cruelty in Perfection ' shows Nero as a prisoner
brought to view the body of his murdered mistress.
The last scene, ' The Reward of Cruelty,' requires
some fuller comment, although it is singularly
repulsive.

The scene of the dissection of Tom Nero takes
place in the theatre of the Barber-Surgeons Company
in Monkwell Street.   It was built in 1636-7 after the
design of Inigo Jones.   It was restored under the
direction of the Earl of Burlington in 1730-1, and
pulled down in 1783.   It has been supposed by some
that the dissecting theatre represented the Surgeons'
Hall in the Old Bailey, and there is this reason for
the opinion that the surgeons separated from the

barbers in 1745. Although this was the case, the surgeons had not a dissecting theatre ready, and it was necessary for a time to continue at the old theatre. The first Court of Assistants of the Surgeons Company was held at their new theatre in the Old Bailey in August 1751, but it was not until 1753 that the first Masters of Anatomy were selected and the first dissections were undertaken in accordance with the Act of 1752.

Mr. Marks gives in his *Tyburn Tree* an illustration of the body of a murderer dissected according to the Act of 1752, which is inscribed ' The Body of a Murderer exposed in the Theatre of the Surgeons' Hall Old Bailey.' This is a different building from that represented in Hogarth's print, which has two windows at the back that are not seen in the other engraving. John Ireland suggests that the President in the Chair much resembles the eminent surgeon John Freke.

CHAPTER XIII

THE SUBURBS

THE suburbs of Hogarth's day have now become an integral part of the town, and in some cases almost its heart. Marylebone and Tyburn were in his time country villages, and in the *Evening Post* of March 16, 1715, we read that ' On Wednesday last, four gentlemen were robbed and stripped in the fields between London and Marylebon.'

The New Road (now the Marylebone, Euston and Pentonville Roads) was formed in 1756 through a rural district, and all north of the road was country. The Duke of Bedford, who then lived on the north side of Bloomsbury Square, unsuccessfully opposed its construction on the ground that the dust created by the traffic would completely spoil the gardens at the back of his mansion.

Tottenham Court Road was quite rural until the beginning of the nineteenth century, and on the east side of the road there was an extensive farm.

Hogarth has immortalised the upper part of the road where it joins the Hampstead Road, and the turnpike was placed in one of his finest pictures, presented by the artist to the Foundling Hospital, and known as ' The March to Finchley.'

"The March to Finchley." 1750.

After the Jacobite rising in 1745 a camp was formed at Finchley, and the Foot Guards represented in this picture, who had been hurriedly recalled from the Low Countries and Germany, are bound for Scotland and on their way to the camp.

Mr. Stephens gives a very full description of the incidents in the picture in his *Catalogue of Satires in the British Museum* (vol. iii. p. 512).

The two public-houses form the prominent features in the picture, viz. the Adam and Eve on the west side and the King's Head on the east side. The Adam and Eve still stands at the corner of the Hampstead and Marylebone Roads, and the King's Head was only taken down in the summer of 1906 in order to allow of the widening of the Hampstead Road. The Adam and Eve was originally the manor-house of the prebendal manor of Tothill, Totenhall, or Tottenham Court, described in Domesday and originally appertaining to the Dean and Chapter of St. Paul's. The first notice of it as a place of public entertainment is contained in the books of the parish of St. Giles's in the Fields under the year 1645, when Mrs. Stacye's maid and two others were fined a shilling apiece 'for drinking at Tottenhall Court on the Sabbath daie.' Ben Jonson, however, appears to allude to the place at a rather earlier date, when he makes Quarlous say to Win-Wife in *Bartholomew Fair*, 1614, 'Because she is in possibility to be your daughter-in-law, and may ask your blessing hereafter when she *courts* it to *Totnam* to eat cream.'

The tea-gardens were for many years a popular resort, and here on May 16, 1785, Vincent Lunardi effected the second descent from his balloon.

In course of time the gardens lost their credit and became the resort of highwaymen and footpads, when about 1811 the music-room was abolished, the skittle-grounds destroyed, and the gardens dug up for the foundation of the present Eden Street, a name more appropriate to the association with Adam and Eve than to the beauty of the situation.

Under the signboard of the inn is inscribed *Tottenham Court Nursery*, in allusion to the boxing-booth at which the celebrated pugilist Broughton exhibited his prowess. In the background beneath the signboard are two combatants. John Ireland says that a little fellow of meagre frame who joins in the fray is a portrait of a well-known man usually styled Jockey James. 'Jockey had a son who rendered himself eminent by boxing with Smallwood, and many other athletic pugilists. The French pyeman, grenadier and chimney sweeper are also taken from the life, and said by those who recollect their persons, to be very faithful resemblances of the persons intended.'[1]

Lord Albemarle Bertie, who is the chief character in the picture of the 'Cockpit,' is also introduced into the 'March to Finchley.' John Nichols informs us that the chimney-sweeper and one of the young fifers were hired by Hogarth, 'who gave each of

[1] *Hogarth Illustrated*, vol. ii. p. 139 (note).

them half a crown for his patience in sitting while his likeness was taken.' [1]

The King's Head on the opposite side of the road has a sign of the portrait of Charles II., but the house that has lately been destroyed had the head of Henry VIII. On the roof of the King's Arms is a meeting of cats, which is intended to give a key to the character of the women who fill every window of the house and are presided over by the infamous Mother Douglas.

This picture, which represents a scene of confusion and disorder, is a triumphant example of Hogarth's supreme power in the arrangement and grouping of his characters.

Arthur Murphy in an article in the *Gray's Inn Journal* draws attention to the dramatic power of the picture, and to the genius of Hogarth in speaking directly to the spectator by means of the eye alone— he, at least, uses a universal language: 'The æra may arrive, when, through the instability of the English language, the style of *Joseph Andrews* and *Tom Jones* shall be obliterated, when the characters shall be unintelligible, and the humour lose its relish; but the many personages which the manner-painting hand of Hogarth has called forth into mimic life will not fade so soon from the canvas, and that admirable picturesque comedy, *The March to Finchley*, will perhaps divert posterity as long as the Foundling Hospital shall do honour to the British nation.'

[1] *Biographical Anecdotes*, p. 246.

An account of how the picture came into the possession of the Foundling will be found in Chapter XI. (Hospitals).

Hogarth wished to dedicate the print of his great picture to George II., and arrangements were made for the King to see the painting. The incident of its reception by the man who hated 'bainting and boetry' is too well known to be repeated here in its entirety. Suffice it to say, that George II. ended his inspection of the picture with the indignant speech, 'What! a bainter burlesque a soldier? he deserves to be bicketed for his insolence! Take his drumpery out of my sight.'[1]

Hogarth was so chagrined that in revenge he inscribed the engraving to Frederick the Great, the King of Prussia, as 'an encourager of Arts and Sciences.' The 'March to Finchley' was engraved by Luke Sullivan, who is described by John Ireland as follows: 'Sullivan was so eccentric a character that while he was engraving this print Hogarth held out every possible inducement to his remaining at his house in Leicester Square night and day, for if Luke quitted it, he was not visible for a month. It has been said, but I know not on what authority, that for engraving it he was paid only one hundred pounds.'[2]

Mr. Austin Dobson refers to the 'March to Finchley' as Sullivan's masterpiece as an engraver.

---

[1] *Hogarth Illustrated*, vol. ii. p. 133
[2] *Ibid*, vol. iii p 353

He also tells us that Sullivan was the angel in ' Paul before Felix.'

Mr. Stephens enumerates nine states of the plate, and adds that the engraver's outline in pencil is in the Print Room of the British Museum.

The States 1 to 6 are as follows :

1. The etching in the British Museum.

2. The finished plate without writing below (very rare).

3. Inscribed 'Painted by Willm Hogarth & Publish'd Dec^br 30 1750. According to Act of Parliament. A Representation of the March of the Guards towards Scotland, in the year 1745. To his Majesty the King of Prusia, an encourager of Arts and Sciences ! This Plate is most humbly dedicated. Engrav'd by Luke Sullivan.'

4. The first part of the inscription is changed to ' Painted & Publish'd by Willm Hogarth Dec^br 30 1750.'

3 and 4 constitute what is called ' the Sunday print,' because it was found that the 30th December 1750 fell on a Sunday.

5. The date is altered to Dec^br 31st.

6. The dedication line stopped out, preparatory to correcting the error in spelling the word ' Prussia.'

In States 3, 4, 5 and 6 the word ' Prussia ' has been engraved with one ' s ' only, another ' s ' has been added above the line, but without a caret, with a pen and ink.[1]

---

[1] *British Museum Catalogue*, vol. iii p 517.

Respecting this John Nichols writes : ' I have
been assured that only twenty-five were worked off
with this literal imperfection, as Hogarth grew tired
of adding the mark ~ with a pen over one S, to supply
the want of the other.   He therefore ordered the
inscription to be corrected before any greater number
of impressions were taken.   Though this circumstance was mentioned by Mr. Thane, to whose ver-
acity and experience in such matters the greatest
attention is due, it is difficult to suppose that
Hogarth was fatigued with correcting his own
mistake in so small a number of the first impressions.
I may venture to add, that I have seen, at least, five
and twenty marked in the manner already described ;
and it is scarce possible, considering the multitudes
of these plates dispersed in the world, that I should
have met with all that were so distinguished.' [1]

With regard to No. 6 John Ireland wrote : ' I have
an early impression of this print, in which the dedication to the King of Prussia does not appear, and it
might pass for a proof.   On inquiry I find that upon
one of Hogarth's fastidious friends objecting to its
being dedicated to a foreign potentate, he replied,
" If you disapprove of it you shall have one without
any dedication," and took off a few impressions,
covering the dedication with fan paper.' [2]

7. The spelling of ' Prussia ' is corrected, and the
following   addition   below   the   engraver's   name :

[1] *Biographical Anecdotes*, 1782, p 243 (note).
[2] *Hogarth Illustrated*, vol. iii. p. 353.

MARYLEBONE CHURCH. ("A RAKE'S PROGRESS." NO. 5.) 1735.
From the original painting in the Soane Museum.

' Retouched and Improved by Wm. Hogarth, re-publish'd June 12th 1761.'

Respecting this inscription John Nichols writes: ' The *improvements* in it, however, remain to be discovered by better eyes than mine.' [1]

8. Mr. Stephens says the plate has been worked on by another and less skilful hand.

9. Much worked on and used for James Heath's edition of Hogarth's works. [2]

The subscription ticket for the ' March to Finchley ' represents a trophy of military weapons, tools and musical instruments used in war (bagpipes, etc.) designed and engraved by Hogarth.

The interior of old Marylebone Church (originally built in the year 1400) is seen in the fifth plate of the ' Rake's Progress,' which was published in 1735. The church was then nearing the end of its days, for in 1741 it was pulled down and the old church now in High Street, Marylebone, was built on its site. The Bishop of London of the day gave orders that all the old tablets should be fixed as nearly as possible in their former places, and the inscription on the front of the gallery pews in the picture is still to be seen.

The great Francis Bacon was married in Hogarth's church in 1606, and Sheridan was married to Miss Linley in the still standing church in 1773.   John

---

[1] *Biographical Anecdotes,* 1782, p. 243.

[2] Mr. Stephens's description of the nine states is given in the *British Museum Catalogue,* vol. iii. pp. 517-18.

Ireland says that in Hogarth's time Marylebone Church was at such a distance from London that it became the favoured resort of those who desired to be privately married. The Rake would naturally not wish to show his deformed wife before a large audience. A great change was about to take place in the relative position of the suburbs to the town, for at the end of the eighteenth century London had joined Marylebone. Ireland notes that while at the date of the Revolution (1688) ' the annual amount of the taxes for the whole parish was four and twenty pounds ; in 1788 the annual amount was four and twenty thousand.' [1] There are three satirical points in the picture which should be noted. The Commandments are broken and the Creed is destroyed by the damp, but the third is the most striking—the poor-box is covered with a cobweb, so that alms-giving evidently had been neglected. Ireland suggests that the broken Commandments ' probably gave the hint to a lady's reply, on being told that thieves had the preceding night broken into the church, and stolen the communion plate and the Ten Commandments. " I can suppose," added the informant, "that they may melt and sell the plate ; but can you divine for what possible purpose they could steal the Commandments ? " " To break them, to be sure," replied she ; " to break them." ' [2]

The Rev. William Gilpin points out that the church

[1] *Hogarth Illustrated,* vol. i. p. 46 (note).
[2] *Ibid,* vol. i. p. 47 (note).

is too small, and that it is divided disagreeably down the centre; but he was answered that, although he is right in his criticism, Hogarth painted what he saw.

A dog making friends with a one-eyed comrade is said to be drawn from the painter's favourite Trump.

The outside of Marylebone Church is supposed to be represented in the Third Stage of 'Cruelty,' or 'Cruelty in Perfection,' where the vile Tom Nero is taken prisoner for the murder of the girl who trusted in him and robbed her mistress for his sake.

'To lawless love, when once betray'd
Soon crime to crime succeeds;
At length beguil'd to theft, the maid
By her beguiler bleeds.'

There is little of the church to judge from, and it may, as some suggest, represent old St. Pancras Church.

The scene of the 'Idle Apprentice at Play in the Churchyard during Divine Service' (Plate 3) has not been identified, but it is either in London or the suburbs. Mr. Stephens, as previously noted, suggests that there are points of resemblance to the churches of St. Michael, Crooked Lane, and St. Paul, Shadwell. The parish beadle in the background, dressed in his gown and gold-laced hat, as well as the shield bearing the arms of the City of London over the door, seem to point to its being a City church.

Mr. Austin Dobson writes: 'There is no more eloquent stroke in the whole of Hogarth than that by which the miserable player at " halfpenny under the hat," in Plate 3, is shown to have but a plank between him and the grave.'

Tyburn was an extreme western suburb of London, and executions took place there for many centuries. The last person executed at Tyburn was John Austin on November 3, 1783, and although the executions before Newgate remained for many years a gross scandal, the scenes exhibited there never equalled in atrocity those which continually occurred at Tyburn.

Tyburn gallows was a triangle in plan, having three legs to stand upon. The Elizabethan writers constantly alluded to it and used it often in an idealised form, as Biron in *Love's Labour's Lost*:

> ' Thou mak'st the triumphery, the corner cap of society,
> The shape of Love's Tyburn, that hangs up simplicity.'

The Triple Tree first came into existence in 1571 at the execution of Dr. John Story, and Hogarth's picture (referred to in the last chapter) of the execution of the Idle Apprentice shows it not long before its abolition. It was fixed in the open space at the end of Edgware Road, formed by the junction of the roads near where the Marble Arch now stands. Between June 18 and October 23, 1759, the old triangular gallows, in use for nearly two hundred years, was removed, and the new movable gallows superseded it. This was ordinarily set up near the union of Bryanston Street and Edgware Road. The site of the fixed gallows was afterwards occupied by the toll-house of the turnpike removed from the east corner of Park Lane.[1]

Spitalfields, situated in the east of London between Bishopsgate and Bethnal Green, has been the favoured home of the silk weavers since the French Protestant refugees settled in this country after the iniquitous revocation of the Edict of Nantes in 1685. This suburb is the scene of the first plate of the 'Fellow Apprentices at the Looms,' where Thomas Idle is asleep and the cat on the floor is playing with his shuttle, while Goodchild is busily engaged in his proper occupation.

The two chief places of entertainment of eighteenth-century London were Ranelagh and Vauxhall Gardens. To the first Hogarth does not appear to have made any allusion, although he must have been an attendant of the Gardens. The Rotunda was a favoured scene of the masquerades arranged by the famous Heidegger, about which something has been said in a former chapter. Ranelagh flourished from 1742 to 1803, but no traces of it exist now. The site is included in Chelsea Hospital Garden, between Church Row and the river to the end of the hospital, the roadway, and the barracks.

Hogarth was intimately connected with Jonathan Tyers and Vauxhall Gardens. Although he did not make any sketch of them, or introduce them into any of his pictures, he suggested their decoration by paintings, and helped that object forward.

---

[1] Alfred Marks, *Tyburn Tree*, pp. 69, 70, 249.

South Lambeth (which included Vauxhall) was considered to have a pleasant climate, and many Londoners went there in the summer for change of air. Hogarth married in 1729, and soon afterwards went with his wife to South Lambeth. In 1733 he settled in Leicester Fields. When he was in the country he made the acquaintance of Tyers. Vauxhall Gardens had a long life, for we know that it was a favourite resort in the time of Samuel Pepys, although its real period of success was inaugurated by Tyers, who took a lease of the place in 1728, and eventually acquired the freehold of the original Gardens and of some acres of land which he added to them. For a time he did little with the place until in 1732 he started his famous *Ridotto al fresco*.

There is a tradition that Tyers was becoming tired of his venture when he took Hogarth into his confidence, with the result that on the painter's advice steps were taken which assured the success of the Gardens. There is no definite authority for this, and it seems strange that Hogarth, who was so violent an opponent of Heidegger's masquerades, should have suggested their adoption at Vauxhall. It may be, however, that his objection was chiefly to the close rooms of the Opera House, and that he saw no harm in a modified form of the same amusement in the fresh air. We do know, however, that Hogarth was a friend to Tyers, and enthusiastic in the support of his friend's management of Vauxhall Gardens.

On Wednesday, June 7, 1732, Tyers held his first

grand *Ridotto al fresco*, the price of admission to which was one guinea. About four hundred of the *élite* of London Society came in boat-loads from town, and Frederick, Prince of Wales (who continued a patron of the Gardens till his death) came down the river from Kew in his barge.

Thus set in the prosperity of the Gardens which continued well into the nineteenth century. Then came a time of decay and a discreditable old age ending in 1859.

For a century the Gardens filled a distinguished place in English life—the novelists and the essayists are full of its glories ; the letter-writers also, for is not Horace Walpole's description of the supper-party at Vauxhall, of which the writer, Lady Caroline Petersham, and the ' Pollard ' Ashe were the principal characters, one of the most brilliant and delightful pages in the correspondence of that most charming of gossips ?

Mr. Warwick Wroth tells us that ' when Tyers leased the Gardens there was in the dwelling-house a " Ham room," so that this famous Vauxhall viand must have been already in request. The thinness of the slices was proverbial. A journal of 1762, for instance, complains that you could read the newspaper through a slice of Tyers's ham or beef. A certain carver, hardly perhaps mythical, readily obtained employment from the proprietor when he promised to cut a ham so thin that the slices would cover the whole garden like a carpet of red and white.'[1] It was considered unsafe to carry a plateful of ham from one box to another in case the slices were blown away.

There must have been a long succession of these ham-cutters, for Thackeray speaks of 'almost invisible slices of ham,' and a friend of the writer's tells how his father enlarged on the wonderful performances of this artist.

Why was it that these Gardens kept up their character for so long a period of time ? It was because the respectable classes continued to visit them, and their presence kept the vicious in order. Families went there in glass coaches or boats and kept together the whole evening. The novelists are full of the dangers attending those who strayed and found themselves unprotected in the dark walks.

Mr. W. B. Boulton writes : ' During the height of their vogue there was a certain etiquette at the Gardens ; ladies came in full evening dress, and the men walked bareheaded, with their hats under their arms. A stately promenade of the main walks of the garden was usually a function which began the delights of the evening for the more fashionable of the company. Then followed the concert, invariably composed of sixteen pieces, songs alternating with instrumental performances—the songs of a very sentimental cast—the sonatas and symphonies for the band being often of a higher musical quality. Tyers, however, engaged the finest voices of his day

[1] *The London Pleasure Gardens*, 1896, p. 299.

to warble the tender ballads for which the place was famous ; and men like Thomas Lowe and Vernon, and lady singers like Mrs. Arne, Miss Stevenson, Miss Wright, Mrs. Baddeley and Mrs. Weichsell, no doubt supplied the charm which the songs themselves—all about Strephon and Delia and Cupid—seem to lack to-day.'[1]

To return to Hogarth. He painted for one of the larger saloons the picture of Henry the Eighth and Anne Boleyn, which was engraved by the artist himself and published in 1729. He is said to have drawn the King from Frederick, Prince of Wales, and Anne Boleyn from the Prince's mistress, Anne Vane.

'Yet Vane could tell what ills from beauty spring.'

This was not one of the pictures sold in 1841 at the sale of movable property in the Gardens. Hogarth allowed his 'Four Times of the Day' to be copied by Hayman. At the sale just referred to, five pictures attributed to Hogarth were sold at the prices here noted : ' Drunken Man,' £4, 4s. ; ' A Woman pulling out an Old Man's Grey Hairs,' £3, 3s. ; ' Harper and Miss Raftor (afterwards Mrs. Clive), as Jobson the Cobbler and his Wife Nell in Coffey's farce of the *Devil to Pay*,' £4, 4s. ; ' The Happy Family,' £3, 15s. ; 'Children at Play,' £4, 11s. 6d. Whether any of these, or any part of them, were by Hogarth it is impossible to say. Mr. Dobson states that the picture of ' Harper and Mrs. Clive' is attributed to Hayman

[1] *The Amusements of Old London*, 1901, vol. ii. p. 27.

in L. Truchy's contemporary print from the painting.   Certainly they were in a bad condition from
constant exposure; the canvas was nailed to boards,
and little remained of any beauty they once may
have possessed.   The free pass presented by Tyers
to Hogarth, which now belongs to Mr. Fairfax
Murray, has already been referred to. (See *ante*,
p. 40.)

In the eighteenth century tea-gardens were to be
found all over the suburbs, and the author of an
article in an old magazine estimated that the
number of visitors to these gardens every Sunday
amounted to at least 20,000, and the money spent
in the course of the day on refreshments to about
£25,000.   In fine weather these gardens were not
large enough to accommodate all the people that
came out of the town for entertainment, and the
fields around were also crowded.

Hogarth has taken Sadler's Wells, or rather the
New River opposite Sadler's Wells, as the subject of
'Evening.'   This place was opened in 1684, in which
year was published, by Dr. Thomas Guidott, a
pamphlet setting forth the virtues of the medicinal
water; and for a time the gardens were styled New
Tunbridge Wells, but the latter designation was
given up when the Islington Spa took the additional
name of 'New Tunbridge Wells.'   The natural
confusion between Islington Wells and Sadler's Wells
shows how close to each other these tea-gardens were
placed.

Sadler, who gave his name to the gardens, made the most of the virtues of the waters, so that Epsom and Tunbridge Wells found them to be a formidable rival, and a pamphlet was published in the interest of the country wells protesting against the horrid plot to injure them. This may have had some effect, for the Clerkenwell Gardens went out of fashion for a time; but in the eighteenth century the water-drinking was discontinued and the Gardens became a favourite resort of the Londoners.

Hogarth's picture was engraved in 1738, and is described as follows by Mr. F. G. Stephens in his *British Museum Catalogue* (vol. iii. p. 268): ' This engraving represents a rural suburb on the north side of London, with the entrance to a building marked " Sadler's Wells " over the porch, a covered gateway in the garden wall on our left ; on our right, nearer the foreground, is a public-house with a sign, comprising in an oval medallion a portrait of " Sr Hugh Midleton." Through a window open in the side of the house a party of men appear within, smoking most energetically. The background is a landscape including two cottages, one of which has a pendent signboard, and hills and trees.'

The building at Sadler's Wells was at this time a music house; and it was not turned into a theatre until later in the century, although miscellaneous entertainments of rope-dancing and tumbling took place in the old house.

The rural character of the Gardens continued for

many years, and the man and his wife who are walking in the heat along the road one would expect to be eager to rest themselves under 'the shady trees' in a scene which is enthusiastically described in a 'New Song on Sadler's Wells, 1740':

> 'These pleasant streams of Middleton
> In gentle murmurs glide along,
> In which the sporting fishes play
> To close each wearied Summer's day.
> And Musick's charms in welling sounds
> Of mirth and harmony abounds;
> While nymphs and swains with beaux and belles
> All praise the joys of Sadler's Wells.
> The herds around o'er herbage green
> And bleating flocks are sporting seen,
> While Phœbus with its brightest rays
> The fertile soil doth seem to praise.'

Mr. Wroth, who quotes this song, adds: 'As late as 1803 mention is made of the tall poplars, graceful willows, sloping banks and flowers of Sadler's Wells.'[1]

The man and his wife and children in the foreground of the picture are in fact turning their backs on Sadler's Wells. The artist goes out of his way to show contempt for the unfortunate husband by making the horns of the cow behind fit upon his head. John Ireland says of them: 'It is not easy to imagine fatigue better delineated than in the appearance of this *amiable pair*. In a few of the earliest impressions, Hogarth painted the man's hands in blue, to shew that he was a dyer, and the woman's face in red to intimate her extreme heat. The lady's

---

[1] *London Pleasure Gardens*, 1896, p. 45.

aspect at once explains her character ; we are certain that she was born to command. As to her husband, God made him, and he must pass for a man ; what his wife has made him, is indicated by the cow's horns, which are so placed as to become his own. The hope of the family, with a cockade, riding upon papa's cane, seems much dissatisfied with female sway. A face with more of the shrew in embryo than that of the girl, is scarcely possible to conceive.' [1]

Mr. Stephens describes three states of the plate. Of the first, three copies only are known ; in this the figure of the scolding girl does not occur, nor the inscription over the door of 'Sadler's Wells.' On the margin of the copy in the Print Room of the British Museum is the following MS. note : ' This proof was deliver'd by Mr. Baron to Mr. Hogarth, & it being told him, this boy has no apparent cause to wimper (*sic*) he put in his sister, threatening him to deliver his gingerbread King, now he put in Cause. The character Hogarth altered where he is crying.' Also ' Engrav'd by M. Baron price 5 Shillings.' [2]

It is worthy of mention that, although the New River is only indicated by a few lines in the foreground, yet its object is clearly indicated by a piece of wooden piping on the bank, such as was used to convey the water to the waterworks and houses.

Although Southwark was not strictly a suburb, Hogarth's great picture, ' A Fair, the Humours of a

[1] *Hogarth Illustrated*, vol. i. p. 142.
[2] *Catalogue of Satires in the British Museum*, vol iii. p. 269.

Fair,' which presents one of the finest of his arrangements of a crowd, naturally comes in for notice in this
chapter.   Walpole refers to it as Bartholomew Fair,
but this is a mistake on his part by reason of his
confusing the two fairs.

Southwark Fair was called also Our Lady Fair, and
St. Margaret's Fair.   It was held in the highway of
the borough, and in the courts and inn-yards between
the Tabard and the church of St. George the Martyr.
It was one of the three great fairs of importance
described in a Proclamation of Charles I. as 'unto
which there is usually extraordinary resort out of all
parts of the kingdom.'   The others were Bartholomew
Fair, and Sturbridge Fair near Cambridge.   Our
Lady's Fair was of considerable antiquity, and liberty
to hold it on September 7, 8, 9 was granted to the
City of London by the charter of 2 Edward IV.
(November 2, 1462).   It had probably been held
informally long before this.   Although the time
allowed by charter was only three days, the fair
continued, like other fairs, for fourteen days.   The
amusements of Southwark Fair were much the same
as those at St. Bartholomew's, and the booth proprietors moved from one to the other, but at Southwark the acrobat and rope-dancer were the most
popular among the performers.

Pepys went to Southwark Fair on September 21,
1668, where he saw a puppet-show and was much
interested in Jacob Hall's dancing on the ropes—
'mightily worth seeing.'   He asked Hall 'whether he

Southwark Fair

had ever any mischief by falls in his time. He told me " Yes, many, but never to the breaking of a limb." He seems a mighty strong man.' Rather later than this, but before Hogarth's time, William Joyce, a strong man, exhibited here. Ward describes him as ' the Southwark Sampson, who breaks Carmen's Ribs with a hug, snaps Cables like Twine Thread, and throws Dray Horses upon their backs, with as much ease as a Westphalia Hog can crack a Cocoa Nut.' When he exhibited before William III. he lifted 1 ton and $14\frac{1}{2}$ lbs. of lead, tied a very strong rope round himself to which was attached a strong horse, and although the horse was whipped it failed to move him ; the rope he afterwards snapped like packthread. ' We are credibly inform'd that the said Mr. Joyce pull'd up a tree of near a yard and a half circumference by the roots at Hampstead on Tuesday last in the open view of some hundreds of people, it being modestly computed to weigh near 2000 pounds weight.' [1]

When Hogarth painted his picture, which was in 1733, the Fair was nearing its end, for in 1762 it was suppressed. The engraving, although dated 1733— ' Invented, Painted and Engrav'd 1733 '—was not printed and issued until June 1735, having been kept back for the purpose of securing the protection afforded by the Act of Parliament known as Hogarth's Act.

In the *London Evening Post* for June 3 and 14,

[1] J. Ashton's *Social Life in the Reign of Queen Anne*, 1882, vol. I. p 267.

1735, it was announced that the nine prints ('A Rake's Progress' and 'Southwark Fair') were 'now printing off and will be ready for delivery on the 25th instant. N.B.—Mr. Hogarth was, and is, obliged to defer the publication and delivery of the aforesaid Prints till the 25th of June in order to secure his property, pursuant to an Act lately passed both Houses of Parliament to secure all new-invented prints that shall be published after the 24th instant, from being copied without the consent of the proprietor, and thereby preventing a scandalous and unjust custom (hitherto practised with impunity) of making and vending base copies of Original Prints to the manifest injury of the Author, and the great discouragement of the Arts of Painting and Engraving.'

'Southwark Fair' is one of the most valuable of Hogarth's pictures as a vivid representation of a phase in the life of his times, and one in which he must have been unusually interested, as he has filled it with an immense amount of detail. He was most careful in representing the different groups, but the topography is not very clear—in fact, some critics have expressed doubts as to the locality.

Pervading the whole scene there is so general a feeling of varied life and action that it has been described as 'painted noise.' Hogarth's amazing power in harmonising the miscellaneous groups into one consistent whole is here displayed in an equal degree to that in the case of the 'March to Finchley.'

The chief figure in the centre group of the picture

is a buxom young woman beating a drum to draw an audience for the entertainment with which she is connected. She is deservedly admired by the men around her, and moreover she is a worthy representative of the painter's favourite style of beauty. Samuel Ireland tells that ' the heroine of this print . . . is a portrait of whom Mrs. Hogarth gave me the following particulars, that H. passing through the fair, on seeing the master of the company strike her and otherwise use her ill, he took her part and gave the fellow a sound drubbing ; whether this chastisement arose from a liking to her person or respect for the sex we know not, but it is certain that she was the kind of woman for whom he entertained a strong partiality. A proof of this may be adduced in many of his works ; where he has occasion to introduce a good-looking female he has generally given us a form not unlike hers, and it must be confessed that her face and figure seem to be of that attractive quality which will never fail to gain admirers in this country.' [1]

Mr. Stephens, after quoting this passage, adds that ' the strongest proof of this figure exhibiting something not remote from Hogarth's ideal of English beauty is to be found by comparing the model's aspect and physique with the like in his portrait of Mrs. Hogarth.' [2] A striking scene is being acted at the left of the picture, where an insecure scaffolding has given way, and the actors are falling

---

[1] *Graphic Illustrations*, 1794, vol. i. pp. 110-11
[2] *British Museum Catalogue of Satires*, vol ii. p. 836 (note)

in confusion. A lantern hanging beneath the stage is inscribed 'Ciber and Bullock,' and 'The Fall of Bajazet.'

John Ireland tells us that a booth was built in the year that this picture was painted (1733) 'for the use of T[heophilus] Cibber, Bullock and H. Hallam, at which the tragedy of Tamerlane, with the Fall of Bajazet, intermixed with the Comedy of the Miser, was actually represented.' [1]

We thus see that Hogarth transferred Cibber's booth from St. Bartholomew's to Southwark, although it is possible that Cibber may (as was common then) have removed from Smithfield to Southwark Fair. The show-cloth above the scaffolding is a copy of 'The Stage Mutiny,' etched by John Laguerre, which has already been referred to in Chapter x. (Theatrical Life). This represents the secession of some actors from Covent Garden under the leadership of Theophilus Cibber.

In the middle of the picture but in the background is one of the chief booths ornamented with a show-cloth on which the Trojan Horse is painted with an inscription announcing *The Siege of Troy is here.* This was a droll written by Elkanah Settle. Beneath the show-cloth is a company rehearsing some parts of the play. A lantern affixed to the booth is inscribed 'Lee and Harper's Great Booth.' Mr. Stephens quotes an advertisement from *The County Journal, or The Craftsman,* September 8, 1733:

---

[1] *Hogarth Illustrated,* 1793, vol. i. p. 72 (note).

' At Lee and Harper's Great Theatrical Booth, on
the Bowling Green behind the Marshalsea in Southwark during the Fair, will be performed that celebrated Droll, which has given such entire satisfaction
to all that ever saw it,' etc., etc. The entertainments
are not the same as are shown in the picture, but
Hogarth gave the correct representation of the booth
quite up to date. In a later advertisement notice is
given of ' a Grotesque Pantomime Entertainment
call'd, The Harlot's Progress or The Ridotto al
Fresco,' which was performed at Lee's booth. This
was a piece by Theophilus Cibber, first acted in
April 1733 at Drury Lane.

In connection with *The Siege of Troy*, J. Ireland
quotes the following interesting information from
Victor's eulogium on Boheme the actor : ' His first
appearance was at a booth in Southwark Fair, which
in those days lasted two weeks, and was much
frequented by persons of all distinctions, of both
sexes. He acted the part of Menelaus, in the best
droll I ever saw called the Siege of Troy.' [1]

To the right of the Trojan Horse are show-cloths
representing Adam and Eve, and the puppet-show
of Punch wheeling Judy into the jaws of destruction.
At the extreme right of the picture is an alehouse
with the sign of The Royal Oak, and chequers over
the door. On a paper lantern is written, ' Royal
Wax Worke,' and ' The Whole Court of France is
here,' and at an open window above is a dwarf

[1] Victor's *History of the Theatres* (1761), vol. ii. p. 74.

drummer and a little wax figure. Below hangs a show-cloth, and a juggler stands in front with a bird in his hand. This was a famous performer named Fawkes, who is said to have acquired £10,000 by his dexterity of hand. He is introduced into the print of *Masquerades and Operas*, already alluded to in Chapter x. (Theatrical Life). Mr. Stephens refers to James Caulfield's *Portraits, Memoirs, and Characters of Remarkable Persons* (1819, vol. ii. p. 65), where there is a portrait of Fawkes standing at a table, and in the act of shaking balls from a bag. Below this is a representation of three men tumbling, one of them being like the tumbler painted on the show-cloth of Hogarth's picture. Fawkes died May 25, 1731, so that according to strict chronological accuracy he should not have been included in a drawing taken in 1733.

In this representation of all the fun of the fair we find two well-known performers on the rope. To the left of the Trojan Horse is the celebrated Violante, and to the right of the church is a rope fixed from the tower of St. George's Church to the Mint, which is out of the picture. The performer on this rope was Cadman, or Kidman as he is named by John Nichols. Cadman later came to a sad end by attempting a similar feat of flying across the Severn at Shrewsbury. The unfortunate man was buried at that town, and on his tombstone were these lines inscribed:

'No, no, a faulty cord being drawn too tight,
Hurried his soul on high to take her flight,
Which bid the body here beneath, good-night.'

A similar performance took place at St. Martin's in the Fields when an acrobat descended a slack rope from the steeple of the church to the Royal Mews, which stood on the site of the present National Gallery. There is some doubt whether this feat was due to Cadman or Violante. John Nichols and John Ireland both give the credit to Cadman, but later writers say it was Violante. If we consult Walpole's Letters we shall find that the doubt is unsolved.

Walpole, writing to Sir Horace Mann respecting balloons (December 2, 1783), says : ' Very early in my life I remember this town at gaze on a man who flew down a rope from the top of St. Martin's steeple ; now late in my day, people are staring at a voyage to the moon. The former Icarus broke his neck at a subsequent flight : when a similar accident happens to modern knights errant, adieu to air-balloons.'

John Wright, in editing Walpole, wrote : ' On the 1st of June 1727, one Violante, an Italian, descended head-foremost by a rope, with his legs and arms extended, from top of the steeple of St. Martin's Church, over the houses in St. Martin's Lane [1] to the furthest side of the Mews, a distance of about three hundred yards, in half a minute. The crowd was immense, and the young princesses, with several of the nobility, were in the Mews.' Here is a definite statement, but it will be noticed that Walpole says that the rope-flier subsequently broke his neck,

[1] It must be remembered that at this time St. Martin's Lane, instead of stopping, as now, at Chandos Street, passed the church and led to the Strand opposite Northumberland House.

and he would therefore probably be thinking of Cadman.

John Nichols records that the latter applied to a bishop for permission to fix a line to the steeple of his cathedral church. The prelate replied that the man might fly *to* the church whenever he pleased, but he should never give his consent to any one's flying *from* it.

The Weekly Miscellany for April 17, 1736, notices that 'Thomas Kidman, the famous flyer, who has flown from several of the highest precipices in England, and was the person who flew off Bromham steeple in Wiltshire, when it fell down, flew on Monday last, from the highest of the rocks near the Hotwells at Bristol with fireworks and pistols; after which he went up the rope, and performed several surprising dexterities on it, in sight of thousands of spectators, both from Somersetshire and Gloucestershire.' It will be seen from this that Nichols had authority for his form of the man's name, viz. Kidman.

One figure of special importance at the Fair is James Figg, the 'Master of the Noble Science of Self-Defence,' who, sitting complacently on his horse and holding his sword with the point upwards, is seen at the extreme right of the picture. His booth is round the corner, and he is about to ride through the fair to gather those sightseers who are desirous of witnessing a fight between himself and some other professor of the art. He has his coat off and his bare head is covered with black patches, indicating the scars left from former combats. A fuller description of James Figg will be found in Chapter IV. (Low Life).

We have now considered the more important of the incidents illustrated in this remarkable picture of Southwark Fair, but it is so rich in the illustration of London life that more might be added. Sufficient for our purpose has, however, been said, and those who wish for a complete account of the picture can refer to Mr. Stephens's full description in the *British Museum Catalogue* (vol. ii. pp. 832-9).

Other amusement-providers might have been introduced into the picture had there been room, such as Timothy Fielding, the actor (often confused with Henry Fielding, the author), who had a booth in the Fair. Greater actors, such, among others, as Powell, Booth, and Macklin, were introduced to the stage in these public and by no means select scenes.

As to the visitors, many men of distinction have figured here, and John Ireland tells an anecdote of Samuel Johnson on one occasion visiting the Fair in company with Mallet.

' When the Doctor first became acquainted with David Mallet, they once went with some other gentlemen to laugh away an hour at Southwark Fair. At one of the booths where wild beasts were exhibited to the wondering crowd, was a very large bear, which the showman assured them was catched in the undiscovered deserts of the remotest Russia. The bear was muzzled, and might therefore be approached with safety, but to all the company, except Johnson, was very surly and ill-tempered : of the philosopher he appeared extremely fond, rubbed against him, and displayed every mark of awkward partiality, and subdued kindness. " How is it," said one of the company, " that this savage animal is so attached to Mr. Johnson ? " " From a very natural cause," replied Mallet, " the bear is a Russian philosopher, and he knows that Linnæus would have placed him in the same class with the English moralist. They are two barbarous animals of one species." ' [1]

Johnson never liked Mallet, and if this anecdote is true it is not probable that after this outrageous expression of contempt Johnson had any further intercourse with the man whose name was introduced into the Dictionary as an illustration of the word *alias*.

J. B. Nichols in his *Anecdotes of William Hogarth* says that the picture was sold in 1746 at the sale of Mrs. Edwards's effects for £19, 8s. 6d. It was afterwards at Valentines, Ilford, Essex, and was sold in 1797 and again in 1800, but the price it realised is not mentioned. Nichols says that the picture was destroyed in the fire at Colonel Thomas Johnes's mansion at Hafod on March 13, 1807 ; but this is a mistake, for it was saved from the fire, and after Mr. Johnes's death Hafod having come into the possession of the Duke of Newcastle, his son exhibited the picture at the Manchester Art Treasures Exhibition, 1857. In the catalogue of that famous exhibition

---

[1] *Hogarth Illustrated*, 1793, vol. i. p. 89 (note).

there is the following note : ' Painted in 1733. Formerly at Valentines in Essex, afterwards the property of Johnes of Hafod (the translator of Froissart), from whom it passed with the Hafod estate to the father of the present possessor.'

Johnes himself lent it to the Exhibition of Hogarth's Works at the British Institution in 1814.

Here ends the notice of Hogarth's pictures of the suburbs, but there are three pictures that may be mentioned here. Chiswick and Twickenham may be treated as suburbs, although some may think Cowley is too far from town to be mentioned in this chapter.

Mr. Dobson gives the following notice of Hogarth's etching of Mr. Ranby's house at Chiswick : ' There is a copy in the British Museum without the writing, but with the manuscript title " A view of Mr. Ranby the Surgeon's house. Taken from Hogarth's window at Chiswick." It is there dated 1748.'

John Nichols writes : ' This view, I am informed, was taken in 1750 ; but was not designed for sale.' [1]

It was ' publish'd as the Act directs by Jane Hogarth at the Golden Head, Leicester Fields, 1st May 1781.'

Mr. Dobson mentions the picture of ' Garrick's Villa ' in his list of paintings of uncertain date, and there are some further particulars in J. B. Nichols's *Anecdotes* (p. 368) as follows: ' Garrick's villa by Lambert, with figures of Mr. and Mrs. Garrick by Hogarth, was bought by Colnaghi at Gwennap's sale

---

[1] *Biographical Anecdotes*, 1782, p. 341.

April 5, 1821, for £7, 17s. 6d., and a companion to
the above, a villa near Blackheath, was bought in
the same sale by Adams for £3, 3s.'

Samuel Ireland has given, in the second volume of
his *Graphic Illustrations* (1799), a pretty engraving
of a ' Garden Scene at Cowley, the residence of the
late Thomas Rich, Esq.,' [1] which he dedicated to
Abraham Langford, the auctioneer, the possessor of
the picture. Cowley is situated near Uxbridge, and
not far from Hillingdon, the residence of Mr. Lane the
original purchaser of the *Marriage à la Mode*. Cowley
has also an interesting association with the great actor
Barton Booth, the original ' Cato ' in Addison's play
of that name, who was buried there. Two well-
known streets in Westminster, Barton and Cowley
Streets, were named after the actor, who possessed
property in Westminster. Rich the manager, already
referred to in Chapter x., died at an advanced age
in 1761, and Ireland supposes that the picture was
painted about the year 1750. It contains portraits
of Rich and his wife, and Mrs. Cock to the left of
the picture, and to the right are portraits of three
men. Cock, the auctioneer, is admiring a picture
held up by a servant and explained by Hogarth
himself. Ireland describes the picture at the time of
the publication of his book as in as fine preservation
as when it left the easel. At the Garrick Club
there is a small picture by Hogarth of John Rich
and his family.

---

[1] This is a blunder made by Samuel Ireland. It should be John Rich.

We here come to the end of these desultory chapters on the associations of Hogarth with the life of his time. I trust that something has been done to elucidate the most interesting incidents of the London of the eighteenth century, which he did so much to make live in his pictures, and also to prove by examples the enormous labour devoted by the artist to his work. The more we study the outcome of Hogarth's life the more we must admire his single-minded devotion to his studies. It was some time before he found his place, but when he did so he ever pressed forward, labouring hard in taking pains, which, with ordinary ability, in the end always achieves success. He was, however, guided through all this hard labour with the spirit which we call genius—a something we know exists but which we cannot well define. This genius is sometimes attributed by enthusiastic admirers to those who have it not; but every one who studies the life and work of this great man, to one side of whose large heart and mind this book is devoted, must know that it existed in no small measure in William Hogarth.

A trivial anecdote sometimes tells more of the life of the subject than others apparently of more importance. Such is one related by John Ireland: ' Hogarth never played at cards, and while his wife and a party of friends were so employed he occasionally took the quadrille fish, and cut upon them scales, fins, heads, etc., so as to give them some degree of character. Three of these little aquatic curiosities which remained in the possession of Mrs. Lewis, she presented to me, and I have ventured to insert them as a Tailpiece.'[1]   This corroborates what is otherwise evident in every incident of the painter's life— that he never was idle.

The fame of Hogarth sprang into life immediately the public had the opportunity of admiring his engravings and seeing what a wealth of meaning there was crowded into the designs, but it has taken many generations to arise and pass away before the world has awakened to the undoubted fact that he was one of the greatest painters of the modern school.

That position he has now attained, and he can never lose it while the love and understanding of art still exist in our land.

[1] *Hogarth Illustrated*, vol. iii. p. 377.

CHAPTER XIV

LITERATURE OF HOGARTH

MR. AUSTIN DOBSON has compiled so comprehensive 'A Bibliography of the Principal Books, Pamphlets, etc., relating to Hogarth and his Works' that it would be useless to attempt to form a new one. Those who want to know all the literature of Hogarth must consult his volume. It seemed, however, advisable to say a few words as to the authorities which will be of most use to the student of Hogarth's works.

First, Mr. Dobson's *William Hogarth* is indispensable. This was originally published in 1879 and since that date has gone through several editions, being continuously improved and enlarged. The last edition (1907) is published at the small price of six shillings; it is fully illustrated and has an excellent index, supplying the reader with the information it contains in a thoroughly handy form.

The most important contemporary account of Hogarth's Pictures and Engravings is the *Biographical Anecdotes of William Hogarth ; and a Catalogue of his Works Chronologically Arranged, with Occasional Remarks*, published by John Nichols, 1781,

Nichols himself explains the origin of this book in his *Literary Anecdotes of the Eighteenth Century*, 1812 (vol. iii. p. 9), as a note on the reference to Trusler's *Hogarth Moralized* (1768) : ' Of this great, this inimitable Artist, I had (more than thirty years ago) collected some materials with a view to an article in the first edition of these *Anecdotes*.   But my intelligence (aided by the acute and elegant criticism of the late George Steevens, Esq.) was so greatly extended beyond the limits of a note, that I formed from them a separate publication, intituled, " Biographical Memoirs (*sic*) of William Hogarth, 1781," which by the indulgence of the publick, arrived at a second edition in 1782, and to a third in 1785 ; and at a distance of 25 years, having been revised and new modelled, was again re-published in two handsome quarto volumes, illustrated with CLX. beautiful Plates in 1810 ' [1808-10].

In the Library of the British Museum is a thin volume of sixty-four pages, bound in russia and lettered, *Anecdotes of Hogarth, a Fragment*.   At the beginning is the following MS. note by Isaac Reed : ' This imperfect Pamphlet is curious as being the first Essay towards the Life of Hogarth.   About half a Dozen were printed and all destroyed except this copy.   Whoever will take the pains of comparing this with the published one will observe some very material alterations.   See particularly P. 22 where the severe reflections on Mr. Walpole were almost wholly omitted.   That part of the Pamphlet

was written by Mr. Steevens, much of the rem[ainder]
by myself, some by Mr. Nichols and many corrections by other hands.   I^{c.} REED.'

The paragraphs alluded to are offensive remarks
to prove that Walpole is ' unfortunate in his attempts
to expose the indelicacy of the Flemish painters by
comparing it with the purity of Hogarth.'

The following note on page 23, which was modified
in the published work, is interesting :

' Might we not however, on this occasion compare the manner of the Artist with that of his
Biographer, who talks of " eyes red with rage and
usquebaugh," and of a " maudlin strumpet's fingers
blooded by the sheep's heart designed for her dinner."
It is whispered (we know not with how much truth)
that even the delicacy of Mrs. H. was shocked by this
description, and that she returned no thanks for the
volume that contains it, when it was sent to her as a
present by its author.'

Nichols, in the *Genuine Works of William Hogarth*
(vol. i. p. 437), referring to Reed's note, writes :
' Preparatory to the First Edition, an impression of
only *twelve copies* was printed for the purpose of
obtaining correct information from those who were
best able to communicate it.'   He further expresses
surprise that Reed should have written as he did.
' The above note (the more curious as Mr. Reed was
always extremely averse to his name appearing in
print),' etc. etc.

The author of this book possesses Horace Walpole's

copy of the first edition which is embellished with one of his bookplates (containing a view of Strawberry Hill) and annotated with his manuscript criticisms. The printed note in Reed's fragment was only partially omitted, and the paragraph beginning 'It is whispered' is retained. Opposite this, on page 44 of the first edition, Walpole inserted a 'Copy of my letter sent with the 4th vol. of my Anecdotes of Painting to Mrs. Hogarth, to which she returned no answer.—H. W.'

The letter is as follows :—

'Mr. Walpole begs Mrs. Hogarth's acceptance of the Volume that accompanies this letter, and hopes she will be content with his Endeavours to do justice to the genius of Mr. Hogarth. If there are some Passages less agreeable to her than the rest, Mr. Walpole will regard her disapprobation only as marks of the goodness of her heart and proof of her affection to her Husband's memory—but she will, he is sure, be so candid as to allow for the Duty an Historian owes to the Public and himself, which obliges him to say what he thinks ; and which when he obeys, his Praise is corroborated by his Censure. The first page of the Preface will more fully make his Apology ; and his just Admiration of Mr. Hogarth, Mr. W. flatters himself, will, notwithstanding his Impartiality, still rank him in Mrs. Hogarth's mind as one of her Husband's most zealous and sincere Friends.'

The original letter is in the British Museum Library.

The second edition of the *Biographical Anecdotes* (greatly enlarged) was published in 1782. Mr. Austin Dobson possesses Nichols's own copy of this edition filled with the MS. corrections and addenda subsequently inserted in the third edition of 1785. A slip pasted at the beginning is inscribed : ' This Vol. belongs to Mr. Nichols, Printer, Red Lion Passage, Fleet Street.   G[eorge] S[teevens].'

There is a copy of the third edition (1785) with a large number of MS. notes, in the British Museum (Add. MSS. 27,996), in which the latest note is dated 1819.

' *The Genuine Works of William Hogarth ;* illustrated with Biographical Anecdotes, a Chronological Catalogue, and Commentary.   By John Nichols and George Steevens,' 2 vols. 4to, 1808-10, and vol. iii., 1817, is practically a fourth edition of the *Biographical Anecdotes* greatly enlarged, and with the addition of plates engraved by T. Cook from the original pictures or proof impressions of the original engravings.

These books are full of valuable information, and the original compilation of the *Anecdotes* has a curious history.   The idea of the book was entirely John Nichols's, but he was considerably assisted by the Shakespearean commentator George Steevens, with great advantage to the literary value of the book, but with considerable injury to its amenity.   Nichols was himself a courteous and considerate man, but Steevens was reckless in assertion and determined to have his own way. Therefore if Nichols desired the help of his friend he was forced to take it in whatever form Steevens was inclined to present it. Two illustrations of Steevens's venomous character may be here given.

On page 30 of the third edition he goes out of his way to make a spiteful remark respecting Nicholas Hardinge, Joint Secretary of the Treasury, which was singularly untrue. He is referring to an 'elegant Sapphic Ode,' by Benjamin Loveling, and adds: 'His style, however, appears to have been formed on a general acquaintance with the language of Roman poetry; nor do any of his effusions betray that poverty of expression so conspicuous in the poems of Nicholas Hardinge, Esq., who writes as if Horace was the only classic author he had ever read.'

Hardinge, a friend of Nichols's master Bowyer, was educated at Eton and became a Fellow of King's College, Cambridge. Nichols says of him: 'At Eton and Cambridge he had the fame of the most eminent scholar of his time; and had very singular powers in Latin verse, perhaps inferior to none since the Augustan Age.'[1]

The brutal allusion to Mary Lewis (Mrs. Hogarth's cousin and executrix) on page 114, where she is likened to the old maid in Hogarth's 'Morning,' is so disgraceful that the author is forced to bear some of the obloquy attached to its appearance in

---

[1] *Literary Anecdotes*, vol. v. p. 339.

his book. Steevens died July 1800, and when Nichols was free to deal with his text as he wished these references were expunged. John Nichols is held in so high esteem by all literary men that we cannot but regret that he allowed such a scandalous attack as that on Mary Lewis to be printed. Steevens's character was, of course, well known, as may be seen by the observation of two distinguished men.

When Lord Mansfield remarked that one could only believe half of what Steevens said, Johnson retorted that the difficulty was to tell which half deserved credence. If the collector possesses a set of the original plates of Hogarth's Works he is fortunate, but the fame of the artist has been sadly dimmed by the large number of worn impressions of his plates in circulation.

George Steevens collected the first and best impressions of Hogarth's plates, and also the last and worst of re-touched plates, so that the contrast between them might be seen, and the good ones might gain by comparison with the common ones.

Those, therefore, who cannot obtain the best impressions of the original plates will be wise to content themselves with the three volumes of the *Genuine Works*, published by John Nichols, 1808-17, especially in large paper, as in this form the impressions are better than in the small paper.

John Bowyer Nichols, son and successor of John Nichols, published in 1833 a very useful handbook to the study of Hogarth, entitled, ' *Anecdotes of William Hogarth*, Written by Himself ; with Essays on his Life and Genius, and Criticisms on his Works, selected from Walpole, Gilpin, J. Ireland, Lamb, Phillips, and others. To which are added a Catalogue of his Prints, Account of their variations and principal copies ; Lists of Paintings, Drawings, etc.,' 1833.

The next book of importance in the literature of Hogarth, after Nichols's *Biographical Anecdotes*, is John Ireland's *Hogarth Illustrated* (2 vols. 8vo, 1791, and Supplement, 1798, vol. iii.), which contains a large amount of valuable matter. The Supplement contains Hogarth's autobiography. The first and second volumes were reprinted in 1793. The whole work was reprinted in 1806 and 1812.

The plates are too small to be of much use as pictures, although they are useful for identification. This is, however, a valuable work, full of important information, and written with much discrimination and some authority ; but it sadly needs an index.

John Ireland was originally a watchmaker in Maiden Lane, Covent Garden, and was employed by Messrs. Boydell to produce this book.[1] He frequented the Three Feathers Coffee-House, and was a friend of John Henderson the actor.

' *Graphic Illustrations of Hogarth*, from Pictures,

[1] The third volume is described as ' Published March 1798 for John Ireland, Poet's Corner, Palace Yard, Westminster.'

Drawings and Scarce Prints in the possession of Samuel Ireland, Author of this work,' is a book of considerable interest, and contains much useful information respecting Hogarth, as well as many illustrations not elsewhere to be found.

Knowing Samuel Ireland's character and his connection with the Shakespeare forgeries of his son William Henry Ireland as we do, it is impossible not to feel considerable doubt respecting the genuineness of many of his ascriptions. It would be of much value if some authority would make a searching investigation as to all the plates that do not occur in other books on Hogarth. This would help the student greatly, and would doubtless, in many instances, restore confidence in the illustrations to this book. Mr. Laurence Binyon's valuable 'Catalogue of Drawings by British Artists, etc., preserved in the Department of Prints and Drawings in the British Museum,' contains references to such of the originals of the engravings as are in the British Museum.[1] There is no index to S. Ireland's book. The 'Catalogue of Prints and Drawings in the British Museum : Division I. Political and Personal Satires,' with full and most elaborate descriptions by the late Mr. Frederic George Stephens, forms a most valuable help to the study of a large number of Hogarth's works, but it is not so well known to the public as it deserves to be. I am greatly indebted for much information contained in it which I have been able

[1] Volume II. (1900), pp. 316-26.

to utilise, as will be seen from many notes in this book.

Mr. Dobson writes of this Catalogue: 'These volumes are, in truth, as far as the subject comes within their scope, a vast storehouse of Hogarthiana, not to be safely neglected by any student of Hogarth's work and epoch.'[1] Having mentioned the books that are positively necessary to the Hogarth collector, we may return to make a rapid survey of the general literature of the subject.

The first book referred to in Mr. Dobson's Bibliography is '*Three Poetical Epistles.* To Mr. Hogarth, Mr. Dandridge, and Mr. Lambert, Masters in the Art of Painting. Written by Mr. Mitchell,' 1781; which is of considerable interest, as Hogarth is called in the Epistle to him, 'Shakespeare in Painting.' This is dated June 12, 1730, just before Hogarth had begun his triumphant career as social satirist by the publication of 'The Harlot's Progress.' The first commentator on Hogarth was Jean Rouquet, a Swiss of French extraction, settled in England as an enameller, who published in 1746 'Lettres de Monsieur . . . . à un de ses Amis à Paris pour lui expliquer les Estampes de Monsieur Hogarth.' In this pamphlet the two 'Progresses,' 'Marriage,'

---

[1] The Hogarth items will be found in volumes ii., iii., and iv. Vol. ii. (1873), No. 1722, first entry of Hogarth's 'South Sea Scheme'; No. 2012, 'Mr D——s ye Critick,' the last. Vol. iii. (pts. 1, 2, 1877), 2018, 'The Complicated R——n,' first entry, 3743, 'Sir Francis Dashwood,' the last. Vol. iv. (1883), 3808, 'Frontispiece to the Catalogue of Pictures,' the first; 4106, 'Finis,' the last.

and nine other prints are described. Walpole says that it was drawn up for the use of Marshal Belleisle, who was then a prisoner in the Round Tower at Windsor Castle ; but Steevens, in Nichols's *Biographical Anecdotes,* corrects this statement by saying that it was the 'Description du Tableau de M. Hogarth, qui représente la Marche des Gardes à leur rendezvous de Finchley, dans leur route en Écosse,' published a few years later, which alone was the letter intended for the Marshal. Steevens also states that the Letters (1746) were 'certainly suggested by Hogarth, and drawn up at his immediate request'; and he further says : 'He [Rouquet] was liberally paid by Hogarth for having clothed his sentiments and illustrations in a foreign dress. This pamphlet was designed, and continues to be employed, as a constant companion to all such sets of his prints as go abroad.' [1]

Rouquet also printed in 1755 another work entitled *L'État des Arts en Angleterre,* in which he alludes to Hogarth's pictures. It was not until after Hogarth's death that the notorious Dr. Trusler compiled the pretentious commentary which he contributed to the first collection of Hogarth's Works, issued in 1766-68.

Hogarth Moralized is a foolish attempt to point out not the philosophy of the painter's art, but that which is on the surface and evident to the most unimaginative of observers. The constant reprint

---

[1] *Biographical Anecdotes,* ed. 1785, p. 103.

of his vapid remarks has lowered the value of much
of the literature of Hogarth, and the unfortunate
circumstance of a cadging bookmaker having by a
bit of sharp practice become the first to publish a
popular edition of these masterpieces has given his
commonplace criticism a certain amount of vogue.
One can only imagine how much disgust Hogarth
himself would have felt if he had had the misfortune
to live to see the publication of this book.

It was issued in fourteen parts at varied prices,
and the cost of the bound volume was one pound
sixteen shillings.

George Steevens gives in *Biographical Anecdotes*
(1785, p. 105) the following notice of the book:
' *Hogarth Moralized* will . . . in some small degree (a
very small one) contribute to preserve the memory of
those temporary circumstances, which Mr. Walpole
is so justly apprehensive will be lost to posterity.
Such an undertaking, indeed, requires a more intimate acquaintance with fleeting customs and past
occurrences, than the compiler of this work can
pretend to.'   In a note the history of the work is
thus given : ' The Rev. John Trusler engaged with
some engravers in this design, after Hogarth's death,
when they could carry it into execution with impunity. Mrs. Hogarth, finding her property would
be much affected by it, was glad to accept an offer
they made her, of entering into partnership with
them ; and they were very glad to receive her,
knowing her name would give credit to the publica-

tion, and that she would certainly supply many anecdotes to explain the plates. Such as are found in the work are probably all hers. The other stuff was introduced by the editor to eke out the book. We are informed, that when the undertaking was completed, in order to get rid of her partners, she was glad to buy out their shares, so that the whole expense which fell on her amounted to at least £700.'

Mr. Dobson quotes from Mrs. Hogarth's own advertisement of the first number of *Hogarth Moralized* in the *London Chronicle* for August 16-19, 1766, where she says that she has 'engaged a Gentleman to explain each Print, and moralize on it in such a Manner as to make them as well instructive as entertaining.'

For those who desire a fair selection of Hogarth literature a good copy of the first edition of *Hogarth Moralized* is worth adding to their collection, as is also Major's beautiful edition, 1831, 1841. There is a special interest in Major's edition in that it contains George Cruikshank's woodcut copies of the four groups—'The Laughing Audience,' 'The Company of Undertakers,' 'The Oratorio,' and the 'Public Lecture.' It is therefore possible to compare our two great satirical artists.

The first collection of Hogarth's Works in atlas folio was the *Original Works*, published by Boydell in 1790. The next collection was almost contemporaneous with the publications of John and

Samuel Ireland, and emanated from Germany. It was in octavo and was commenced in 1794, being continued for some years. This was ' G. C. Lichtenberg's ausführliche Erklärung der Hogarthischen Kupferstiche, mit verkleinerten aber vollständigen Copien derselben von E. Riepenhausen,' published at Göttingen.[1]

Then came ' *Hogarth Restored. The Whole Works* . . . as Originally published. Now Re-engraved by Thomas Cook. . . . London (G. and J. Robinson),' 1802. Atlas folio.

The *Genuine Works*, already referred to, were published in three volumes, dated respectively 1808, 1810, and 1817. 4to.

The *Works* were published in two volumes 8vo by Thomas Clerk, London (R. Scholey), 1810.

Another edition of the *Works*, ' from the original Plates restored by James Heath, Esq., R.A.,' was published in 1822 in atlas folio: 'Printed for Baldwin, Cradock & Joy, Paternoster Row, by J. Nichols & Son.' This has continued to be re-issued and reprinted until there is little pleasure to be obtained from looking at the worn plates.

Several quarto editions of Hogarth's re-engraved works have been published. One of these is worthy of special mention, as it contains a very interesting Introductory Essay by James Hannay, entitled ' Hogarth as a Satirist.' This is ' *The Complete*

---

[1] An article on Lichtenberg and Hogarth was published in the *Foreign Quarterly Review* (No. xxxii., 1836).

Works of William Hogarth : in a series of one hundred and fifty steel Engravings. . . . London : Richard Griffin and Company.' The book is undated, but Mr. Dobson supposes it to have been published in 1860. The descriptive letterpress is not of much value, as it consists of Trusler's vapourings and some rather odd imaginings of E. F. Roberts.

Another edition, 'reproduced from the Original Engravings in permanent Photographs,' was published by Bell and Daldy in 1872 in two volumes quarto.

The last folio edition of Hogarth's Works is the special issue in 1902 of Mr. Austin Dobson's *Memoir* by Mr. Heinemann as one of his art monographs. This handsome volume contains a large number of photogravures from the original pictures.

There is a considerable literature of pamphlets (mostly catchpenny publications) containing accounts of the various series of engravings by Hogarth, of some of which the following is a list :—

Harlot's Progress. The Lure of Venus ; or a Harlot's Progress. An Heroi-Comical Poem by Mr. Joseph Gay [Captain John Durant Breval], 1733.

Rake's Progress. Explanation of the Eight Prints copied from the Originals by Thomas Bakewell, Printseller, Fleet Street, 1735 (broadside).

The Rake's Progress, or the Humours of Drury Lane, a Poem. (J. Chettwood), 1735.

Marriage a-la-Mode : an Humorous Tale, in six Cantos. (Weaver Bickerton), 1746.

Industry and Idleness. The Effects of I. and I. Illustrated. . . . Being an Explanation of the Moral of Twelve celebrated Prints. (C. Corbett, 1748.)

Gin Lane, etc. A Dissertation on Mr. Hogarth's Six Prints lately publish'd, viz. Gin Lane, Beerstreet, and the Four Stages of Cruelty. . . . (B. Dickinson), 1751.

An Election. A Poetical Description of Mr. Hogarth's Election Prints, in four Cantos. Printed for T. Caslon and sold by J. Smith, at Hogarth's Head in Cheapside, 1759.

Roast Beef of Old England. A Cantata. Taken from a celebrated Print of the Ingenious Mr. Hogarth. (John Smith), *n.d.*

Enraged Musician. Ut Pictura Poesis ! or the Enraged Musician. A Musical Entertainment Founded on Hogarth. Written by George Colman. T. Cadell, 1789.

In the first two volumes of the *Cornhill Magazine* (1860) George Augustus Sala contributed a series of nine interesting articles on Hogarth as Painter, Engraver and Philosopher, which were republished as a book by Smith, Elder and Co. in 1866. There is a good deal of conjecture and not much new matter, but the book is well worth reading.

Mr. Dobson's Bibliography fills thirty-five pages of his work, and contains a full description of a large number of books and pamphlets as well as references to articles in reviews and magazines.

In spite of the magnitude of this literature, there is still no absolutely exhaustive account of all Hogarth's engravings and their various states. A reprint of the entries in Stephens's British Museum Catalogue, with a description of all those engravings which do not come under the division of Satires added, would be of great value; it would, however, be a work of considerable labour.

A rigid examination of some of the pictures attributed to Hogarth which have no authenticated history is also much required, and a search for painted portraits by Hogarth is imperative. There seems to be good reason for the belief that there are still many in private hands which have not yet been registered.

INDEX

Printed by T and A CONSTABLE, Printers to His Majesty
at the Edinburgh University Press

Lightning Source UK Ltd.
Milton Keynes UK
UKOW07f1908210116

266845UK00014B/687/P